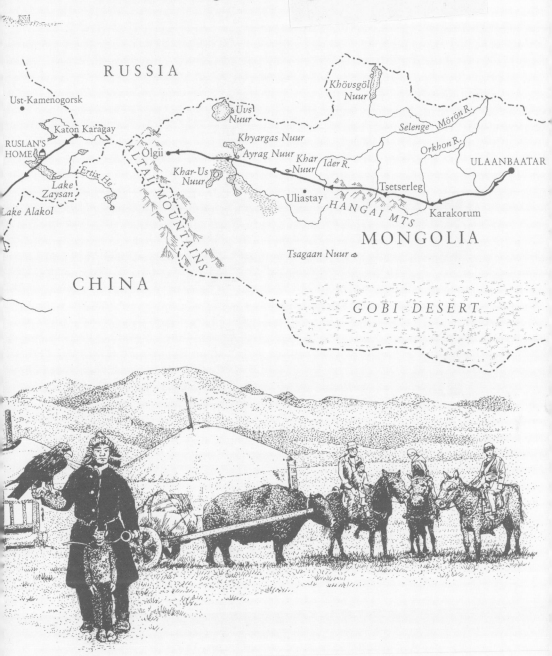

RUSSIA

Ust-Kamenogorsk

Katon Karagay

RUSLAN'S
HOME

Ertix He

Lake
Zaysan

Lake Alakol

ALTAI MOUNTAINS

CHINA

Khövsgöl
Nuur

Uvs
Nuur

Selenge   Mörön R.

Khyargas Nuur

Ölgii

Khar-Us
Nuur

Ayrag Nuur

Khar
Nuur

Orkhon R.

ULAANBAATAR

Ider R.

Uliastay

Tsetserleg

HANGAI MTS

Karakorum

MONGOLIA

Tsagaan Nuur

GOBI DESERT

SILK ROUTE
ADVENTURE

The trouble about journeys nowadays is that they are easy to make but difficult to justify. The earth, which once danced and spun before us alluringly as a celluloid ball on top of a fountain in a rifle range, is now a dull and vulnerable target.... All along the line we have been forestalled, and forestalled by better men than we. Only the born tourist – happy, goggling ruminant – can follow in their tracks with the conviction that he is not wasting his time.

Peter Fleming

SILK ROUTE ADVENTURE

On Horseback in the Heart of Asia

CLAIRE BURGES WATSON

ROBERT HALE · LONDON

ISBN 978-0-7090-8061-9

Robert Hale Limited
Clerkenwell House
Clerkenwell Green
London EC1R 0HT

A catalogue record for this book is available from the British Library

2 4 6 8 10 9 7 5 3 1

Map by Leslie Robinson

Printed in China by
New Era Printing Company Limited

CONTENTS

ACKNOWLEDGEMENTS

Thanks are due to Berlinn Ltd for permission to quote from *News from Tartary* by Peter Fleming and to AMS Press Inc. for *Mongol Journeys* by Owen Lattimore.

This journey would not have been possible without the generosity of hundreds of poor families in Central Asia who shared their precious rations with me and once even borrowed from a neighbour to feed me. Hospitality is central to nomadic culture but the more the area opens up to tourism, the more likely it is that their hospitality will be abused. I did my best to put something back consistently, not least by delivering US$16,000 worth of aid to Mongolian herders during one of the worst winters on record. The Mongolians have a saying, 'help comes from help'. I hope that they continue to believe in this maxim.

Crucial to the success of the journey were my guides Batbaatar, Tamir, Baatsaihan, Ruslan, Rassul, Ravshan and Durgmoot and my local fixers, Bayarbaatar in Mongolia and Serdar and Kootlebai in Dashoguz in Uzbekistan. Thanks, too, to Wilfred McKie for his help in Mongolia both before and after the journey. Thanks to Fraser Wilson, Ambassador in Ashkabad who saved me from a nasty run-in with the Turkmen authorities. I owe a special debt to Richard Lewington, Ambassador in Almaty and his wife Sylvianne for consistently getting me out of scrapes in Kazakhstan and to my neighbours in Bishkek – Dinara, Boris, Sveta, Ira and Yelena – for their friendship and support. I was also glad of the company of Rupert Eastwood, James Robertson, Dominic Nisbett and Rebecca Carey who joined me on various legs of the journey and brought vital supplies. Thanks too to Ruth and John Carey for looking after Jilda for six months during the final leg of my journey.

Thanks to my sponsors, personal friends and family friends whose generosity helped me to raise over US$50,000 for a number of charities. Llewellyn Juby from ADRA oversaw the funds raised to help Mongolian nomads after one of the worst winters on record. The Christina Noble

Foundation was given money to help street children in Mongolia. The British Embassy in Almaty helped me to raise money for those who had suffered physical deformities as a result of nuclear testing in Kazakhstan. Pamela and Robert Gordon, Martin Garrett and John Daniel helped me to build and sponsor an orphanage in Burma. That project is on-going.

My sponsors included many of my close friends as well as colleagues at Jardine Fleming. I am particularly grateful to Jardine Fleming and my boss Mark Dowie. I am also highly indebted to Iridium, Star TV, Dragon Air, Singapore Airlines, Kim Eng Securities, Berry Brothers, Jardine Logistics, the Rotary Club in Hong Kong, Crossroads and to the staff at Cameron McKenna, especially Ian Sepion for their enormous support while I was in Uzbekistan. Thanks too to William Benter and Andrew Stinson from Quantrix for setting up a live website.

Many thanks to Miles and Justin Geldard for lending me their beautiful house in Cortona to write this book and to his mother, Betty for her companionship. I am also grateful to the Royal Society for Asian Affairs for allowing me to spend much valuable time researching this book in their library and for excusing me when I returned my books late!

I could not have got this book to print without the dedication and wise alterations from my agents Doreen and Caroline Montgomery. I am grateful to John Hare for introducing me to them. Thank you Maya for editing the text and to the editorial staff, particularly Susan Hale, at Robert Hale Ltd, for smoothing the publication process. Finally thanks to Leslie Robinson and Vera Brice for their tireless work on the map of Central Asia, and to Rex Nicholls for his illustrations.

I would like to highlight the particularly important contribution of my family who were enormously supportive both during and after the journey. My mother and father flew to Mongolia to see me off and supported me throughout the journey. My father tirelessly helped edit this book and helped my cousin Susan Maher maintain my website. I am highly indebted to both Susan and my sister Mini who looked after correspondence relating to the charities while I was away. My siblings Mini and Mark were very generous when I got into financial scrapes. Thanks, too, to my sister Sarah for her support and to my brother Tom who visited while I was sitting out the winter in Bishkek.

Finally I would like to thank my devoted companion, Jilda, who protected me through much of the journey and dutifully followed the horses for three thousand kilometres. Sadly she died last year.

This book is dedicated to Jilda

PROLOGUE

All good journeys begin with a map. It is just a shame that in my case I barely knew how to read one. When I decided to ride a horse across Central Asia, my route-planning consisted of spreading a map in front of me and making some rudimentary calculations with a piece of string. I worked out that the journey would be about six thousand kilometres. A back-of-the-envelope calculation concluded that if I rode fifty kilometres a day and rested two days a week, it would take about six months; in the end it took sixteen. I made up the rest as I went along.

I couldn't ride. I thought about riding lessons; my only experience had been a couple of pony treks on Dartmoor. I decided that I would have plenty of time to learn. I didn't know how to use a compass, I had had no survival training and I couldn't speak any of the languages of Central Asia.

However, as a diplomat's daughter, I could relate to the rootless existence of nomads. Packing up and moving on every few years was in my blood. I was used to making friends with people from different cultures – even in situations when we didn't share a common language. I wasn't worried about the privations of the trail. I was pretty resilient – you have to be if you are to hold your own in a family of five children. I had also survived what some would regard as the horror of being sent to boarding school aged nine – except in my case I happily trotted in to school on the first day and never looked back. I got reasonably fit in Hong Kong, completing a marathon and a triathlon. I had saved enough money to finance the journey and, as a former stockbroker, I had a well-practised ability to spin a yarn and fly by the seat of my pants.

Most importantly, I have always enjoyed a challenge, particularly one for which I have no qualifications. One of my proudest moments at Oxford was beating both the President and the Vice-President of the beer society in a pint-drinking competition. It was only the third time I had drunk beer but my three-second performance (which I had to reproduce five times that night) earned me a place in the beer society, an all-male bastion. An ability to drink people under the table would stand me in good stead in Central Asia.

I inherited my sense of adventure from my parents who relished the opportunities for exploration which my father's final posting to Nepal afforded. They initially went into denial when I told them of my intended journey but they quickly sobered up when I resigned and shifted all my worldly possessions to a warehouse in London. While their friends told them they should forbid me from going, they knew that any attempts at dissuasion would only encourage me more. Fresh from a holiday in Iran, they made a last-minute decision to fly to Ulaanbaatar to see me off.

When I told my boss in Hong Kong that I was resigning to ride by horse and camel across Central Asia, it seemed to confirm all of his doubts about my suitability as a corporate financier. It wasn't a complete surprise to him – he had frequently caught me secretly reading Victorian travel escapades under my desk when I was supposed to be crunching numbers. He had been remarkably patient when I had requested an extended holiday to accommodate a spot of camel-trekking in the Gobi desert or got back to work several days late after deciding to see if I could make the sixty-six-hour (each way) train journey to Ulaanbaatar in a long weekend.

In the end, even extended holidays weren't satisfying enough. I was fidgety. I had gone to Hong Kong to expand my horizons but now I felt hemmed in. I wanted my life to add up to more than 'banker'. I was fed up with the self-indulgent Hong Kong rat race. My twenty-ninth birthday was looming. At some point I might get married and have children – if anyone was mad enough to have me. This could be the last chance for a real adventure.

Much of Central Asia was waiting to be rediscovered. It had been submerged under the control of the USSR for the best part of a hundred years and largely forgotten about in the West. With the collapse of the Soviet Union, Central Asians were trying to recover their identity. Now was my chance to explore it on horseback and camel as had been done a century earlier. I looked forward to a year with no responsibility and no commitments besides saddling and unsaddling my horses. My heart sang when I thought of an uncomplicated year with no clutter – no bills, no bank statements, no need for frantic conversations with utility companies after being cut off yet again. I would live off the land, camp anywhere and shake off the predictability of my life.

I decided that my definition of Central Asia would start in Ulaanbaatar in Mongolia. I would ride across Kazakhstan, Kyrgyzstan, Uzbekistan and finish in Ashkabad in Turkmenistan. The route across Mongolia didn't look too difficult; the terrain would be hilly rather than mountainous. Once in Kazakhstan, I would head south-west to the Kyrgyz border. The line down through Kazakhstan was less direct, on account of the Chinese border. That stretch looked pretty bleak: 1,400 kilometres of monotonous steppe. In southern Kazakhstan I would meet the Tian Shan mountains, cross a small pass into Kyrgyzstan where I would skirt Lake Issyk-kul and turn west across the mountains – another 1,000 kilometres as the crow flies but probably considerably more on horseback. Kyrgyzstan would be tough; I would have to cross several mountain ranges before dropping down into the Ferghana Valley in Uzbekistan. From there I would continue 800 kilometres west to Samarkand. Turning due north, I would take in Bukhara and Khiva – another 700 kilometres which would involve crossing the Kyzylkum desert. Finally I would cross the 'black sands' of the Karakum desert to Ashkabad, the capital of Turkmenistan, some 600 kilometres away.

I sourced most of my equipment in the YHA camping shop in London. Health insurance took several weeks to organize; even the more adventurous insurers claimed reassuringly that I was 'uninsurable'. There were some tricky decisions to make about personal security. I entered into secret negotiations for kidnap insurance and compromised on a rape alarm and a hunting knife for protection.

ILLUSTRATIONS

1
PREPARATIONS

My fixer in Mongolia was a man of forty-something named Bayarbaatar, whose name means 'Happy Hero'. A Marlboro permanently hung from his lips and his Levi's strained at the girth. He seemed to have a finger in every part of the new capitalist pie and a girlfriend in every port. We had met a year earlier in a train corridor, on my weekend excursion to Mongolia from Hong Kong. I had been taking a break from a rather intense political debate with my fellow cabin mates – two North Koreans. At the time I'd been poring over a diagram on the correct way to cut up a sheep and he'd offered to explain it.

Bayarbaatar invited me to his office where I found six men sitting around a table. One would be the driver of the support vehicle, 'for the generator' and five others would be for personal protection and pampering. Gently, I persuaded Bayarbaatar that the luxury safari that he was planning wasn't quite what I had in mind: I wanted simplicity and peace without the intrusion of modernity.

'I understand. But you must take at least four guides. You are a woman; you need protection. They can help you with the horses, cooking, setting up the tents.' How could I explain that I had the luxury to choose to throw away my pampered existence for the hardship of the road? I wanted to struggle; to feel alive after the torpor of western life; to test faculties which would otherwise have remained dormant all my life. It would have been self-indulgence if I had said this to Bayar. I knew he was disappointed. In the end, I settled for two guides.

The first was Tamir, a wiry bespectacled, middle-aged intellectual with a slightly morose expression. He wasn't exactly built to be a bodyguard but he spoke good English and threw himself into the spirit of the adventure from the start. He assumed control of the preparations, shepherding me around Ulaanbaatar, 'like a daughter'. The other guide, Bayar's brother, Baatar, was a sturdy young man of about thirty. He had a proud, handsome Mongol face: high, prominent cheekbones, flat nose and narrow eyes. He was dressed in fake designer jeans and a pressed white shirt and seemed attached at the hip to his young Chinese girlfriend with doe-like eyes.

We sourced our supplies from the local bazaar, known as the black market, on the side of a hill on the outskirts of the city. Old men squatted down, fingering hinges, cogs, screws, bolts, little pieces of string, which were laid out on sheets of canvas. Baatar's ancient uncle, a former lorry driver with bottle-end glasses and a pronounced stoop, helped choose our equipment. He didn't want payment, just a few bottles of vodka to share with his friends. He led us into a sloping, cobbled square surrounded by old train carriages, now canteens, serving boiled dumplings, fried dumplings, tea and copious quantities of *airag* – fermented mares' milk.

In the centre of the square, bow-legged, seasoned riders haggled over ropey-looking tack, spread out on small wooden tables. My eye was drawn to rows of simple wooden orange arches, a little over a foot square, which I realized, to my horror, were saddles. High in the front and the back, shaped in a deep 'U', the Mongolian idea of comfort being a thin square of felt or carpet stuck to a wooden frame. A few were inlaid with imitation silver studs and tacky rubber side-skirts. Nevertheless we ordered four saddles; two for the guides, fitted with canvas cushions to protect soft city bottoms, and two for baggage. We found some tough Russian canvas which we gave to a herder's wife to sew saddlebags, and about twenty yards of felt to protect the horses' backs. Finally we bought three pairs of old Russian army officer boots and three sets of long army capes with matching galoshes.

Bayarbaatar directed us to a friend's home, a round-topped felt tent known locally as a *ger*, an hour's drive from Ulaanbaatar, where he assured us we would find horses. We followed Mongolia's main western artery, a small, two-lane tarmac road. Accidents were common and we were barely out of Ulaanbaatar before we encountered a Russian Jeep on its side in a ditch, the windscreen shattered, the driver, who had been propelled through it, lying beside the road. Miraculously, his only ailment was severe whiplash.

'Herders think that driving is like riding a horse; they are used to the freedom of the steppe and find it hard to live in a city and obey the rules,' explained Tamir. 'My family has been in Ulaanbaatar for two generations, we understand city life. My son won't even eat meat from the countryside: he says it smells. Everyone is moving to the city now; they don't understand that life is different. The old order of society doesn't work in the city.'

We continued along the road for an hour and pulled up beside another Russian Jeep. A family had just arrived for the summer. A *ger* lay stacked behind them, the wooden frame in three neat rectangles, the felt rolled up like a carpet and the white canvas for the roof folded on top, to keep off the

Mongolian felt tents known as 'gers'

rain. They were constructing a raised platform of wooden planks, which would serve as a base. We asked the owner about horses. He pointed over to his huge herd. He singled out the only stallion in at least thirty mares. His horses were all mares which he needed for *airag*.

The average Mongolian family of five drinks 200 litres of fermented mares' milk per week. Fruit and vegetables simply do not appear in the local diet. *Airag* contains six vitamins, including B-complex, nineteen amino acids and many minerals. It is an essential part of the Mongolian diet. Even the Russians recognized the wholesome nature of *airag*, using it in their sanatoria as a cure for tuberculosis, consumption, debility, digestive disorders and nervous illnesses.[1]

Turning off the main road we headed along a dirt track on the crest of a long ridge. A limitless swell of hills floated on the skyline. I could understand why the Mongolians revere Tengri, the god of the heavens; he seemed that much closer. I watched in awe as the evening light played on the green crests which purpled as the colours on the horizon intensified, once pale blue then lavender to fuchsia. Later the sky turned black, the wind picked up, driving dust from the floor of the valley into eddies. The driver could barely see and slowed down to a crawl. We pulled up outside a *ger*. The strong wind whipped dust and grit into our faces as we hurried for shelter. Old hubcaps, designed to weigh down the canvas, were tested by the gusts.

An old man ushered us into the *ger* and assumed his position on a small stool at the head of a low table facing the door, while his wife motioned us to sit us on small stools to his right. She sat on a bed on the right hand side of the *ger* next to her two young grandchildren, who giggled and whispered inquisitively. A young girl in her early teens gave us a shy smile, hurriedly scraping back her hair into a neat bun and covering her working clothes with an elegant turquoise silk *del*, an ankle-length, quilted, loose-fitting jacket. She placed a huge metal cauldron on a cylindrical metal stove, the size of a large waste-paper bin. She tossed a few crusty pieces of cow dung through a small door in the side of the stove, poured a bucket of water into the cauldron and added a few cupfuls of milk. Extracting a handful of tea from a cotton bag, and a small handful of salt, she stirred them into the brew. The tea comes from China, made from the cheapest leaves available, which are wetted and pressed into a solid block and sold in Mongolia by the brick.

Tamir explained our business: we were looking to buy horses. The old man's heavily-lined face briefly lit up when Tamir said that we wanted five horses. However, he recovered himself, his face assuming a suitably inscrutable expression which betrayed only a casual interest in making a transaction. He pulled out a small green silk pouch from the front of his *del* and extracted a jade snuff-bottle. Baatar hurried forward and proffered his, which was carved from yak's bone – an heirloom from his grandfather. The exchange is an art form: Baatar held his out in his right hand, supported under the elbow by the left hand, the old man did the same as they performed a one-handed swap. Holding the bottle in his left hand, he unscrewed the top carefully, scooped a small amount of snuff on to the little spatula attached to the lid and pinched it between the thumb and forefinger of his right hand. Replacing the lid, the swap was reversed. He sniffed the powder and nodded his head in thanks.

After a bowl of tea, we braved the elements. It was cold and the wind was still up. I could see, in the half-light, that we were perched on a bank overlooking a small river, across which several hundred horses were being driven. From the *ger* we could hear the occasional whistle and whoop from the boys as they drove the herd into a tighter pack. After several minutes, they galloped up the steep bank; the younger boy was standing in his stirrups, carrying a huge pole – about ten feet long – on the end of which was a small leather lasso. The two boys set about trying to contain the horses and catch those that were being singled out by the old man. The horses charged around us snorting and trying to avoid the lasso pole.

Each Mongolian family has an average of nine horses, one of which is permanently tethered outside the *ger*. The others run wild with the rest of

the herd and fatten up for the winter. A lassoing horse is specially trained
to recognize the horse that his master is seeking to catch so that the rider
can concentrate all his efforts on lassoing his prey, rather than steering his
mount. Once the horse is caught around the neck, the noose is tightened
and the rider's horse digs its hooves in to stop the other horse's momentum; a bulb at the bottom of the pole stops it from slipping out of the
rider's hands.

Tamir and Baatar tried out the horses, as I hadn't worked up the courage.
The horses met with universal approval and they picked out four geldings
over the age of five. The stud was good; one of the owner's horses had come
eighth in the annual horseracing competition, known as *naadam*. We went
back inside to discuss terms. He wanted $125 per horse. I bargained as was
expected but was secretly pleased to be getting such a good deal.

For the next few days, we set up a temporary campsite twenty kilometres
outside Ulaanbaatar so that we could test the equipment and watch the
horses. It was a good chance for me to make sure that the guides and I
worked well together. Tamir was keen to ensure that we had an impressive send-off; he had persuaded Bayar to organize a brass band and
insisted that we should start our journey in the main piazza, Sukhebaatar
Square.

'Sukhebaatar is like your Nelson,' he explained. 'He is our hero, he saved
us from the Chinese who would have destroyed our culture; he persuaded
the Russians to be our protectors.'

Sukhebaatar, whose name means, 'axe hero,' was a communist print-
worker who played an important part in the liberation of Mongolia after
200 years of Chinese rule. In 1921, he was part of a delegation sent to
Moscow to seek Russian help. He carried a secret appeal to Lenin from the
Kutukhtu, the head of the Buddhist church, hidden in the butt of his whip.
Mongolia turned to the Russians as protectors after the collapse of the
Manchu dynasty in 1911. However, after the Russian Revolution, the
Chinese seized the initiative and embarked on an aggressive policy of sini-
fication, actively encouraging Chinese immigration into Mongolia. The tax
burden became unbearable.

The Russian intervention marked the start of a monumental transformation of Mongolia from a medieval theocracy, in which forty per cent of
the male population were monks known as lamas, into a literate nation in
which an equivalent percentage became factory workers. Mongolia was not
exactly Marx's ideal model; it had no industry, no capitalists and no prole-
tariat. Different class enemies had to be created. The obvious target was the
church. There was good reason to attack the Buddhist church. It was a

decadent, diseased institution sapping the country of all its male labour. Usury, drinking and all-embracing sexual depravity were rampant throughout the lamaseries as was syphilis. Even the head of the Buddhist Church, the seventh Kutukhtu, was a sex-crazed syphilitic.[2]

It took fifteen years before the communists dared to attack the church. When they did so, it was with Soviet troops. The threat from the Japanese provided a good excuse; any enemy could be labelled as a Japanese collaborator. After 1935, the Communists, directed by Stalin, stepped up their efforts and began an extermination campaign against the church, which has been compared with the Reformation in England under Henry VIII. About seven hundred monasteries were destroyed and three per cent of the national population was executed. It was not until 1953 that the Mongolians were collectivized. Mongolian herd numbers plummeted by 7 million – the herdsmen preferring to slaughter their animals rather than hand them over to the State. And so Mongolia was dragged kicking and screaming into the twentieth century.

By coincidence, our departure date was set for 4 July 1999. I went out for a 'last supper' with my parents. Our nerves were stretched to breaking point. We ate pizza washed down with liberal quantities of red wine and vodka. I slept badly; I knew it was the last night for a long time that I would have the comfort and security of four walls and a door to protect me. I had no idea what to expect or what might happen to me. I knew that there was a chance that I wouldn't make it back. I had been having recurring nightmares, in which my assailants slit my tent open with a knife. The voice of reason kept telling me to quit; no one would hold it against me. But my pride would not let me. Besides, I was also excited; I was turning my back on civilization and I had no commitments; my life stretched out ahead of me, limitless as the steppe.

> My father was a beautiful singer
> He serenaded me while he was herding
> I still remember his voice from my childhood
> He had a very deep voice.
>
> My father was a herdsman
> My father was a singer.
>
> My father was a strong man
> He cradled me as we galloped along
> He was a clever man
> He rocked me to sleep with long songs.

My father was a herdsman
My father was a singer.

He never lost the rope on the horse's neck
As he lassoed his catch
He was a famous singer
I love him very much.

Mongolian 'Father Song'

2

ULAANBAATAR – KARAKORUM

I awoke at five. It was drizzling when we arrived in Sukhebaatar Square and there was no sign of the horses or my guides. I sat underneath the statue of Sukhebaatar, seated on his rearing horse, for what seemed an eternity, breathing deeply as I tried to control my butterflies. Finally I heard the sound of an engine. A small van appeared in the square containing Baatar's relatives. Our send-off had begun: Baatar's 70-year-old mother, a petite but formidable woman who had been a journalist in her youth, stepped gracefully out of the car, dismissing the hand Baatar put out to help her. She was dressed in an elegant green *del*, fixed at the waist with a bright blue sash. The material was shot with flowers, embroidered with silver

The final send-off. The brass band in Sukhebataar Square

thread. She was wearing a dun-coloured camel-hair beret and a pair of oversized dark glasses. Bayar finally appeared with a motley brass band, which looked as though they had come straight from an evening in a local night-club. Still dressed in black tie, the players started warming up underneath Sukhebaatar's statue. Puzzled commuters stopped to ask what the celebration was about.

Baatar saddled our 'fill-in' horses, one of which was blind in one eye. The 'real' horses were at the campsite. Tamir led his son around the square on one of the horses. He had splashed out on a camouflage waistcoat, a Don Quixote straw hat, military fatigues and prescription sunglasses. His mother, sporting an electric-blue silk *del*, fastened with a white leather belt, clutched a leather vat of milk to her generous stomach. Baatar was wearing a rusty cotton-padded *del*, which concealed his Levi's. A maroon silk pouch containing his snuff-bottle swung at his side, attached to an apricot silk sash. He held the horses while his mother daubed their foreheads and backs with milk and sprinkled our path ahead. She offered each of us a bowl of milk. Baatar took his, Marlboro in one hand. Just as we mounted our horses, my mother rushed up and placed a blue silk scarf, a *khatagh*, around our necks. The guides were evidently delighted that she had remembered their tradition.

We circled the square three times to the strains of the 'Mongolian Last Post'. The band was in time by the third lap. We posed for photos. By coincidence I could just make out the word 'start' on the cobbles beneath us; I have no idea how it got there, but it was nothing to do with us. Finally we waved goodbye, trotting off around the corner. I clung to the saddle, petrified of falling off. Once we were out of sight, we dismounted and hurried off for a blessing.

The head of the Gandang Monastery, the most important monastery in Mongolia, was waiting for us in a spartan room in a low-rise apartment. Clad in his saffron robes, he was seated on a cushion behind a cloud of incense, wafting up from a low table in front of him. Motioning us forward, he tapped us in turn on the head with his beads and muttered a series of Tibetan prayers. I gave him a small offering of thanks and he presented me with some incense. He wished me luck in a flawless English accent and reassuringly squeezed my shoulder as he gathered his robes before him and left the room.

We moved on to Tamir's home, a large flat in an old block in the centre of town. His father had been deputy head of the Mongolian KGB. We sat down at a table piled high with small pastries, curd, clotted cream and wild strawberry jam, trying not to get sticky fingers on black and white photos, many of which dated back to the 1930s. The pictures were fascinating: Communist military parades, trips to Moscow, youthful grandparents

The 'start'. The author with Baatar and Tamir in Sukhebaatar Square

posing for what must have been some of the first cameras in Mongolia. Tamir's elderly father was still an imposing, fearsome man, despite the debilitating sickness which confined him to his bed in a next-door room.

Finally we came to the moment I had dreaded. My heart fluttered as we drove in silence out to the campsite. I tried not to look at my parents as we dismantled the tents, saddled our horses and loaded the baggage. The guides struggled with the weight of the bags, some of which had to be balanced precariously on the top of our neat, new saddlebags. Bayar produced a bottle of Genghis Khan vodka and we all took a grateful sip.

My mother's mouth began to twitch but she never got as far as tears. As I moved away from my father, he pulled me back and I had to shelter his head on my shoulder as he tried to regain his composure, catching his breath between sobs. My father told me later that he had had a premonition, happily wrong, that he would never see me again. My mother bit her lip and gave me a swift kiss. I climbed on my horse and shook Bayar's hand. I nodded to the guides and we started to ride. After one hundred metres, all the bags fell off one of the horses. The guides got off to re-arrange them and Bayar drove up in his Jeep to help. My father and mother wandered over again. I stayed on my horse, staring awkwardly at the ground. When we were far enough away, I stared back at the white van shrinking as it drove off towards the horizon. The belching smokestacks and enormous squat

*The author on the first day of
her journey*

chimney of Ulaanbaatar's power station remained on the horizon as we
rode over a hill and down into a valley below.

Our immediate target was Karakorum, 378 kilometres west of
Ulaanbaatar. We reckoned that it would take us about a week if we covered
fifty kilometres a day. The ground ahead would be fairly easygoing and
Tamir and Baatar knew the way. Tamir rode ahead and Baatar brought up
the rear. I hummed in my saddle, trying to ease the large lump which was
hurting the back of my throat. I quickly discovered that the Mongolians
love singing and their songs are very moving. One of Baatar's favourites,
which I was to hear throughout the trip, was the 'Mother Song'. Every
Mongolian has dozens of mother songs in his repertoire.

> If people are flowers,
> I was born in the hand of my mother
> I am a wild young rose in the vast steppe.
> I grew in the hand of my mother
> Which is like the earth.
> I cannot promise her eternal happiness

But I will take care of her for the rest of my life.
Her love is as big as the world
My respect for her is as great as the earth.
I will always love my mother
We will be together forever
Like a tree with its roots.

As we rode, Baatar explained that he had had a strange upbringing. His parents already had six children when Baatar was born so he was given to a friend who was unable to have children. While his real mother was a well-travelled, sophisticated journalist, his adoptive mother lived in a *ger* in the countryside. He began his education in a village school and finished it at the Russian school in Ulaanbaatar. As he grew older, he spent more time with his real family and his 'number one mother'. Despite his evident love for his adoptive mother, I got the impression that he felt like the poor relation, cheated out of his real family.

We stopped for a snack at five and Tamir produced a bottle of vodka. The guides had already taken to Worcester Sauce, which we dribbled on bread and processed meat. We camped quite late and had to put up the tents in the dark. I set my tent up at a respectable distance from that of the guides to make sure that they didn't get the wrong idea. I had great difficulty getting my stove to work. A few inquisitive herdsmen from a nearby *ger* came to help, sporting a large hammer. I managed to persuade them to let me finish reading the instructions and found a small safety-pin catch, which had been keeping us from our supper. Unfortunately, the only fuel we could find at the last minute was diesel; the black fumes put me off the gruel and left me breathless. Tamir insisted on cooking next to the tents and took great umbrage at being told to move the stove because it was a fire hazard. It was the last time we bothered with the stove.

That night I wrote my first impressions in my diary:

> I had always thought that the nomads would be in a perpetual state of motion and expected to find a horizon littered with caravans of yaks, camels and horses. Instead, I've seen carpeted green prairie dotted with mushrooming white specks which, on closer inspection, are clusters of felt tents. I expected a barren, harsh, monotonous landscape and have found myriads of streams, marshes speckled with wild flowers and tree-covered mountains.

Later I lay in my sleeping-bag listening out for strange noises, alert to any movements that Tamir or Baatar might make. I didn't feel I could trust them yet. I shifted around, trying to get comfortable in my sleeping-bag while remaining on my small mat, and puffing up my jacket, which I had folded up into a pillow. Faint wafts of cigarette smoke drifted up towards my tent. After a while, the guides stopped whispering. All I could hear was the breeze gently buffeting my tent and occasionally, a thudding sound as the horses shuffled in their hobbles. Conscious of the need to remain on my guard, I fought to stay awake but within a few minutes I had slipped into a deep sleep.

In nomad-land the spaces belong to the tribes, and the Mongol rides over them singing and shouting, free as the air he breathes, tied to no building and confined by no walls of city or of home.

Mildred Cable

3

THE GATHERING STORM

The next day, I tailed behind the other horses. The guides seemed to be able to keep their horses moving at a fast walk; I kept trotting to catch up. I tried to practise my rising trot but the quick gait of my Mongolian pony was unsuited to this and I held on tightly to my saddle to avoid being shaken off.

We spent the morning naming the horses. Despite the obvious appendage between its legs, Tamir was adamant that his should be called Michelle, after his daughter. Baatar's dappled grey pony became 'Harley' after the motorbike he longed to own. Mine, a dun, was christened Lavgagh after the Mongolian world featherweight boxing champion. The feisty, cunning, chestnut baggage horse, which Tamir was leading, earned the name Nazarbaev, after the president of Kazakhstan. Baatar's baggage horse was yet to be named. Tamir decided that it should be named after the new Wimbledon champion. I hoped that we would be able to call him Henman but we ended up having to call him Peter (after Sampras).

Throughout the day, we stayed in the same valley flanked by treeless hills, which rose to about a thousand metres. Occasional clouds drifted over the changing steppe, mottling it with patches of shadow. The valley must have been five or ten kilometres across, but it was impossible to train the eye to distance on the steppe. *Gers*, little mushrooms in the distance, never seemed to get any closer and it seemed to take hours to reach them. The terrain was tricky for the horses; they stumbled over clumps of tundra grasses and I steered them carefully around minefields of dozens of marmot burrows. Occasionally we came across a femur sticking out of one the holes, a stern reminder of what could happen if we didn't watch where we were going.

When the ground became even, I fell in with Tamir who was looking wistful. I asked him what he was thinking about.

'My son, I miss him. I see him so little now that I have split up from my girlfriend, his mother. She looks after him and I only see him in the holidays.'

'What about Michelle?'

Tea in a ger

'Her mother was my wife. She left me and took our daughter with her; I haven't seen them since.'

As he became more morose, I tried to change the conversation.

'Your son's name is Temujin. How did you chose the name?'

'We consulted the chief lama from the Gandang Monastery. He chose the name.'

'Are Mongolian children christened like they are in England?'

'Yes, it is similar. We have a "first washing" ceremony when the child is one month old. We invite all our family to the celebration. Once we have chosen a name, we whisper it into our child's ear before telling anyone else.'

'Wasn't Genghis Khan called Temujin?'

'Yes,' he said proudly. 'Temujin means "Man of Iron".' He smiled. 'It is a lucky name for my son. The Russians and the Europeans do not like Genghis Khan. He conquered their countries. But for us, he was a hero. Mongolia was a great nation with a huge empire; only you British had a bigger empire.'

I had read up on Genghis Khan and knew that he was born near the inter-section of the Onon and Balj rivers in 1167, the year of the wild boar, something we have in common. According to Mongolian legend, his mother was impregnated by a moonbeam. At birth, he was clutching a blood clot the size of a knucklebone, an auspicious sign which earned him the name Temujin. It is appropriate that he should share his name, at least in translation, with Attila and Tamerlane. When Temujin was eight, his father, a minor clan leader, was poisoned in a tribal feud with the Tatars. Not wishing to be led by a minor, his tribe, the Bjorjin, abandoned him.[3]

Temujin, still heir to his father's tribe, went on the run. Inured to hardship, he lived off whatever his bow landed him. Privation may have caused his ruthless streak; he murdered his half-brother over a few birds they had shot. As he grew older, he cultivated a following. Allying himself with his father's friend, the chief of the Kereyids, and with Chinese help, he conquered the Tatars, the leading tribe, and avenged his father's death. Tribal alliances were always shifting and were often short-lived. Temujin was to fight his blood brother, Jamuqa and his father's friend and former ally, the Kereyid chief, before he conquered the steppe.

Tamir was delighted to give me the full picture.

'He united those he conquered into a meaningful force and invested himself with the title of Genghis Khan or "oceanic ruler". Genghis Khan organized his army in such a way that it cut across traditional clan loyalties. Those he conquered were split into different regiments, organized on a decimal basis. The tradition of absolute clan loyalty in Mongolia did not apply in peace-time. In order to prevent his newly-acquired army from simply disintegrating in the steppe, it was necessary to create a perpetual state of war. A sharp fall in the average annual temperature of Mongolia and the subsequent deterioration in the quality of grazing land may have made the search for pasture a motive for conquest.

'Genghis Khan's army was a formidable fighting machine,' Tamir went on. 'His men were unrivalled as mounted archers. The Mongolian herdsman, riveted to his steed from birth, would have been given his first bow when he was four. By the time he was an adolescent he would be firing arrows, from a range of 200 metres, at his quarry at a full gallop from any position in the saddle. Genghis Khan did not invent a new form of warfare but he honed the natural fighting skills of his men. The main peacetime pursuits were huge hunts, known as *gorugen*. Pursuing gazelles, wild boar and kulan (wild donkey), a beat would often be organized over thousands of kilometres but with a huge degree of precision. The animals were driven into an area about fifteen square kilometres, hemmed in by felts. Once Genghis Khan gave the order, a massive cull would start which could last several days. Each soldier was restricted to one arrow and if any archer missed, he would never live it down. Encirclement was one of the Mongols' favourite battle tactics.

'Each horseman in the army, about 129,000-strong, would have at least a couple of spare horses and was armed with two bows, three quivers, a sabre, an axe and a hooked lance to pull the enemy off his horse. Their armour was made of leather, toughened with animal urine and lined with silk, which made it easier to extract enemy arrows. The armour was noticeably thinner on the back, according to some, to discourage flight. The mounted archers were able to fire arrows facing forward or backwards standing in the saddle, their disk-shaped stirrups providing a platform for stability. They often travelled for ten days without a hot meal, covering one hundred kilometres per day and surviving on dried curd; each man was rationed to five kilos. Occasionally, a soldier would make a small incision in the jugular of his mount and drink its blood. Herds to sustain the troops and camels pulling carts, mangonels, catapults and felt tents would follow the riders. The Mongols were used to moving at least four times a year with their herds; supply-line drill was in their blood.[4]

'The first campaign outside Mongolia was against the Tangut kingdom, near modern Tibet. The Mongols constructed a massive dam and attempted to inundate the city but succeeded in flooding their own camp. Finally Genghis Khan sent a message to the Tangut leader asking for a peace tribute of 1,000 cats and 1,000 swallows. These poor animals were then set alight. They fled home, spreading the fire wherever they went. Once again, Genghis Khan claimed victory and the Tangut kingdom was absorbed into his growing empire.'[5]

When it came to relating the history of the defeat of the Chinese, Tamir became highly animated and talked excitedly – the Mongolians still hold a strong dislike for the Chinese.

'It took twenty-three years to defeat the Chin dynasty. While the Mongols had no problem overpowering the Chinese in the open, they had to learn about siege warfare. Recruiting engineers from China and Persia, they acquired an arsenal of incendiary devices, fireworks, mangonels and catapults. Chung-tu (near modern Peking) was finally torched with incendiary arrows. According to a witness, the streets were greasy with human fat. Genghis Khan considered annihilating the conquered Chinese and turning their land over to grazing. His adviser, Yeh-lu Ch'u-ts'ai, suggested instead that he tax the peasants and use the revenue to finance his campaigns. Despite the narrow escape, censuses of the Chinese population reveal that they did not get off lightly. The population fell from 100 million during the Sung dynasty to 70 million by 1290.'[6]

As he talked, Tamir insisted that it is unfair to mention only the bloodthirsty characteristics of Mongolia's hero.

'In 1206, Genghis Khan instituted some basic laws, including a 'blue book' which evolved into a case law system. Mongols were encouraged to be hospitable in peacetime but in war they had to become 'like a hungry falcon'.[7] Drinking was only allowed three times per month. Adultery (within the clan) and paedophilia were punished. A man caught over-eating would be dragged through a hole in the *ger* and killed. Urinating on or stepping over a fire was punishable by death. It was also a serious crime to defile a river or a spring. Thieves, spies, deserters and those who had been declared bankrupt more than three times were given the death penalty. A taxation system was introduced to fund campaigns and a postal system to speed up communications. The yam system ensured that every twenty miles there was a *darogha* (the Russian word for road) or post where there would be fresh horses and fodder. Those on government business were armed with a special seal ensuring them safe passage and free horses. In China alone, there were reckoned to be at least 50,000 yam-system horses. Normal traffic would travel about twenty-five miles a day but urgent missives could go 200 miles a day and a single rider might go as much as 1,000 miles, jumping from horse to horse without stopping.

Despite his search for the elixir of life, I had read that Genghis Khan eventually succumbed. His death, by some accounts, was far from heroic. A victim of lust, he is reputed to have stolen the beautiful, virginal daughter of a Tangut king as part of his booty. She was not compliant and some say she castrated him with her teeth or possibly something sharper. The blood from his wounds ran white as milk and within three days he was dead.

Tamir was horrified at this version; he insisted that he had died a warrior's death.

'A solemn procession escorted his body back to Mongolia,' Tamir said wistfully. 'It has never been found. Such was the desire for secrecy of the burial area of the great khans that all who witnessed his body in transit were slaughtered, to serve the master in another world. His tomb is supposed to contain the bodies of forty moon-faced virgins and forty of his finest horses. The sacred ground was trampled by thousands of hooves, to make detection impossible.'

Nobody knows where he is buried. Tamir reckoned that Genghis Khan's burial chamber was hidden near his birthplace somewhere in Bayan Ovoo, a complex network of valleys, covered by Taiga forest, near the Siberian border. Many groups of archaeologists have searched in the area for his tomb. Tamir hoped they would never find it.

In fact many nations are fighting over the legacy of Genghis Khan. The Chinese Communist Party recognizes him as the man who built the Chinese nation, incorporating Tibet and Mongolia into the mainland. They say that Genghis Khan's body never left China and assert that his tomb is in Xinjiang, possibly in the Tien Shan mountains. The Chinese will claim that, when Genghis Khan died, the Mongols were not using embalming techniques. Genghis Khan died in August; if it had not been embalmed, the stench from the body would have been unbearable within a matter of days. A journey back to his birthplace would have taken two or three weeks. The mausoleum in China does not contain the remains of Genghis Khan; its most important relics are the tufts of camel hair which they believe were held over Genghis Khan's lips as he died, capturing his eternal spirit. In the 1930s the Chinese had jealously to guard the camel hairs from the Japanese who would have liked to prove their claim to his ancestry. In the last decade the Japanese have led many high-tech expeditions to Mongolia to find the body. A Turkish expedition has also been looking for the Khan's tomb in the Orkhon River valley, near Karakorum, and recently uncovered what they believe to be the tomb of Bilge Kagan, an eighth-century Mongolian ruler who was later overthrown by the Uighurs. If the tomb of Genghis Khan is ever discovered, the Mongolians will have to make a difficult decision as to whether to risk destroying the spirit of their most revered ruler in the interests of much-needed hard currency and tourism.

'Tourism may bring Mongolia riches, which we need, but we mustn't sell our culture,' Tamir warned. 'We may only have memories of Mongolia's former greatness, but at least we can still keep our pride. We mustn't allow foreigners to excavate his tomb. Besides, it may be cursed. We call Genghis Khan's tomb, Ikh Khoring, or the "Great Taboo". We believe that when you disturb a man's body after it has been laid to rest, you kill his soul. It is said that birds flying over his standard drop dead.'

The light was fading and we fell silent, picking our way around a ravine in the dark, trying to find the *ger* of the man from whom we had bought the horses. I was thrown three times; my horse shied at the slightest excuse. At midnight, we were still stumbling around. I lost my temper, shouting at Tamir for leading us on a dangerous wild-goose chase in the dark. I wanted to stop; he wanted to go on. Luckily we met a young boy who led us to the *ger*. I had difficulty getting off my horse, sliding inelegantly over the side holding on to the saddle for support. The pain in my legs was excruciating and for a few minutes I couldn't stand up. I angrily brushed tears away as I hobbled off. Our host gave me a bed; I unrolled my sleeping-bag, curled up and passed out.

I awoke to the giggling of a couple of young children. Threaded into the spokes, wooden struts supporting the roof above my bed, were school satchels, pencils, and a home-made cotton bag for toothbrushes, which looked as though they had been used for polishing. The children followed me down to the river, still giggling and staring as I washed my face and brushed my teeth.

I decided to amuse them with a spot of fishing. I hadn't fished since I was a teenager, tagging along behind my brother whenever he went trout fishing. My first cast caught a thistle several metres from my feet. The second hit the opposite bank and snagged. I waded across the river and managed to unsnag my spinner, only to find that I was stuck in thick mud. The only method of escape was to step out of my galoshes and tug them out by hand; soon I was covered in sludge. Later, the young boy tried on my muddy galoshes over his Wellingtons and stumbled around, clasping them over the tops of his thighs and imitating my flailing performance earlier, much to the amusement of his sister, who was making a daisy chain. As I watched, I felt something large dive into the side of my jumper. I recoiled in horror, only to find that I had snagged myself. I had one 'bite' and gave up.

After a late lunch of traditional Mongolian noodle soup, we rode until early evening when we felt the first drops of rain. We reckoned that we were about a hundred kilometres from Ulaanbaatar. The leaden sky looked

My fishing companions

ominous and a strong wind made the horses skittish. We spotted spirals
of smoke puffing from the chimneys of a cluster of *gers* and rode towards
them. As we approached, several dogs ran towards us barking furiously
and looking ready to tear us apart. A stocky young man wearing a leather
trilby and a long brown *del* secured with a mandarin sash called off the
dogs. On one side of the tents, a cart with wooden wheels lay on its traces,
on the other stood a battered Russian Jeep. A couple of toddlers ran
round the side of the *ger*. When they saw us they abandoned a rusty metal
hubcap, which they had been chasing with a bent metal rod, and ran
inside the tent.

The stocky young man approached Tamir's horse. Tamir leaned out of
the saddle and shook his hand. Erdene, as he later introduced himself,
insisted that we stay and ordered his younger brother to unload the horses
and hobble them. The guides sat outside on their haunches smoking; the
man's wife, who was wearing a *Titanic* T-shirt underneath a blue silk *del*,
invited me into the family *ger*. She was a pretty woman, her thick black hair
tied back to reveal high, flattened cheekbones and a ruddy complexion. She
was boiling tea on a simple wood-burning stove. Shafts of sunlight poured
through the hole in the roof, catching the smoky haze escaping from the
fire. Smiling bashfully she whispered something and motioned me to sit on
a small stool, beside a low table facing the door. The warmth of their
welcome astonished me and for the first time I felt relaxed and sure that I
had made the right decision to undertake the journey.

While the tea boiled, Erdene leaned over a large blue vat on the left-hand
side of the door, churned it a few times and ladled out a bowl, which he
offered to me using his left hand to support his right arm at the elbow. It
was fermented mares' milk. I sipped it gingerly, prepared for the worst.

'Mongolian white beer,' Tamir suggested. It was slightly beery but also a
bit cheesy.

'Perhaps a cross between feta and beer?' A few flies floated on the top,
which our host blew to the side of his bowl. I followed suit.

His wife disappeared, reappearing an hour later with a huge metal washing basin full of lamb. It smelled enticing, until I saw it: every innard
imaginable stared up at me from the bowl. Having spent hours in childhood having tantrums over lumps of fat and pieces of gristle, I didn't think
I could eat it. The guides fell upon the bowl with their penknives, sucking
and chewing as though they hadn't seen food for weeks. Tamir looked up
from his food and gave me a look which said 'what are you waiting for?'

'I can't eat fat, it makes me sick,' I half-mimed, half-whispered, check-
ing our hosts couldn't see me.

'Try the heart,' he advised. 'It tastes like meat.'

I cautiously nibbled on a little heart, liver and kidneys. I couldn't manage the stomach, the lungs, or the intestine oozing congealed blood.

As we ate, our hosts talked animatedly to Tamir about our journey. I didn't understand any of their conversation except that when he said we were planning to ride to Bayan Olgii, our host's father looked astonished.

'What did he say?'

'He asks why a rich lady like you is travelling in a poor country like Mongolia when you have so many comforts at home.'

'Tell him I want to learn about the Mongolian people and their traditions.'

'Why don't you travel in a Jeep? It is much more comfortable.'

'Because you can see more on horseback. In a Jeep, you go too fast and you miss opportunities like this to stay with Mongol families.'

A family on the move

Nodding pensively, he drew hard on his pipe and said, 'It is good to see the world. In Mongolia we have an expression – a fool who has seen much is better than a wise man who sits and wears holes in the mattress.' Baatar had his own explanation and rolled up his sleeve.

'Look!' He pointed to a large birthmark on his forearm.

'It looks like the map of Mongolia. It is fate; this journey was printed on my arm from birth.'

After supper our host Erdene's wife motioned me to the bed at the top of the *ger*. Next to the bed was a large bright orange chest, decorated with Chinese dragon motifs in reds, greens, blues and black. A picture of the Dalai Lama was attached to the side of a mirror above the chest. On the dresser was a *dorje*, a small brass ornament, slightly larger than a fist, composed of two adjoining sceptres, and a brass bell with a sceptred handle. Beside them stood some china horses. The *dorje*, which means 'indestructible' in Tibetan, symbolizes the male aspects of fitness and action, the bell the feminine qualities of wisdom or supreme knowledge. The union of the two is said to lead to ultimate enlightenment.

Next to the ornaments was a large plastic frame containing school photos, a picture of Erdene and his wife; two shy newly-weds holding hands in Sukhebaatar Square, his photos from military service and some well-thumbed pictures of deceased relatives. The inside walls of the *ger* were covered in brightly coloured silk and the toothbrushes sat in a smart yellow plastic container over a portable sink. A jagged saw was threaded into the wooden spokes above the door to ward off evil spirits.

We set off the next morning under a sweltering sun. At lunch, we stopped beside a river for a swim. While I battled the currents, Baatar lay in the shallows in his blue Y-fronts and Tamir stayed in the shade of the trees. Further downstream, a large herd of horses stood cooling off in the water.

After lunch, I lay under a tree reading about Mongolian etymology. Mongolian belongs to the Altay-Uralic language group, which includes Turkish, Korean, Japanese, Finnish and Hungarian. However, Central Asia was also a melting pot of shifting populations outside the Altay-Uralic group, a cradle for many of the principal language groups. Some time before the third millennium BC, a large area with indefinite borders from the Carpathians, north of the Black Sea, to Eastern Afghanistan contained the language groups Uralic, Altayic, Dravidian and Indo-European. Neighbouring Uralic nomads brushed shoulders with Altayic nomads; Indo-European with Dravidian. Likewise, Uralic had more similarities with Indo-European and Altayic with Dravidian. In the third millennium BC, huge migrations, probably caused by population pressures and changes in climate, forced the Indo-Europeans out in all directions, driving a wedge between the Uralians who moved north and the Altayans who went east to Mongolia. The Dravidians migrated southeast, into India. [8]

The Mongolians gave the English the word horde from the Mongolian *ordu*, meaning 'camp'. In India, the *ordu* became the military language, Urdu. The Russians adopted *darogha* from the Mongolian for 'staging post'. The Indians took *bahadur* from the Mongolian *baatar*, meaning 'hero'. The Hungarians have taken *alma* from the Turkish meaning 'apple'; the Mongolian word is *alimaa*. The Finnish word for 'sister-in-law', *ķaly*, is very similar to the Uighur, *ķalin*, meaning 'bride' or 'daughter-in-law'. Given how keenly the Russians feel the humiliation of Mongolian domination, it is surprising that words like *ķremlin*, which comes from the Mongolian word for 'castle', and Moscow, the Mongolian for 'meander', should have been kept for posterity!

I grew weary of etymology and turned to names. Mongolian names are exquisite, funny, lucky, superstitious and in some cases, downright rude. A name may be an everyday object or the first thing the mother sees after giving birth: such as Cholon, 'stone'; Sukhe, 'axe'; Khongordzol, meaning 'thistle', or Tolui, 'mirror'; Qadan, 'cliff', or Checheg, 'flower'. A name can be a blessing: Monke, 'eternal'; Cheren, 'long life'; Delger, 'abundance'; Dash, 'good luck'. Some children are given wonderful names like Shurentsetseg, 'coral flower'; Mugentuya, 'silver ray'; or Bolorerdene, 'crystal treasure', while others are simply numbers such as Jirghadai, 'sixth child', or Nayan, for one fathered by an 80-year-old! Far and away the most interesting names are the rude ones, designed to fool the spirits: Muunokhoi, 'vicious dog'; Khasar, 'terrible dog'; Bujir, 'filthy'; Khoonbish, 'not a human being'; Khenbish, 'nobody'; Enebish, 'not this one'; Terbish, 'not that one', or Nergui, which means, 'no name'. I was christened Tonga, short for Tongaluck, which means 'clear, straightforward and pure'. While the former is evidently an appropriate tag, I have to confess that the name is a translation from the French for Claire!

The following day, in the late afternoon, we climbed a small pass, surrounded by craggy rockfaces. The horses picked their way over rough ground covered in scrub, long thick grass and clusters of bright alpine flowers: edelweiss, gentians, saxifrage and wild jasmine. As the horses trampled the grass underfoot, wafts of artemisia, which the Mongolians use to make perfume, rose from the ground. Baatar reached down from his saddle and presented me with a bright pink flower, which looked like a foxglove. I blushed as I realized that far from being an amorous gesture, he wanted to show me how many bees could settle on one stalk. I dropped it in a hurry and he trotted off, chuckling at my reaction.

At about seven, the wind picked up and it started to rain hard. We donned our Russian capes, which we tucked in under our legs so that we wouldn't scare the horses. The capes reached our ankles and kept the worst of the rain off. My horse didn't like the driving rain and kept dancing around. From our vantage-point near the top of the mountain, we could see a storm approaching: lightning flares illuminated the tops of the nearby mountains and electrical storms flashed in several other distant valleys.

Soon there was almost no gap between the lightning and claps of thunder, which kept sending my horse off into a nervous trot. There was no cover and the storm was directly over us. Shouting to be heard over the wind, we agreed that it was best to continue down the mountain rather than camp, exposed on the hill. We hurried on; the wind kept whipping my cape up around my ankles, causing my horse to shy. I held on and gradually we lost height and left the worst of the storm behind. At dusk we spotted a couple of *gers* in the distance. It took several hours to reach them and by the time we got there, it was dark. After a bowl of hot milk we set up our tents, as there were at least a dozen bodies sprawled on the floor of the *ger*.

In the morning, a couple of mischievous children with runny noses tapped the side of my tent and invited me to breakfast. The small table was piled high with delicious fried pastries on to which we spooned home-made clotted cream, known as *urum* and surprisingly good rancid butter. We washed it down with fresh creamy yaks' yoghurt, which was delicious.

We continued on through a wide valley, five or six kilometres across. The chameleon steppe kept changing its hues under the cover of passing clouds. The colours were never uniform but mottled, blotched and striped: bleached green, lime green, silvery-green, iridescent green. Over-grazed tops of hills, grooved with deep fissures, cut by fresh springs, were a kaleidoscope of khaki, dun, tawny, orange, dusty-pink and clay. Tiny birds flirted with our horses, darting out from under their hoofs; chipmunks scurried for cover into their burrows and large, winged crickets purred and looped around us like miniature Tiger Moths. Several hundred feet up, huge kites

A random collection of old Mongolian tanks in the steppe

glided lazily on the up-draughts. The sky cast its own colours over hilltops on the horizon: blue, lilac and lavender. Patches of firs, navy in the distance, were restored to their rightful colours as we approached them.

After covering much ground, we stopped for lunch in a dust bowl over-looking a wide river. The area around the *ger* was dark with sheep and goat droppings. The young men of the family demonstrated their prowess chasing several hundred sheep and goats into a pen with a lasso pole. Riders and goats stirred up so much dust that I could barely see. A bashful young girl, with thick black hair and pink chapped cheeks, wearing a green silk *del*, was kneeling in a corner making lunch. She poured flour into a bowl, added a little water, a pinch of salt and kneaded it into small balls which she rolled out like very thin pizza bases and draped on a cloth over the end of a bed. While the dough was drying, she picked off a few pieces of dried meat, which were dangling on a line threaded through the spokes of the *ger*. After hammering these for several minutes in a soften-ing process, she chopped the meat into small pieces and tipped them into a bowl of boiling water. After about twenty minutes, she cut the pastry into thin strips and added them to the boiling meat. I would love to be able to say it was good, such was the generosity with which it was provided. The meat, despite the pounding, took ages to chew, so I gave up and swallowed it whole. I managed to pass the gristle to Baatar when our hostess wasn't looking. The soup tasted like washing-up water and was full of grit which had blown in from outside.

I gave some colourful velvet hair bands to the little daughter and found out, much to my embarrassment, that the toddler, with its hair in purple ribbons, was actually her son. Before the age of five, Mongolian herders do not cut their children's hair. Hair cutting is an important nomadic tradition which is performed when the child has survived its infancy. The hair-cutting ceremony is an important family occasion which is celebrated with a big feast to which all of the family are invited. Tamir explained that the young infant's hair would be cut in the autumn when the family had finished making their preparations for the winter. Her husband beamed when I presented him with a farewell gift: a Swiss army knife. I was rather surprised when he handed me a hundred Tugrig note in return. Baatar explained that it is bad luck to receive a knife as a gift and you must always pay a token sum towards it. They wished us well on our journey and his wife scooped handfuls of curd into our hands while he obligingly pointed us in the direction of a path which wound up the side of a hill behind the *ger*.

Half an hour later, the track we were following petered out. I checked my compass and pointed in the direction we needed to be going. Tamir ignored me and rode off in the opposite direction. I tried to explain, riding after him and pointing at my compass.

'Are you sure we are going in the right direction. It looks like we are heading back to Ulaanbaatar.'

'I see, I see,' he kept saying, his face set in an unbreakable expression, riding on as if he hadn't heard me. We trotted up behind him and tried again to persuade him. But it was useless; as far as Tamir was concerned, there was to be no discussion.

'Your compass is wrong.' He quickened his pace, leaving Bataar and me behind. Baatar examined my compass and together we eventually persuaded Tamir to change course.

We continued up a small track past a couple of grazing camels. Tamir wasn't talking to me and I rode on my own, pretending to enjoy the sunset. We were still lost by nightfall and I began to wonder whether Tamir had indeed been right. My map was useless, the scale was about one centimetre to ten kilometres and all the hills looked the same on the contours. We divided up a stale loaf and the last of a smelly sausage. I retired to my tent, and wrote my diary to the sound of clinking as Baatar and Tamir hammered in the tethering posts.

Throughout the following morning we failed to get our bearings and wandered up and down the hills, tiring the horses unnecessarily. The one bright spot was that we sighted two Marco Polo sheep, known in Mongolia as *arghali*. They were jumping with agility from rock to rock, their heads steady despite enormous horns, which can weigh over twenty kilos, curled around the sides. Apparently, the horns can inflict severe damage in their sexual jousting matches. They have evolved with extra strong skulls to survive the head butting. While it is the Venetian explorer who claims credit for the name of the species, it was the Flemish Franciscan monk Friar William of Rubruck – who was renouned for his detailed descriptions of the court at Karakorum – who described them in detail after a journey he made twenty years earlier.

By midday, we still hadn't seen any *gers*; our horses hadn't been watered in over twenty-four hours. The heat was draining. I was hungry and worried and Baatar was grouchy; he had run out of cigarettes. I suggested we ride down into the next bowl, where several valleys intersected, in the hope that there might be a stream. As we led our horses down the steep slope, we spotted tiny black specks in the distance and drawing closer, we could see yaks grazing near a group of *gers* below. I felt we were returning to civilization.

Relieved, we hurried in the direction of the *gers* and stopped outside a small wooden hut. It was bustling with activity: two young boys, in vivid silk shirts, matching trousers and peaked coronets, were getting ready for the horse race in the local *naadam* festival, which was starting the next day. Normally, the race takes place over a thirty-kilometre stretch of steppe. There are no special breeds and the riders are light enough not to tire their horses and strong enough not to fall off. The majority of the jockeys are children below the age of twelve and some are as young as four or five. The boys' older brother was shaving in front of half a mirror with the communal razor. A mousy young man with long Turkic features and sea-green eyes, he scraped at a few bits of fluff on his top lip, when he saw that I was looking.

Not one to be left out, the grandfather, a burly man, who would have been tall (for a Mongolian) were it not for a stoop, dug around in a battered leather suitcase which was stacked in a corner of the room. He flourished a worn photo of a handsome, muscular man, wearing skimpy blue and red embroidered briefs and a waistcoat and holding aloft a wide, leather belt with an enormous brass buckle. He beamed, pointing at the photo and beating his chest as he explained that in his youth he had been local wrestling champion for three years in a row. For a Mongolian man, to be wrestling champion is the ultimate accolade. I watched the guides' reactions change towards him. Previously an old man to be respected, he was now a hero to revere.

I drank bowlful after bowlful of *airag*, an incredibly refreshing drink after hours in the saddle. My eyes began to droop. A leathery old lady plumped up some pillows and I lay watching her cutting up a few pieces of fresh meat and a few precious shallots. I awoke to a steaming bowl of noodles. The fresh meat made such a difference.

After lunch, the grandfather sped off on a shiny Yamaha, the two young boys clinging on behind him. Their horses had already gone ahead. We followed his motorcycle tracks under a brilliant sun, which was soon blotted out by thunderous clouds, casting dark shadows over the steppe. After a heavy shower, shafts of golden light broke through the storm clouds, casting bright pools over the prairie.

At sundown, we met up with our host and his two young nieces, who were camped on a hill overlooking Erdinsen, the village where the *naadam* was to be held. Anxious to return their generous hospitality, I sent Tamir off on the motorbike to buy 'supplies'. He returned with five litres of vodka, a cake of soap, and a bar of chocolate. The grandfather fished out a lump of congealed lamb fat from the front of his *del*, which we washed down with the vodka. I set up my tent, at a reasonable distance from the party. The inquisitive children amused themselves enormously, crawling in and out of

alliance between the church and state but this concept was never refined to a great degree. The Buddhist Church was favoured but not very strongly and the presiding religion in Mongolia remained Shamanism or animism.

Under Altan Khan (1507–82), Buddhism in Mongolia finally took off. The Khan invited the third lama from the Tibetan yellow sect into Mongolia, taking precedence over the hitherto dominant red sect. Altan Khan was recognized as an incarnation of Khubilai Khan and he in turn recognized the Lama as the incarnation of Phagspa, Khubilai Khan's head lama. The Buddhist Church now became a potent force. Shamans were outlawed, their properties and livestock confiscated. Monasteries swallowed manpower, land and flocks, creating a class of ecclesiastical serfs. Ordinary Mongolians clung to Buddhist or Bon elements from Tibet. The amulets, rosaries and pre-mystical trances and spells of the Buddhist monks were easy for a formerly Shaman populace to understand.

Abdai Khan (1554–88), who ruled Outer Mongolia in the same period, followed Altan Khan's example. Although unable to persuade the yellow sect to recognize him, he established Erdene Juu, the jewel monastery, on the rubble of Ogedei's city. Chinese architectural motifs fused with Tibetan and Newari carving. In its heyday, it was home to ten thousand monks. Now the visitor to Erdene Juu must resort to a fair amount of imagination.

Erdene Juu, Altan Khan's monastery built on the rubble of Ogedei's famous city, Karakorum

Surrounded by walls made of 108 interlinking stuppas, the monastery is a sad reflection of its former glory. First ransacked by the Chinese and later by Stalin's cronies, who breached the walls with high explosives, only three of its one hundred temples have been left standing. Clay tiles, which once graced the roofs of the monasteries, litter the ground. A joint German-Japanese team of archaeologists is digging within the walls in the hope of discovering more about the Khan's ancient city. One of their most important discoveries to date is an underground heating system. In the centre of the walls they have also found a depression, which might once have been a pool in front of Altan Khan's *ger*. The team has also uncovered two copper plates, thought to date back to Genghis Khan's time and many Persian, Chinese and bronze coins.

I returned to my guides who met me at their *ger* doorway in their underpants, reeking of booze. In my absence they'd run up a $70 bar bill in a local hostelry; an incredible feat in a country where vodka is a dollar a bottle. They expected me to pay; I wasn't pleased as I had already given them a special holiday bonus which they had drunk. While Baatar was apologetic, Tamir was unrepentant. The next day, Tamir produced another tab.

'We can't go tomorrow,' he slurred mutinously, 'one of the horses is very sick.' I inspected the horses and found that Baatar's horse, Harley, had a sore on his back. I tried my best to clean it with disinfectant and treated it with a strong antibiotic cream.

I decided to ride Harley as my saddle would not rub the infected area. We left Karakorum and rode through the Orkhon valley, which is at least 25 kilometres across. We headed towards Tsetserleg, 120 kilometres north-west of Karakorum. Baatar said that he had relatives there and that we would be able to swap Harley for another horse. Harley's sore hadn't affected his gait and he tugged eagerly on the reins. Tall trees defined the path of the river, which joins the Selenge, the largest river in Mongolia, emptying into Lake Baikal, on its way to the Arctic Ocean. Groups of *gers*, white pincushions from afar, speckled the valley at intervals of several hundred metres. Outside each *ger* stood a simple wooden sheep pen and a tethering line, secured by two thick wooden posts, for the family horses. Every so often we passed a dark brown circle on the ground surrounded by sheep droppings, the only evidence of a family that had since moved on. As evening drew in, we found ourselves in a small valley dotted with pools of water. Graceful demoiselle cranes paddled beside a molten reflection of the evening sky. A couple of young boys were rounding up a flock of cashmere goats.

Escaping from a storm. This kind man offered us tea and shelter

Baatar was flirting and singing love songs. He insisted that the words weren't insulting but I had to wait until Tamir had stopped sulking to get a translation. While the words clearly weren't designed for me, they were nevertheless very pretty.

> You have a soft character
> Like spring water.
> You have a curved eyebrow
> Like a swallow's wing.
> You were born
> To attract me
> You add to the beauty
> Of the Mongolian race.

The following morning, the weather turned and we were forced to seek refuge from the wind and rain in a weather-beaten *ger*. Various children were bustling around lowering the sides of the *ger*, which had been raised to let in the breeze. The wife drew in the chimney, a long stove pipe which protruded through a hole in the roof, and laid it on the floor, pulling a small square of material over the hole in the roof. The tent heaved and flapped but I was soon oblivious to everything around me, curled up underneath one of the beds.

After the storm cleared, I inspected Harley's sore. It was writhing with maggots and stank of rotting flesh. No one seemed able to suggest any local remedies. The only advice I was given was to douse the wound with petrol. That evening, we managed to buy a bottle of vodka, which I used to clean the wound. By torchlight, I picked out at several dozen wriggling maggots with a pair of tweezers. I have since found out that this was completely the wrong thing to do: the maggots clean the wound and prevent the onset of gangrene.

At daybreak, I sent Baatar off on the back of a motorbike, in search of a vet. He returned in the evening with a man in a flat black leather cap and checked shirt undone to the waist. I had hoped it was the vet but he turned out to be a drinking partner. Baatar produced a few vials of penicillin, one of which we injected into Harley's neck, and strange brown powder wrapped in newspaper, which we sprinkled on the sore.

Baatar and his carouser were armed with several bottles of vodka and I wondered if the medicine was bought with the change from the booze. Like bees to honey, all the likely lads from surrounding *gers* turned up to join in the drinking games. They sat in a small circle, one knee up in the chest, the other on the ground, long reins casually draped over one arm. Baatar and another young man were soon locked in the 'fingers game'. The two men chanted a song and while singing, each extended his right hand into the

Mr Sleaze and likely lads

middle, varying the number of fingers put forth. Tamir explained that each player must add up the combined fingers and shout it out without losing track of the song. The first to shout out the answer wins the round; the game continues until someone has won five times. Mongolians pride themselves on their ability at this game and I can see why. It was conducted at a vigorous pace, which left my head swimming. Later in the evening they played a Mongolian equivalent of 'stone, paper, scissors', involving much chanting and copious drinking forfeits.

We decided to rest for a few days while we waited for the antibiotics to take effect on Harley. Baatar's drinking partner invited us for lunch. His *ger* stood in a wide bowl beside a sea of wheat, ploughed in what seemed to be alternate light and dark green stripes. Lush green hills rolled up behind the *ger*. Small patches of firs, which almost exclusively cover the northern slopes in Mongolia, broke the monotony of distant hills. A timid woman, whose sleepy expression made me feel that she had just emerged from hibernation, greeted us at the doorway in a shabby dark-grey T-shirt and leggings, which had seen better days. Two baby goats bleated from somewhere underneath one of the beds. A cheery young girl in a light green towelling-dress and red Alice-band swayed bashfully from side to side, holding on to the bed rail. Baatar smacked his lips, 'Arkhangai is my home. We have the best *airag* in Mongolia.'

Baatar and our host announced that they were off in search of marmot. Slinging a couple of .22 rifles over their shoulders, they hopped on to a motorbike and disappeared off into the distance. While they were gone, we had a wonderful afternoon: with her husband absent, the shy wife, Checheg, came out of her shell. Language was no barrier; we had an impromptu gymnastics session practising cartwheels, forward rolls and handstands against the *ger* wall. Egged on by the children, the baby goat kept trying to steal things from my bag and lifting the lid off the teapot. Prompted by Checheg, the little girl performed ballads, nervously shifting her weight from one foot to the other in time with the music, an arm around her bemused younger brother who tickled her in revenge. Despite a few pregnant, forgetful pauses, she sang like a cherub. Her younger brother, determined not to let his sister steal the show, showed his prowess riding a baby yak bareback without a bridle, his hands and feet flapping nonchalantly at his sides.

Several hours later the men returned, three plump marmots dangling from the side of the motorbike. They gutted one on the grassy floor of the kitchen tent. Checheg collected a large bowl of stones, which she loaded on to the fire. After removing the head and all its innards, the men placed

Cooking marmot

the meat into a small bowl filled with freshly chopped wild onions. Using a pair of tongs, they shovelled the red hot stones down through the headless neck of the empty skin and squeezed them into the feet amid squeaking flatulence, as air inside the animal escaped. The good meat was replaced in the marmot skin; the guts full of half-digested grass were tossed to grateful dogs.

Once full, they tied the neck with a piece of wire and dunked it in the fire. Every so often, the wire was untwisted to allow air to escape. Partway through the cooking process, we took turns plucking off the fur; the rest was singed with a blowtorch. Suddenly there was a loud bang, the marmot exploded and was deemed ready and placed on its back on the ground. It looked as though it had bitten through a 20,000-volt cable. A small bowl of fatty, gamey juice was handed around. It was by far the best bit and it soothed my chapped lips. Next we each received a greasy stone from inside the marmot, which we tossed hurriedly from hand to hand. As I winced at the heat, Baatar assured me that handling the hot stone would relieve tiredness. The meat, known as *bordog*, was good: gamey and rich. The skin looked like whale blubber, tasted of nothing except the charred outside and was harder to chew than a Lego tyre.

*

of some of the ordeals we had endured. It was the first time that I had been able to talk to anyone about what I had felt and it came pouring out, scattergun, for the best part of an hour. I think he was quite shocked at what I had put up with from Tamir. I tried to explain that when you are alone in a strange place with no one really to talk to, it is easy to lose all sense of perspective. I was their hostage and I had to put up with them and occasionally stand up to them; it was difficult – one woman against two men. Usually, I would succeed in talking Baatar round – I think he was frightened about what his brother would do – but Tamir had been a law unto himself.

Look this way! Milking goats in Zavkhan Province

Despite the harrowing tales, Milo asked to join us for a while and I gave him Tamir's horse. His riding holiday didn't work out quite as we'd planned: Baatar's girlfriend trailed behind on a motorbike and seemed intent on sticking around. The passes ahead were not motorbike territory and Baatar was in no hurry to travel. With Tamir gone, Baatar changed. Perhaps he was showing off or maybe he found Milo a threat. He was no longer the quiet, unquestioning, supportive man I had known. He became difficult and loutish, succumbing to frequent drinking bouts.

One of the horses, Lavgagh, had developed a small sore on his side. Conspiring with a group who had gathered around our horses, Baatar insisted, 'This horse no good, maybe die.'

I begged to differ. So he then consulted an old woman who informed us that, 'Today, Wednesday, no good day travelling.'

I might have given him the benefit of the doubt if he had consulted the cracks in a sheep's shoulder-bone, but to suggest that Wednesday was an inauspicious day for travel was absurd. Baatar remained petulant and argumentative in front of a gathering audience. He told us to ride on ahead, saying he would catch up on his friend's bike. I took his horse and left with Milo. Baatar never caught us up. I felt betrayed and angry; I couldn't understand what had brought about this sudden change in behaviour. Milo was sure that I was well rid of Baatar.

We camped for the night. Milo and I worked well together unloading the baggage, setting up the tents, unsaddling and tethering the horses and doing the reverse in the morning. We ate a delicious vacuum-packed camping meal and chatted around the campfire. It was nice to have a proper conversation that wasn't in pidgin English. We decided that night we could manage on our own. I could get a new guide when Milo left.

The next morning Milo kept hurriedly dismounting and darting behind bushes. By midday he was doubled over with cramps. By lunchtime, he had decided to go back to Ulaanbaatar for medical attention and suggested that I go back with him.

'You'll never manage the horses and all the baggage on your own. It was difficult enough for the two of us. You don't speak the language. Why don't you come back to Ulaanbaatar and look for a new guide?'

I couldn't bear the idea of such an early defeat. I had given up everything for this trip. I couldn't go back. If I lost momentum, I knew that there was a risk that I would give up. I had to keep going, no matter how desolate and defeated I was feeling. I didn't want to hang around. The longer I waited, the more likely it was that I would give myself away. If Milo realized how fragile my state of mind was, he would try to talk me out of continuing.

I mounted my horse. Despite the gathering clouds, I put on my sunglasses so Milo wouldn't see the tears in my eyes. He passed up the leading reins, two on each side and I set off. I made a kilometre before Lavgagh stopped to pee. Stopping sharply in his tracks, he tugged the leading rein out of my hand. I got off my horse and picked up the reins. Several hundred metres on, Nazarbaev jerked his head back, eyeing me sideways, showing me the whites of his eyes and stopped in his tracks. I dropped all the reins. A couple of young men from a neighbouring *ger* came to my rescue and tied the horses together at the neck so that I was leading two pairs.

The system worked well and I covered about ten kilometres. Driving rain soon ended my progress; the horses stopped, turning away from the wind so that I couldn't get them to move. I got off my horse and led them for several hours. Despite my cape, my legs were soaked. At dusk, I sought shelter in a nearby *ger*. I tried in vain to hire a guide but no one wanted to come with me as there was a *naadam* in two days. All the top seeds in Mongolian wrestling were attending. To suggest to a Mongolian that he should miss it would be tantamount to telling a football fan that he could not watch the World Cup. A couple from one of the surrounding *gers* offered to put me up while I tried to find a guide.

My host, Tonga was straight as an arrow. He had a handsome face: high cheekbones, dark almond eyes and neatly cropped hair. His clothes were spotless, well looked after and looked pressed although I never saw an iron in the *ger*. He and his wife were incredibly hospitable and generous, he in a no-nonsense kind of way, setting my equipment right, letting me rest and then gently persuading me that I needed to get on my way. After a couple of days with him, he asked when I was planning to go and suggested a solution. I should ride alone to the *naadam* at Tsakir Soum – a day's ride from his house. Once the festivities were over, I would be able to find a guide. Tonga couldn't ride with me as his son was competing in the *naadam*. I sketched plans with him, communicating with hand-signals and with the use of my phrasebook as he explained the best way to lead four horses; I should lead two, the other two would be tied to the others by the neck. He

Tonga and his family preparing for the Naadam race

drew me a map of the route to Tsakir, where the *naadam* was taking place. It was thirty kilometres away. If I started early, I would be there by night-fall. Looking back, he was the perfect tonic. Any over-indulgence would have killed my will to continue.

> If you've begun – finish.
> If you've sought – find.

Stanley N. Frye, *Two Hundred and Fifty Mongolian Proverbs*, 1967

6

GOING SOLO

Tonga's family were up at dawn. The surrounding steppe was bathed in a crisp, brilliant light. We sat outside at a small red wooden table, piled high with fried pastries, cream, curd and tea. Their son, a nervous 6-year-old, was decked out in a gaudy, checked, red and yellow racing shirt; it was his second *naadam*. After breakfast, Tonga helped me load the horses.

I was barely out of sight when Nazarbaev decided to be obdurate and stopped. I dropped the reins. As I tried to get back on Michelle, his saddle slipped and he bolted, bucking out of his saddle. One of the girth straps broke. I fastened the saddle with a piece of rope and remounted. The going was good for a kilometre or so but torrential rain put paid to further progress. I couldn't control five horses on my own. They danced nervously, turning their backs to the driving rain and tangling their reins round my middle. As they panicked, it was all I could do to stay in my saddle. I decided to walk, trying to reassure myself with every step that I took that I would be able to manage somehow. I tried to sing hymns to myself but I couldn't control my trembling voice: a large lump in my throat blocked the passage of many notes. Soon tears were trickling down my face as I felt a growing sense of panic at the awfulness of my situation; I was completely isolated, friendless and unable to communicate with anyone. Home seemed a million miles away. Had my parents learned of my predicament, they would have been horrified. What if something happened to me? What if I were attacked; how would they find out? Would they ever find me? Could I really put them through the pain of never knowing what had happened to me, of endlessly searching?

Feelings of guilt turned to anger: why was Tamir an alcoholic, how could Baatar have deserted me? Why should I give up because of them? Why should they ruin my plans? I had given up everything to do this. Anger became defiance: I would not let them win. Chiding myself for being so pathetic, I tapped into hidden reserves of self-control and stopped crying.

Refusing to be beaten by the horses I managed to remount Michelle and ride on.

We came to a small dirt track which cut across the steppe toward Tsakir Soum. As we headed along the track, out of nowhere a van appeared at high speed and hooted 'hello'. Pandemonium broke out. Lavgagh bit Mickey who shied, frightening and scattering the other horses. Lavgagh charged off in one direction, bucking out of his saddle and trailing it around his bloodied back legs until it lay in pieces on the steppe. Mickey, whose saddlebags contained all of my valuables and most of my money, was a moving dot on the horizon. A car stopped and a few passengers got out. It was impossible to communicate. All I could say was 'help, help', and point to Mickey, who was still running. One of them rubbed his forefingers with his thumb, his eyes bulging in anticipation. He tore across the steppe on Michelle, returning triumphantly twenty minutes later. I paid him $10. He wiggled his little finger in disappoint-ment, got back in the car and drove off.

I tethered the horses, sat on my bags and cried until I felt totally drained. And then I just sat on my saddlebags staring at nothing. Several hours passed before I eventually stood up and wandered around the steppe, pick-ing up bits of baggage and saddle while the horses calmed down. I loaded the horses; it was tough on my own, each saddlebag weighed about forty kilos and it was extremely difficult to steady the horses and load the baggage: every time I got the baggage near the saddle, Nazarbaev danced away, the whites of his eyes showing in fear. I was quite proud of my efforts; the bags looked reasonably steady. I had just started to get the hang of leading the four horses, when I came to a log bridge. The horses refused to cross. I got off and tried to coax them across. A lorry came up close behind, honk-ing its horn impatiently. I was petrified that one of the horses would jump into the river. When I reached the opposite bank four men jumped out. One lurched towards me and tried to reach for my knife, which was poking out of the top of my boot. My heart started hammering against my ribs. Were they going to beat me up, or worse? I hurriedly stepped back and, trying to remain calm, I suggested a photo to distract him and dispel the friction. It did the trick; their vanity got the better of them – they were all smiles for their photocall, after which they all shook my hand and drove off.

Once they had driven away, I mounted my horse and continued across the steppe. Within minutes, the heavens opened and the horses stopped in their tracks. Coaxing and kicking to no avail, I was soon drenched. If I attempted to extract my rain jacket I risked the alternative, four startled horses cantering off, so I kept going. The freezing rain had soon soaked several layers of clothing and wet rivulets ran down my trousers inside my boots, drenching my socks. I felt the chill from every gust of wind until my whole body felt numb. I found it very difficult to control the horses; I could neither feel my stirrups nor hold the reins properly.

The wind picked up and the horses began prancing nervously. Nazarbaev tugged on his leading rein; the look he gave me told me he intended to stop in his tracks. The soggy leather reins slipped through my fingers and on to the ground. I tried to get back in the saddle but the horses shifted in different directions and I couldn't control them. I resorted to leading them again. I managed to get my cape on but it was too late. My hair was matted to my forehead, the sharp rain stung my eyes.

Eventually I came to a *ger*. It was deserted save for an old woman, hunched on the edge of a bed, smoking a roll-up. She drew up a small stool beside the fire and draped a blanket around me. After several hours by the stove and copious quantities of tea, I was still shivering. Later, two lorry drivers joined us and I managed to establish that they were heading for Tsakir. The co-driver agreed to come with me, providing that he could sleep off his stomach-ache.

'Bad *airag*,' he complained, rubbing his tummy and collapsing on a bed.

When he awoke, he'd changed his mind: he felt sick and wasn't going anywhere. I kept repeating the word, 'HELP!' in a desperate voice. He looked increasingly guilty as the other occupants of the *ger* stared at him, waiting for a decision. Reluctantly he agreed, helping me load the horses before we set off. Several hundred metres up the valley, he leaned out of his saddle and threw up. I steered my horses sharply away to avoid the volley of vomit. Within half an hour, he lay sprawled by the side of the road, clutching his midriff and moaning. I gave him some rehydration fluid. After drinking a little, he lay down in the grass and passed out. I sat on the damp grass with my head bowed, wondering what on earth had possessed me to undertake such a foolhardy adventure.

After an hour, he woke up and somehow we made it to a nearby *ger*. After tea and a rest, he rallied. I found out that his name was Baatzorig, which means 'strong and courageous'.

As we rode, I patiently took him through the words for 'I am Sailing', which he practised until nightfall, but unfortunately he never managed to perfect it. He couldn't speak any English so he was learning it by rote and the fact that he couldn't hold a tune didn't help. We made it to Tsakir, riding the final few kilometres in the dark.

The small village was overrun with Mongolians at the tail end of a mammoth day's drinking. Cars sped around the surrounding hills like monstrous dragonflies, their lights on full beam. The horses trotted nervously and shied at the slightest provocation. The *naadam* was being hosted to mark the hundredth birthday of Jemyang, a national wrestling hero. Tonga had suggested that I seek out Jemyang's granddaughter, Nara, whom he said might speak English. An excited wrestling fan led me to a simple, two-roomed whitewashed house, near the stadium.

A giant white-haired Mongolian man presided over a charred sheep, which took up the length of the wooden table. He was wearing a camel-wool *del*, fastened at the waist with a large silver buckle, presumably a wrestling trophy, and a traditional pointed skullcap crowned his head. Beside him stood an enormous wooden vat, brimming with fermented mares' milk. Attendants rushed round refilling a silver cup, lined with yak's bone, and circulating it to the guests. Any space on the table was covered with mounds of curd, clotted cream, cheese, pastries and sweets. Nara, whose name means 'sun', was a statuesque woman in her early thirties. She insisted that we join the family feast. Baatzorig was overwhelmed. We gorged ourselves on congealed lamb, washed down with *airag*, while Nara questioned us about our journey and translated to her father. The air was charged; the wrestling would begin the following morning.

I woke early and crawled out of my tent to check on the horses. I found five tethering posts but no horses. I rushed to Baatzorig's tent and found him snoring on his back, surrounded by vodka bottles. I scolded myself for giving him his money the night before. It took me several minutes of violent shaking before he stirred. We recovered four of the horses but Mickey had disappeared. Nara explained that Mongolian horses run home. By now, Orka probably had gained both Harley and Mickey.

Thoughts of Mickey receded in favour of the *naadam*. I heard a woman throat-singing, a strange split-note wailing coming over the stadium sound-system. Outside the grounds, the area was teeming with activity. Hundreds of horses were tethered at a purpose-built stockade and motorbikes and cars stretched as far as the eye could see. Dozens of lorries filled with soap, washing powder, confectionery, cheap Chinese electronics and Russian tinned food were waiting for an active day's trading. Other lorries were being used as extra seating, pulled up alongside the edge of the stadium with dozens of men squeezed together on cabin roofs, straining to get a view of the day's celebrations over the wall.

The small arena was buzzing with excited chatter. Five rows of tiered seats, their occupants wearing white sun-hats and sporting caps, were not adequate, and the crowd spilled out on to the grass where uniformed policemen kept them out of the way of the competitors. A small awning at the north end, crowned with a picture of Jemyang and a large blue '100' sign, was reserved for family and visiting dignitaries. I sat on the grass at the south end, barely ten feet from the action. My camera equipment had convinced them that I must be a journalist.

Most of the day's activities took place outside the stadium. In the morning, we watched dozens of young children make their way to the start line in their bright racing gear, atop horses with plumed manes dancing above their ears. Outside the stadium were a couple of beautiful blue tents decorated with white scroll ornaments and Buddhist coins, reserved for the horse-trainers. Throughout the day there were several races, for geldings and mares of different ages, but the highlight was the 25-kilometre race for mature 6-year-old stallions. The stallions were surprisingly skinny; training for the *naadam* involves both exercise and a strict diet to reduce the horse's belly – a fat horse cannot gallop over a long distance. The riders consisted of girls and boys, the majority under ten and a smattering of toddlers. While some were dressed in racing colours sitting atop fine saddles, others were riding bareback.

After we'd been informed that the race had started, we spent at least twenty minutes waiting for something to happen. I was growing impatient when suddenly there was a murmur and a crowd of excited spectators pointed towards a rising plume at the foot of a hill, ten kilometres in the distance. Gradually dark specks emerged from a gathering dust cloud, strung out at intervals across the steppe. A dozen horses were clear leaders, and as they approached, I could see their young jockeys standing upright in the saddles whipping them furiously and howling like Red Indians going into battle. A boy of nine or ten, dressed in a bright yellow costume, sailed across the finish line about forty minutes after the start and the crowd roared its approval. Each subsequent rider charged at the line as if to run down the mass of spectators and was swallowed into the crowd. It took at least fifteen minutes for the stragglers to come in, some feebly flaying their mounts, rider and horse evidently exhausted.

The highlight of the celebrations was the wrestling competition, which took place on the second day. As master of ceremonies, Nara's father was resplendent in a crimson padded silk *del* covered in a gold Tibetan 'coin' pattern, fastened at the waist by two golden interlocking horses. He exchanged snuff bottles with a man in the crowd while the judges watched from a small table laden with Mongolian delicacies. A forty-litre blue plastic barrel of *airag* stood below the table.

A few wrestlers began to warm up, stripping off *dels* to reveal skimpy blue and red briefs embroidered with silver, and jackets in the same material ending at the midriff, a small piece of string securing the front. Long black boots, decorated with strips of turquoise leather, finished just below their knees and curled up at the toes. Stretching out legs and hips, slapping their bottoms, parading around the national flag, they were a curious assortment of bodies. Some were small and sinewy; others stocky – many had paunches spilling out over briefs and layers of fat folding down their backs. All had brown faces and pasty white legs. As part of the warm-up, members of the crowd challenged their wrestling heroes. Some spectators had their own costumes; others borrowed a sash or boots, which were the minimum requirement to take part. Tossed effortlessly to the ground by the professionals, they took back their hats and hurried back to friends in the audience.

Finally the competition began, the finest wrestlers in Mongolia were on show. Six men jogged out into the centre of the grass. Each wrestler had a second, who took his hat and proffered a shoulder on which the wrestler could lean and dance around, flapping one arm like an enormous eagle. This dance was then repeated around the national flag at the north end of the stadium in front of the VIPs, the wrestlers beating both wings. Two wrestlers then sized each other up. Bending over, they began lungeing at each other, slapping hands out of the way as each tried to gain a grip on his opponent without letting his adversary get a good hold on him. Finally their heads were locked like two rams in the rutting season; one had a grip

Wrestlers in Tsakir celebrating 100 years since Jemyang's birth

on a small piece of string around his adversary's waist, the other clasped the shoulders of his rival's jacket. Seemingly attached at the neck, they stomped around the stadium for about ten minutes without much happening, save for encouraging slaps on the bottom coming from their helpers.

The umpire, dressed in a red silk *del* with gold brocade, stood nearby, occasionally moving the couple towards the centre. Suddenly a foot thrust out, catching one wrestler unawares and he fell to the ground. He was helped to his feet by the victor and passed under his arm in submission before trotting back to his second for his hat. The champion jogged purposefully up to the flag for his victory dance, which involved further unruffling of feathers. One after the other, the competitors tumbled, flipped by a quick foot or were swung around and thrown to the ground. Weight seems to be an important, but by no means decisive factor. Some of the fattest men were out-footed and out-witted by more nimble opponents.

After lunch, there was a break in the wrestling competition to award prizes to the winning horses from the previous day. The young jockeys cantered around the stadium singing and stopped in front of the main awning. A herald presided over the awards ceremony, singing long poems about the admirable qualities of the horses and explaining the background of the owner and the jockey. After the chanting, each horse was anointed with mares' milk on its mane and its rump. I was told afterwards that the winning jockey's prize was a motorbike.

The wrestling began afresh. The crowd cheered as the champion, known as the 'Lion', strutted out. Passing the head table, he took several handfuls of hard curd, which he tossed to his fans who scrambled for the pieces. Nara's brother, Uskul, was one of the top competitors. Tall, lithe, and graceful, my eyes never left him as he limbered up for his match. Towering over his competitors, he had the advantage of a good stretch, which allowed him to get a firm grip on his opponent and his long legs reached that much further to trip his quarry. Finally, the match was down to Uskul, the fifth seed, and the Lion. They didn't wrestle and with a sporting bow, the champion gave way to the grandson of the local hero and the two friends drove off in the prize, a Russian Jeep.

As the crowds dispelled, I caught sight of Baatar, weaving his way through the stadium. I suppose it shouldn't have surprised me: Baatar was a huge wrestling fan. Where else would he have run to? As he caught my eye, he looked shocked, then guilty and hurried away from me. I caught him up and he had to stop and talk. He admitted that he had spotted me earlier and had been reassured that I was OK. He asked after Milo and I explained that he had fallen ill. Baatar was visibly upset when I explained that I had been managing on my own. I was tempted to hurl abuse at him or even hit him but instead I asked him if he had time to talk and we found a relatively quiet spot on the grass. I asked what had made him change, what had I done wrong? It was so out of character, he must have had a good reason for deserting me like that. He admitted that he and his girlfriend had been having serious problems and she had begged him to stay with her. He hadn't dared tell me as he had promised his brother that he would look after me. I told him that forgiveness was important in my culture. If he still wanted a job, I would re-employ him but he must promise that he would never desert me again.

Later he admitted to me that seeing me alone in the stadium, his opinion of me had changed. Before he had thought that I was a spoiled, rich girl on a long holiday and imagined that at some stage, I would give up and turn back. Now he realized that this wasn't the case and he joked that I was a real Mongolian woman. His girlfriend joined us; we let bygones be bygones, and went out carousing with 'The Eagle', the third seed. We sat in his Jeep in the middle of the steppe mixing screwdrivers and other such cocktails until four in the morning.

If a man cannot possibly abstain from drinking, let him get drunk three times in a month; if he gets drunk more than three times in thirty days, he does wrongly, and if he gets drunk twice in one month it is better still; and if a man never gets drunk it is best of all. But where is such a man to be found?

Genghis Khan
(Henning Haslund, *Men and Gods of Mongolia*)

7

BAATSAIHAN – BOLD
AND BEAUTIFUL

The next morning I woke up, startled by Baatar who was violently rattling my tent.

'Claire, come quick. We go to my friend Baatsaihan's *ger*.'

Zipping open the tent, I stuck my head out into a raging blizzard. Snow had blanketed the steppe during my intoxicated sleep. We saddled the horses and braved the bitter wind for five miles to Baatsaihan's *ger*.

Baatar explained that Baatsaihan was a wrestling teacher in the local school; they had been junior wrestling champions together. Although he was the same age as Baatar, greying, cropped hair framed Baatsaihan's face which was heavily lined from years of exposure to the powerful sun and bitter wind. Deep grooves were etched around eyes used to laughter. Everything about him suggested solidity, dependability and wisdom beyond his years. Baatar kept repeating: 'Baatsaihan my very good friend. He very good guide; no drinking.' I couldn't believe my luck: I had stumbled across Mongolia's only teetotaller and he had agreed to be my guide. His name, 'warrior of peace,' was propitious.

Baatsaihan's wife Chisma, a burly, brusque woman with dark sun blotches on her face, was a cook in the local café. She was catering for the *naadam* and cooked us a feast of *horsho*, delicious pasties filled with lamb which we ate while we waited for a marmot casserole. Baatsaihan skinned the marmot carefully and added the skin to a tally of 200, which he modestly told us he sold every year. He was incredibly house-proud, on the alert for any stray ash which he would sweep up the moment it fell from the fire on to the floor. Chisma didn't seem to appreciate these qualities and kept telling me to take him and not to bother to bring him back! It was quite difficult at times to tell whether or not she was joking.

Baatar regaled our adventures to Chisma and Baatsaihan, the latter's rough voice occasionally breaking out into high-pitched, childish giggles.

Later in the evening, various people from surrounding *gers* dropped in to buy things. Chisma rummaged in various rusty trunks piled on top of each other fishing out cigarettes, vodka, sweets, and notebooks. Finally Chisma laid out a dozen quilts on the floor, some serving as mattresses and the others as quilts. Chisma took off her *del* revealing skimpy fashionable underwear and slipped under her quilt. The men in the room didn't bat an eyelid. In a culture where everyone sleeps in such close proximity, you cannot afford to be too body-shy.

We left the next morning. Baatsaihan's horse was an extraordinary creature, which we named Zebra on account of its stripy forelock and prehistoric head. It was the wildest horse I'd ever seen and Baatsaihan kept handing me the baggage horse and galloping up the almost vertical slopes of the valley to try to calm it down. Several days later, Baatsaihan admitted defeat and swapped his horse for a calmer one. Zebra's new owner was thrilled with the bargain. Our new addition had an ample posterior so we christened him Targan Gui, or 'fat bottom'.

Baatsaihan was a great influence. On the first morning we were off at dawn, climbing through a marshy valley, which became progressively more narrow and steep. Soon we had snow underfoot. A chill wind whipped down the valley and by the time we reached the crest, at 3,500 metres, I was numb and ravenous. A promising wisp of smoke, which I hoped might be emanating from a *ger*, revealed itself to be from a small fire, tended by a wizened shepherd with no front teeth. He spoke wearily of his ordeal trying to drive an exhausted yak and its calf to the top of the pass.

We trudged down the other side of the pass, flanked by the dark contours of firs against a brilliant evening sky. Patches of pine and larch on the opposite slopes were pink in the evening sunlight. Camping on the only piece of flat ground on the steep surrounding slopes, we were soon joined by the old herdsman, Baatbold, to whom it was now our turn to be host. He was very grateful for a bed in the guides' tent; the forests were teeming with wolves and bears. He could barely walk; years in the saddle had left him acutely bow-legged, a clear 'O' had formed between his knees. Although he looked about ninety, he was sixty-three. Baatar and Baatsaihan had a grave discussion with him over supper. Baatar diligently translated their conversation into broken English which, over time, I learned to decipher quite well.

'This winter is going to be very bad. The cows are moving on to the higher ground. The rivers are dry in places and we have had a plague of flying locusts. This is a sign of a white *dzud*.'

Baatar explained. A white *dzud* occurs when there is heavy snowfall, at least a metre deep. The snow prevents the animals from getting at the grass.

Many die of starvation, others die of cold in the snowdrifts. Baatsaihan looked concerned, his animals were not far away.

The Mongolians do not tend to prepare and store winter fodder. Traditionally, well-planned summer grazing patterns ensure that the animals gain sufficient body weight to last them through the winter when the animals are turned out on the steppe, pawing at the ground under the snow for tufts of grass to sustain them. The low precipitation means that normally they do not have to dig very far under the snow. By the spring, the animals have lost between twenty-five and forty per cent of their body-weight. However, approximately every decade, there is a *dzud*; in the worst cases it can start in the summer with a drought followed by heavy snowfall in winter or an early spring thaw, which freezes back over, leaving a layer of ice over the grass. These freak weather patterns can be concurrent.

Baatar assured me that Baatbold was a very good herder, a repository of hundreds of years of accumulated knowledge, passed down from generation to generation. Apparently, the last time there had been a *dzud*, he had told his family that they must move to a mountain twenty kilometres from their winter camp. On the day that they moved, there was a heavy snowfall. They took much longer than they had expected to get to their camp; their yak-drawn carts kept getting stuck in deep snowdrifts. By the time they got to the mountain it was almost dark. Baatbold realized that several of the lambs were missing and spent hours searching; he didn't stop until he had found all of them. He placed the lambs in front of the herd to shelter them from the wind. They slept in the cow shelter; there wasn't time to put up the ger and they nearly froze to death. That winter, he only lost three of his herd. Most of his neighbours were lucky if they had three animals left. However, Baatbold was still struggling. Even the best herders cannot get complacent. Their animals frequently die from disease; since the collapse of the Soviet Union, inoculations for farm animals have stopped. If animals survive the winter, they can still end up dying of foot-and-mouth or anthrax; every year there are outbreaks of the latter.

Baatbold explained: 'In the summer, my granddaughters help my wife and me with the herding and help my wife to make butter, cream and *arrol* (curd) for the winter. But then they go back to school and I have to make all the other preparations for the winter on my own. I try to make some hay, but it is hard to do it alone.'

Despite the gravity of our discussions, Baatbold kept his humour and he laughed with Baatsaihan and Baatar late into the night.

*

I went to sleep to the sounds of munching horses; they were tethered so close to us that their shadows danced on the side of my tent. Baatar woke me in the middle of the night rattling my tent, begging for painkillers. I suspected that he had an abscess so I gave him a couple of paracetemol and started him on a course of antibiotics. Half an hour later, he was back for more. I dug around in my medical kit and gave him a couple of diocedene. Several hours' later, he pestered me for a couple more. I found out in the morning that one tablet is the equivalent of ten milligrams of morphine. Baatar was complaining of dizziness, unsurprising since he had taken four tablets! I couldn't give him any more painkillers and he made do with a bag of snow to take the swelling down. Meanwhile, I started feeling very queasy and was running a fever. I suspected that I had amoebic dysentery and started to take a course of flagyll. The tablets left a strong metallic taste in my mouth, which made me retch.

The next morning, we left the snowline and continued down a tiny track through the pines. Baatbold kept pointing out grazing areas to us.

'This is a good spot. Here it is sheltered; there isn't much snow. The horses and yaks can graze here. Just up the hill, it is often quite windy; the sheep need the wind to blow the snow off the ground so that they can graze but they need warmth at night.' Within a few hundred metres of the previous site, he identified a seemingly sheltered spot as one where snowdrifts frequently accumulate. He seemed to know every inch of the valley and how to choose and allocate the pastureland among his herds, with their varying eating requirements. I felt enormous admiration for him. It is easy for a traveller in Mongolia to get a rosy impression of the country during the summer months. Such stories were a potent reminder that winter represents a struggle for survival.

We were now in lush meadowland. The horses forded several rivers, which came up over their bellies; we kept our feet dry by kneeling in the saddle. Coming up in the other direction, several riders were returning home from a local *naadam*. Ribbons and rosettes hung from the mane of one chestnut, which had come third. Baatar's spirits had lifted; his toothache had subsided and within a few days, the antibiotics had worked their magic. It was my turn to suffer. At midday, I lay down in the shade of a bush; the dysentery was giving me terrible cramps.

I woke to the sound of six creaking wooden carts moving down a rough path through a small gorge. A dozen yaks were in their traces, a baby yak tottering behind. In the distance I could hear a cacophony of bleating sheep. Out in front on a small pony was a middle-aged lady in a bright blue head-scarf, her mauve skirt secured to the pommel of her saddle to facilitate riding. She carried a long lasso pole in her left hand. Her husband followed behind, a small child squeezed between his thighs. The family dog trotted out in front, its bushy black tail curled up over its back. A teenage son led the caravan of yaks on foot. On one cart was a neat roll of felt and a bundle of sticks, an orange wheel on the top – their *ger*; others were piled high with tiny chairs, tables, pans, vats, and suitcases. Bringing up the rear, another boy was driving a herd of several hundred sheep and goats.

Many families in Mongolia are losing their nomadic traditions and moving less frequently. This family said that they moved three of four times in the summer in search of the best pastures. The summer grazing grounds tend to be further north, by lakes, river valleys or in high mountain meadows where the animals can feast on lush feather-grasses and put on enough weight to survive the eight-month winter. Travelling anything between 10 and 200 kilometres between grazing grounds, some Mongolians move as many as ten times a year. In the old days, a tribal elder would decide migration routes in accordance with tradition. He would pass down valuable knowledge such as knowing from birdsong where to go in what season, where to go in a dry summer, where to go in a winter with a heavy snowfall.

Unfortunately, the problem is much more than interpreting the weather. Under the communist system, the government was responsible for maintenance of wells, collection of fodder and the vaccination of the

Moving to autumn pastures

animals. Even today the constitution states that livestock should be under government protection. The Mongols don't understand the true extent of their own responsibility now that the communist regime is over. After the collapse of communism, many factory workers were forced to seek a living off the land. According to a recent survey, over a third of Mongolians have little understanding of herding practices and are putting undue pressure on good pastureland. A serious overgrazing problem is developing and the herd of 30 million may be too large for the land resources available. Many of the younger farmers are losing all their herds while their more experienced neighbours are suffering much lighter casualties.

On 14 August, an auspicious day for marriage, we arrived in a small settlement called Ider. We were over 800 kilometres north-west of Ulaanbaatar and I really felt we had well and truly left the beaten track. We were invited to a small wedding near our campsite. By the time we arrived, the formalities, usually brief at a Mongolian marriage, had already taken place and the party was in full swing. The *ger* was heaving with at least seventy bodies. We sat on the right side of the tent, normally the women's side, but in this case reserved for the groom's family. The bride's father and various elders sat in the position of honour, presiding over a charred sheep's head at the north end. The rest of the blackened animal lay on a table piled high with dairy products, home-made biscuits and confectionery.

The father of the bride, already pickled, had to be reminded by his neighbour of the proper order to cut the sheep. As he carved, the meat disappeared into the folds of incredibly generous sleeves before emerging on a plate, frequently after a detour via the floor. The head was placed on the family altar to honour dead relatives and pieces of congealed fatty lamb were handed round the guests. A young man ladled drink from a selection of vats in the centre, handing around alternate bowlfuls of *airag* and Russian vodka. Each guest must drink three bowlfuls of each and one of tea. Unfortunately, I could only drink the tea; the medicine was working, my dysentery had abated but it was prohibited to mix it with alcohol.

The bride stood awkwardly on the left-hand side of the *ger*, receiving gifts from the guests. It was her family's duty to furnish the *ger*, purchased by the groom's father. Folds of silk, new pans, carpets, felt and quilts were accepted by the solemn girl who passed them to her husband, he trying to look manly and suitably grave for the occasion. One of the gifts, a new turquoise *del* embroidered with silver flowers, was donned ceremonially, the mother fastening it with a sash, while others secured a matching scarf at the back of her head. As they worked, they sang, wailing throat singing interspersed with more traditional Mongolian ballads.

I wondered whether Mongolian wedding songs are like their Kazakh equivalents. For if the words are anything like those marital ballads, I can understand why the couple looked so down-in-the-mouth. In one ballad the bride, filled with sadness and loss, sings farewell to her parental home:

'It is as if you shot me through the breast, oh dear father. You sold me for a herd of horses, oh dear father.'

In Kazakh tradition, the song progresses to the marital home, where her in-laws scold her for failing in her conjugal duties:

'She uses the eating-dish for a washing utensil. Her pants hang untidily over her boots, her hair sticks out of her head-dress and her breasts hang down.'[12]

As the singing reached a crescendo, the bride began her first household chores. Gathering up a few pieces of wood, she lit her first fire and placed a new aluminium cauldron on the stove. Once the first tea had brewed, she threw the first cup to the winds. Her father, by this stage, was oblivious to the proceedings. He became hostile, forgetting that he had invited us; we decided to make ourselves scarce.

We spent several days resting the horses and loading up on supplies including a toothbrush, razor, underpants, tracksuit and T-shirts for Baatsaihan, who had only brought the clothes he was standing in. A top priority was a warm blanket for him but the only blankets on sale in the local bazaar were synthetic ones from China.

'How can a country with 15 million sheep and 11 million goats fail to have woollen blankets?' I asked in amazement.

Baatar shrugged his shoulders in resignation, explaining that Mongolia has few wool factories. Before, they had sold their wool to the Soviet Union, now the Chinese buy their wool at rock-bottom prices. I later found out that this was also the case for leather products and most cashmere. The Chinese have a few token textile factories in Mongolia to enhance their quotas but the real value from Mongolia's livestock is extracted outside Mongolia.

In the afternoon Baatsaihan spent several hours peering down barrels of some rusty .22s as we held court to various locals who'd heard that we wanted to buy a gun; Baatsaihan was a crack shot and we all craved marmot. We had great fun test-firing at our target, a dollop of fresh cow dung, smeared on to a sheep's jawbone, before finding one for a $100 which met with his approval. Another man sold us a fine white horse for $60, which we named Tsaagan Turu, the Mongolian for edelweiss. For all their manly qualities, it was my guides' favourite song. Baatar asked me why Europeans have such a beautiful song about such a common flower. I told Baatar that they are very rare in Europe and that you can be fined for picking them. Baatar was incredulous.

'In Mongolia there are so many we shit on them.'

We left Ider and followed a small river in a gently undulating valley. A stallion was leading his herd down to the water, startling hundreds of black cranes and seagulls into flight. It seemed astonishing that Mongolia should host so many seagulls given its distance from the ocean. Deceptively green belts were increasingly broken by dust bowls and the formerly rich turf began thinning out, with blades of grass standing inches apart. A dozen enormous cinereous vultures staggered on a rocky outcrop. Several were still picking at a half-eaten horse carcass, festering nearby.

Baatsaihan asked me to teach him English and so he started by learning how to count, repeating each number after me. We made it to a thousand several times that afternoon. To reduce the monotony, I recalled the song, '1,2,3,4,5, once I caught a fish alive'; the meaning had him in fits. By the end of the first day, he had learned the words, 'good', 'no', 'yes' and 'good morning'. We had a go at 'In Dublin's Fair City', but I decided it was a little premature. Both guides were particularly keen on 'Two Little Boys', a good English song about horses. In return for my English lessons, Baatsaihan began teaching me the words to a Mongolian ballad, 'Chinghing Mongol'.

> I calm a spooked horse by twisting its ear,
> I can ride without a bridle or a halter
> I bear my spouse's love
> I speak bluntly.
> I am a real Mongolian
> A real countryside man.
>
> I can sleep outside on a felt
> I can stay in a field with a saddle under my head
> And breathe freely under the stars
> I tend the fireplace of my ancestors.
> I am a real Mongolian
> A real countryside man.
>
> When I brag, I play the fingers game and drink airag
> When I have a quarrel I go and wrestle
> I love a horse with a fast trot
> I respect our great nation.
> I am a real Mongolian
> A real countryside man.

Lost in song, we found ourselves in a wide valley. Huge waves of green hills rose in the distance, their crests iced with the last of the previous week's snow. A couple of *gers* lay in the bottom of the valley, dwarfed in an enormous sea of green. We stopped for lunch. At first the family were shy, unsure of what they were supposed to do with a foreign guest in their house. I showed them picture books of England. The grandmother gazed at them intently, smoking an old roll-up between third and fourth fingers. The light streaming through the roof of the *ger* illuminated her smooth head and etched face in a youthful glow.

The granddaughters soon went back to their tasks. One was sewing red and gold brocade on to a green silk *del*. Her sister was stirring a huge cauldron of mares' milk. The rising steam coloured her high, delicate cheekbones in her perfectly structured face. The guides were transfixed, watching as she placed a wooden barrel, open at each end, over the boiling milk. Finally she lifted a large bowl of cold water and balanced it on the top of the barrel. As the steam rises, it condenses on the bottom of the bowl of cold water and the milk spirit is caught in a small cup, suspended in the mouth of the barrel and weighed down with a couple of leather pouches.

After lunch, we played a game of knuckles. Almost every Mongolian child has a box of sheep knuckles under the bed. Rather like dice, the bones have four faces on which they can land: horse, camel, sheep and goat. Like finger-billiards, the object of the game is to flick one bone against its twin. After a hit, one bone is removed and gradually the pitch is cleared. A miss turns the pitch over to the opponent. The little boy against whom I played was more dextrous than I, cueing with all his fingers, while I was limited to thumb and middle finger. If there are no matching bones, the knuckles are cast again. The game can end suddenly if all bones land the same way up; the winner is the first to scoop them up.

Once the mares' milk had been distilled, we went outside to watch the youngest member of the family, a 4-year-old girl with a crew-cut, on her first dung collection. Pretty in a frilly red dress, she had a small wicker basket on her back and held a little rake. Crusty cowpats littered the ground. She tottered around in the high wind, seemingly lost for choice, possibly on the lookout for a dry one. Finally, she scooped one up. With great effort, she lifted up the rake and tossed the cowpat over her shoulder; it failed to make the basket. Oblivious to the last miss, she trotted over to a second, which also failed to make its target. Her mother picked up a few, secreted them in the basket and led the little girl home. Dried dung, known as *argol*, is a crucial winter fuel when temperatures can fall as low as minus sixty. While northern Mongolia is part of the Taiga forest belt, much of Mongolia has little tree-cover. Dung collection is therefore a constant preoccupation during the summer months. Large piles of pancake cowpats are piled up outside. The dung does not smell, giving off little smoke and burning like hot coals, retaining the heat for much of the cold winter nights.

After lunch, the horses slogged up a steep hill. At the top we left the steppe behind and desert unfurled as far as the eye could see. Khaar Nuur, the massive 'Black Lake', lay below us, surrounded by sand mountains of light silver and gilt. We needed to ride over one of the sand mountains to reach the next valley. At the top of the hill, we stopped at an ovoo, a large pile of rocks and blue *khatagh* scarves. In the recesses between the rocks was an assortment of votive offerings: notes, some of large denominations, small stones, sweets, vodka bottles and unsmoked cigarettes.

Mountains are very important in shaman culture and the ovoo is the focus of religious rituals. There are 800 venerated mountains in Mongolia and 280 even have their own sutras: Buddhist poems dedicated to the mountain's spirit. Each mountain has a deity; each spring has a spirit. Ovoos are placed at significant points on mountains and it is required to circle them clockwise three times and make an offering for safe passage to the mountain's deity. One famous mountain-goddess in Mongolia resides at Sutai Peak in the Altai Mountains in western Mongolia. The deity is a pale lady, protector of the poor, who is usually depicted on a fierce bull which holds up the heavens with its horns and tramples the earth with its hoofs.

We decided to stop beside the lake for a few days to give the horses a chance to rest before the slog up the sand-mountain. We'd been making good time, covering 160 kilometres in just four days. We were all hungry and negotiated to buy a sheep for ten dollars from a nearby *ger*. The sheep was laid out on its back on a piece of canvas; a sheep should be honourably killed and not a drop of blood should be spilled on the ground. The shepherd sat alongside the animal, one leg over its hind legs to keep it still. Making a small incision in the chest cavity, he slid his hand into the hole, found the heart and squeezed the aorta, cutting off the blood supply. It thrashed around, possibly a nervous reaction, and he finished it off by holding his hand over its nose and mouth. It was over in less than a minute. Breaking off the bottoms of its legs, he proceeded to skin it. Nothing was wasted; the guts were emptied, to make blood sausage and the congealed blood was scooped out into a small vat. They cooked the mutton in a large milk churn filled with hot stones. Closing the flip-lid, it became a pressure cooker, which they rolled around distributing the heat. Before the advent of the milk churn, this delicacy, known as *horhog*, would have been cooked in the sheep's skin, in the same way as they had cooked the

A couple of traders with their camels

marmot. After forty minutes, supper was ready. It tasted like barbecued lamb. Particularly delicious was the Mongolian equivalent of *foie gras*: a slice of liver sandwiched between two pieces of crisp fat.

We ate by the lake, our dried washing still lying all around us on the grass. Several men from the surrounding *gers* came to join the feast. As we were eating, a train of six camels laden with family belongings lolloped by, led by a woman on a tiny pony. A herd of sheep and goats followed, bustling and scampering between our tents, which were pitched at the water's edge. A large silvery tongue of sand jutted out into the water on the farthest shore. Our reflected surroundings floated over the water, clear blue sky, cloud puffs, green hills, sand dunes and finally a dying sun, splashing the dunes red and orange.

While I failed to catch supper in the lake, Baatsaihan showed himself to be a true hunter-gatherer. Donning a white T-shit and whirling a thick length of white yak's tail on a stock, he crept towards a family of loudly chirruping marmots. The curious marmots scampered out of their burrows to investigate the whirling white stick. Baatsaihan dropped on to his front, took aim and shot one marmot, reloaded and caught another as it dashed back to its burrow. After preparing the marmots, he placed the oily skins underneath his saddle to heal his horse's saddle sores. One of our guests from the previous night was Sukh Gerel, 'axelight', a solid man with a dark red, chubby face, which had aged prematurely in the harsh sunlight. He volunteered to show us a route through the desert.

> Dear Blue Eternal Heaven
> Let summer come to us
> Let well-being come to us
> Let winter go away
> Let rain come to us
> Let wind go away
> Let it be wet, and
> Let us have more grassland.
>
> A Mongolian prayer

8

DROUGHT

Early the following morning, we began to slog up the sand-mountain. The horses found the deep sand heavy-going and they panted like overheated dogs as they trudged up the hill. It took several hours to get to the top where we collapsed in the soft sand, admiring the waves of dunes which stretched for a hundred kilometres into the distance.

I rode alongside Sukh Gerel. He chatted away to me in Mongolian. I could only pick up the occasional word but somehow it made sense. We admired the deep blue lake from successively higher vantage-points up the sand-mountain and he pointed things out to me: wolf tracks, insects, small birds and marmots. Quite out of the blue, he presented me with the reins of a 2-year-old charcoal-grey mare with a silver mane, which had been trotting

The author and Baatar near the sand mountains at Khar Nuur

alongside his horse. I assumed that he wanted me to lead it but he kept pointing at the horse and then at me; Baatar explained that he wanted me to have the little horse. I was extremely embarrassed. How could I accept such a generous gift from someone I didn't know? I couldn't refuse it. I would just have to think of a way of paying him back. Sukh Gerel asked me what I planned to call her. I decided on 'Shoni Tenger' which means 'night sky'.

Despite the heat, Sukh Gerel's dog, Puma, spent fruitless hours chasing marmots. Finally he spotted one far from its hole. Bounding after it, he caught it by the throat, killing it instantly. Baatsaihan's face lit up and he charged over to Puma who obediently surrendered his prey. He was too busy chasing marmots to notice the large wolf, which bounded out ten metres in front of us and disappeared back into the dunes. The struggle continued into the afternoon as we laboured through dunes, the baggage repeatedly slipping off the horses. Until that day, Peter, the large horse which had been christened after that year's Wimbledon champion, had been a star performer. The sand-mountain had taken its toll and he began to flag. He sat down several times and Baatsaihan and Sukh Gerel did a sterling job keeping him going.

In the early evening, we reached our campsite: grassy banks, ringed by dunes. A small stream seeped out of the bottom of a 200-foot sand wall. We paddled up to the source of our oasis, past the carcass of a horse. The evening

Relief from the sand mountains, life and death at the oasis

light bisected the sand wall: one-half warm-orange and the other in shadow. Ripples running over the uneven sand on the stream bed glinted peach-pink.

The next morning, as I leant over the bank splashing my face, I watched a herd of horses trot down to the stream, upsetting an avalanche of sand which cascaded down to the water. A herd of cows further upstream was cooling ankles or nibbling at the grass. Later, a biblical picture: a large herd of goats crossed a skyline which was one-third blue, cloudless sky, two-thirds sand. Lambs bleated to their mothers as they floundered in the dunes. We spent the morning running up the sand wall and surfing down several hundred feet on our bottoms.

After lunch, we rode out of the dunes, into flat Africa-type savannah, punctuated by rocky outcrops. I led my new little friend, Shoni Tenger, whose name we changed to Jijig, 'small horse'. It was a sweltering day and the flies plagued us, ringing our heads with haloes and peppering my forehead with vicious, itchy bites. Although we were out of the desert, we were running parallel to the huge dunes. The sands encroached stealthily on to the steppe and the grazing progressively worsened.

We stopped for tea with a portly, handsome lady, who was looking after her grandchildren. Her sons had driven the family herd north. The grass in Zavkhan province had been ruined by drought. She had had no rain for three months. Even the camels were dying. A lengthy discussion started about the impending *dzud*. They were interrupted by the impatient blast of a horn. She rushed out to a truck parked outside and was soon haggling over a new aluminium teapot. Luckily, the elderly in Mongolia still receive a pension of $20 a month, enabling them to look after their grandchildren. She wanted to kill a sheep in our honour, a very generous gift given how hard times were. We gave her some biscuits and a watermelon, which we bought from the passing truck. She insisted on giving us handfuls of dried curd and returning half our biscuits.

For the next few days, the going remained tough. The horses were tired and the lack of grazing was beginning to take its toll. We only managed to cover sixty kilometres in three days. The days in the saddle were long and hot and the flies preyed on us relentlessly. Watching the horses going hungry and suffering from the heat and the flies was very distressing. Despite their hobbles, each night the horses strayed further and further away from our campsite; one morning, we found them five kilometres away. What drove me on was the thought that in Bayan Olgii there would be ample pastureland for the horses; I had to get them away from the drought in Zavkhan if they were to survive. As we limped into Zavkhan

Mandal, a squall stirred up the ground, hiding the town behind a curtain of sand and blowing grit into our faces.

We resolved to stop again to rest the horses. The area around the settlement had been heavily grazed but we found a good spot by the river for them. Happily, our visit coincided with a mini-*naadam*. Women were sitting underneath umbrellas on the green banks of the river. Little girls skipped around in lacy white dresses. A dignified man, resplendent in a Mongolian peaked-hat and burgundy *del*, was hosting the match. A former wrestling champion born in the area, he sat behind a small wooden table, beside a woman in a blue suit and smart shades. The commentator sat next to him clasping a megaphone, hitched up to a couple of speakers. Behind them, the undulating dunes disappeared into the distance. Baatar whispered the prize was twenty-five sheep. I managed to persuade Baatsaihan to enter the wrestling competition by buying him a new pair of wrestling boots. Perhaps the pressure got to him; he was easily defeated in the second round. Crestfallen, he spent the afternoon flicking through my dictionary and writing things down. After at least an hour, he produced a note:

'Thank you for boots. Baatsaihan sorry no good wrestling.'

After the wrestling, we went to a dance in the village hall. At the beginning, everyone sat around fidgeting nervously, waiting to be asked to take

The author with Darima and her son

the floor, but soon our hostess, Darima, was being whirled around by an assortment of dance partners; she and Baatsaihan were masters of the four-step waltz. My attempts were miserable and I hid in a back row, praying that I wouldn't be asked.

We left the village, accompanied by Erunde, a blue-eyed man who had reached the semi-finals in the wrestling. We chatted in pidgin Mongolian, interspersed with Russian words, which I looked up in my dictionary. I made a real effort to chat; he was a big fan of James Bond and all things British.

The dunes shadowed us to the north; the small oases had formed into a river which snaked lazily alongside our track. We stopped for tea with a family making tent-felt for their son, who was soon to be married. Several hides, stitched together, lay spread out by the river. Baatar was careful to flatter the family. 'May your felt be as hard as bone and as white as snow.'

He explained afterwards that had he not flattered them, tradition has it that the family could have said, 'this man has not mouth', and stuffed his mouth full of wool!

Baatar described how earlier, they would have piled wool several inches deep on to the hides and fluffed it with wands. Sprinkling it liberally with water, they would have rolled it up on a large wooden pole and attached it to trail behind a horse. The horse would then have trotted off with its load, bumping it across the steppe for several kilometres until the felt was tightly compressed. Unrolling the felt, a dozen of them now held a corner, or edge, and shook it out, with much merriment. Finally, they handed me a huge pair of blunt scissors and I chopped pieces of horsehair to reinforce areas where the felt was thinning, an old lady following me, sprinkling sugar over the top. Apparently the sugar helps the compacting of the felt.

Baatsaihan stripped down to his underpants and challenged Erunde to an impromptu wrestling match. Baatar acted as umpire, slapping their bottoms and yelling encouragement to Baatsaihan. The first bout was close-run, each man repeatedly whipping a foot out to catch his opponent. Baatsaihan, at least a stone lighter, was more nimble than Erunde but he ended up on his backside, rather downcast. In the second round, they both looked as if they were going to fall into the river. Baatsaihan toppled, recovered himself, and caught Erunde on his back foot. Baatsaihan was vindicated. We had a merry party at our campsite in the dunes. Baatsaihan made stew, which we washed down with liberal quantities of vodka.

We left the river behind and returned to semi-desert. The ground was parched and our path was littered with carcasses of animals, which had starved before winter had even set in. The horses snatched hungrily at any grass underfoot.

The sun sapped away our energy and, each day, we hunted around for shelter from the midday sun. One memorable day, we stopped at a *ger* in the dunes. A man with a long white beard and a severe, piercing gaze sat on a cushion working a piece of hide into a new bridle. The guides hung on his every word as he talked. I tried to appear sociable and to look interested, despite the fact that I couldn't understand what he was saying. Later I woke to find that they had killed a goat in our honour. We ate home-made blood sausage washed down with fizzy goats' milk followed by huge quantities of goats' meat.

Our host, Erdensen, insisted on swapping Fat Bottom, who had developed nasty saddle sores, for one of his horses. I felt humbled by his extraordinary generosity. Erdensen's brother was particularly badly-off. His wife had just died, leaving him with a seven-month-old baby he was rearing on goats' milk. His younger sister was acting as a surrogate mother for the summer holidays but would soon be back at school. I managed to persuade the girl to accept some money for milk powder; I knew that our host wouldn't have accepted it otherwise. I also rustled up a goodbye present for all the family: snuff, penknives, a matchbox dump-truck, notebooks, pencils and earrings and a soft toy – a little Beanie puppy that I had been saving for a special occasion. While the matchbox truck went down well, the little girl didn't know what to do with the puppy; she wasn't familiar with the concept of a cuddly toy. Later that afternoon, I noticed that the children had tied a string around its neck – they were dragging it around on the ground and stoning it.

Before we left, Erdensen performed surgery on our new horse. Apparently he had breathing difficulties. Baatar and Baatsaihan helped his brother hold him down while Erdensen threaded some thick cotton through his nostril. The horse struggled and tried to get up but they managed to hold him steady. Once the thread was through, he yanked at it and pulled a large lump of skin from the nostril, which he said had been blocking the airway. Blood ran down his muzzle. He repeated the procedure on the other side. The horse's nostrils filled with blood, which initially must have made breathing more difficult, but once the blood dried, he was fine. I named him Desert Storm.

At lunch, Baatsaihan shot a hare and Erdensen's sister prepared a delicious stew. Baatar drank a little soup, but refused to eat the meat. Baatsaihan and I polished off as much as we could. Maybe hare isn't fatty enough for the Mongolians. The others stuck to dairy products; everything in Zavkhan seemed to be made from goats' milk. They even fermented and distilled it. The fermented yoghurt tasted as if it was past its sell-by date; the distilled milk was good but bore little resemblance to dairy products.

Baatsaihan gave up leading Peter and had to resort to herding him on foot. The lump on his back had swelled to the size of a small dinner-plate. One night we had to stop in the desert as Peter refused to go on. We had to dig for water and there wasn't any grass, only camel fodder. The next morning, all of the horses had diarrhoea. Jijig, my small horse, kept sitting down. Baatsaihan pointed at her distended belly and said that it was colic. Erdinsen hurried us to his father-in-law's *ger*. A stooped man with a hoary beard appeared with a screwdriver, which he forced between Jijig's ribs. Baatar pointed at the handle, which was twitching: 'This good, gas coming out'.

After thirty seconds, he repeated the process on the other side. A small trickle of blood ran down each side. Jijig rolled around, thrashing from side to side. I walked her round on the grass for about half an hour. Finally she broke wind and discharged a watery green stool. She was lucky; if they'd got to her half an hour later she would have been dead.

That afternoon, the going was tough; our route led us back into the desert. Baatsaihan fell further behind as he tried to keep Peter going, beating him around the legs with a leather hobble. When he was out of sight, I stopped to wait. I could make out a line of houses and *gers*, Zavkhan Soum, on the banks of a river, five kilometres away. Baatsaihan limped up without Peter and cast the hobbles down on the ground in resignation. He pulled up his trouser leg revealing a large red mark on his shin that was smarting and had the makings of a painful bruise. I went back for Peter. He was nibbling at lonely tufts of grass in the sand. I couldn't let him die within sight of the river. Taking up the hobbles, I hit Peter hard on the bottom but he refused to budge. Undeterred, I hit him even harder on the shins, he lashed out at me but I was already round at the front pulling on the leading rein. We made fifty metres before he stopped again. And so we continued for about an hour until he wouldn't go any further and I sat in the sand waiting for Baatar. After about thirty minutes, he staggered over the horizon, leading an exhausted Michelle behind him. A light drizzle began to fall and the wind drove the sand into our faces.

'We have to get him to Zavkhan Soum and find a vet.'

Rather cowardly, I led Michelle leaving Baatar to administer the beating. Several hours later, we reached the river. Leaving Baatsaihan with the grazing horses, we borrowed a motorbike and went off in search of the vet. We found her in a spacious tumbledown wooden house, which must once have belonged to a Russian official. Baatar described Peter's symptoms, cupping

his hands together to indicate the size of the wound. Despite her grand
surroundings, the medicine cabinet was practically empty. She handed us a
razor blade and explained how we should lance the sore and inject the hole
with an antibiotic liquid, which she gave to us in a huge jar. We were also
given a few syringes and some more brown powder. She didn't want
payment but I insisted.

Despite his injury, Baatsaihan volunteered to undertake the operation.
Baatar and our host, Noshi, gripped either side of Peter's bridle while
Baatsaihan slit the bottom of the swelling. At least half a cupful of puss
spilled down Peter's side. He injected the sore with the antibiotic fluid and
sprinkled it with the powder. We decided to stop for a few days to give the
horses some rest.

Baatar found us somewhere to stay: a smart *ger*, with huge sofa beds,
wall-to-wall carpeting and a garish hi-fi, fitted with flashing disco lights
and a plastic ballerina, which waltzed on the top, whatever the music. The
young couple, childhood sweethearts, were married in August on the auspicious fourteenth, the day we had attended the wedding in Ider. His bride
showed us wedding photos. She had painted every facing page in pastels;
two bites of an apple; swans with necks inter-twined; a couple in the sunset.
Noshi called himself a 'commersant': he seemed to buy and sell anything
legal that made him a margin.

That evening the old man next-door rolled a large milk churn through
the door with a great flourish. He had slaughtered a goat in our honour.
The meat was succulent, roasted for several hours in its juices. The men
discussed our journey, wrestling, horse-racing and the health of the old
man's animals, a recurrent topic in every *ger* we came to. The Mongolians
have over three hundred words for describing a horse and at least forty for
camels. A man who is observant of animals is known as a *mal-dur girqai
kumun*. In the case of horses, most of the words are colours but horses will
also be identified by their age, sex and even the thickness of their tail. A
thick tail is apparently very lucky. Peter had a long, thick tail; I hoped that
he would be lucky. Camels are recognized by their humps, front erect,
back floppy, both floppy, bending to the right or left. The old man was
astounded when we told him that we had ridden from Ulaanbaatar. We
had covered 1,500 kilometres since we had left there. People no longer
made discouraging noises about the journey ahead but congratulated us
on how far we'd come.

We breakfasted on cold cuts, staring at a white goat's head, whose horns
were threaded through the spokes of the *ger*. Baatar spent the morning
sitting in the shade with the old man, a large bottle of distilled horse milk
by their side. By lunch, the old man was decidedly morose, weeping into my

shoulder, clutching a photo of his recently deceased brother, the last of his immediate family. His wife was embarrassed, saying something I took to mean, 'he gets like that these days after a few'.

Within a couple of days, Peter's sore was better. The swelling had gone and it was beginning to heal. At dawn, we set off again in the knowledge that there was no grazing or water for forty kilometres. Michelle was sluggish so I walked for most of the morning. By lunchtime, his belly was distended and he kept sitting down. Deciding that it could be colic, the guides punctured his ribcage. After the air was expelled, he perked up. We needed to keep going in order to get to the well by nightfall. We pressed on over the gravel desert, our only company scurrying lizards looking for shade.

In the evening, we accepted defeat. We hadn't found the well marked on the map. The horses picked at scant shoots of wild chives. I was worried; I knew that we would be all right, we had water, but the horses had nothing to drink. As we set off, we spotted a couple of stray camels on the horizon. As we rode towards them, a couple of men on horseback came over the brow of the hill. I felt like kissing them. Within half an hour, 600 camels were grazing around us. We had camped in the middle of a sacred site, where camel owners congregated with their beasts once a year. We weren't far from the well and the herders offered to lead us to it.

Our exhausted horses' burdens were hoisted on to the backs of two moulting Bactrian camels with fluffy dark-brown ruffs. There was no way that my horse's girth would stretch around my brute so they wedged my saddle between its humps and I rode in this precarious position all afternoon. Our party had swelled to a herd of fifty camels, fifteen horses, two baggage camels and my shaggy mount. As we rode along, I learned something of camel folklore. The proud camel used to have enormous antlers. One day, he was approached by a reindeer who asked him if he could borrow his beautiful horns. He was flattered and agreed.

'I'll return them by sundown,' promised the reindeer. 'I'll meet you at the well.'

That evening the camel went to the well to drink. Every so often, he would stop drinking and look up to see whether the reindeer had arrived with his horns. The reindeer never came. To this day, when a camel is drinking, he will always look up every now and then and scan the horizon for the reindeer with his horns.

We left the camels at the well and climbed about a thousand metres up a steep rock-strewn mountain track. From the summit, we had a spectacular view of Shaazgay Nuur, shining like a mirror in the brilliant sunlight. We reached the water's edge at sundown. The streaky rose-capped Altai

The author hitching a lift on a Bactrian camel

Mountains gazed down at their lofty reflections. The end of my Mongolian adventure was in sight. Kazakhstan lay beyond the Altai, running north-south down from southern Russia to China.

Our small caravan drew inquisitive looks in Olgii Soum. The dusty streets and clapperboard fences reminded me of a Western. Baatar bumped into the local bank manager, Delgermaa, a thick-set, intelligent woman who spoke good English. She was another classmate of Baatar from university and we were soon installed in her house, drinking obligatory shots and looking through college photos. As head boy, Baatar had an individual photo in the yearbook. His behaviour that night was anything but exemplary. He was up all night drinking vodka and was in a combative mood by morning. Delgermaa was embarrassed.

'I am sorry, Claire. It is the drink. We have a saying here, "Vodka slips into the mouth like a mosquito but roars out like a wild elephant".'

For the rest of the afternoon, Baatar was all over the place, swaying so badly on his horse that I had to lead it, while he held on to the pommel of his saddle. Eventually he fell off. Baatsaihan set up the tents, realizing that the day's riding was over; we had barely travelled ten kilometres. I looked back at Baatar who was squatting down for all to see, his trousers around his ankles defecating, urinating and vomiting in unison.

That evening we shared a leg of lamb with a young man called Altangerel, 'golden light', who still had an awkward, refreshing naïvety about him. The next morning, he accompanied us to his dilapidated village. Dogs scavenged between crumbling walls of Russian gingerbread homes with no windows, and sunlight streaming through roofs into half-covered rooms. I remember asking a friend some time later, why all of the buildings in the soum centres were in a state of collapse.

'Mongolians like to destroy,' she explained. 'Our ancestors looked on settled life with disdain. They valued their freedom and chose to live away from the grip of the barbarian rulers. They chose marginal land which couldn't be farmed but could be used for pastureland. They knew it was risky. They put up with the drought and the terrible winters. It is the price they pay for their freedom.'

9

THE END IN SIGHT

We lunched with Altangerel's brother who offered to show us a shortcut through a mountain pass to the Khovd River. He reckoned we could wade across it, saving a detour of several hundred kilometres to the bridge. We were willing to give it a try. Baatsaihan was getting agitated; he was late back for school.

We rode up a steep, rough track. Menacing black clouds blotted out the sun. Winter was in the air, blowing up the sleeves and down the neck of my down jacket. At the top, we looked down on our campsite; shafts of sunlight broke through the cloud, illuminating a small opal lake surrounded by inhospitable craggy rockfaces. Behind them loomed larger peaks, sporting zigzagged caps of snow. The guides shared their tent with a shepherd, who was driving several hundred goats and a few horses down into the Khovd valley for the winter. It was 5 September. We had something to celebrate; we had been going for two months and a day. We put on an impressive spread: mouldy bread, Polish pickled vegetables, Russian chocolate and a bottle of beer. The shepherd contributed fresh warm goats' milk.

I awoke that night to shouts and panicked bleating and heard the excited snort of a wolf as it snapped at one of the goats. Baatsaihan let off a few shots in the air; it was pitch black without the help of the moon. The wolf was not deterred and came back four times but, thankfully, it didn't manage another bite. Several hours' later, I was dying for the loo. Gingerly, I crawled out of my tent, anxiously peering into the darkness, expecting it to pounce any minute. I was too ashamed to ask one of the others to stand guard, so I squatted within four feet of my tent and scurried back like a frightened marmot heading for its burrow.

In the morning we led the horses up a narrow track, winding through the rocks, no doubt past the lair of our midnight visitor. As we climbed, the view opened out on to barren boulder-strewn pastureland. An ice wall, 1,000 metres of sheer, slippery peril, glittered at us as we trudged. Numerous false

summits soon took the spring out of our steps. Finally we reached the top
and looked down on the Khovd River snaking below us. Once we got there,
we would be two days' ride from Bayan Olgii and no more than four or five
days' ride from the Kazakh border. We clambered down a steep gully, into
a gentle valley, where we were able to get back in the saddle. Jijig trotted
behind us like a faithful dog, stopping to graze until were almost out of sight
and then cantering to catch up.

Thoughts of reaching our destination soon evaporated. The Khovd
River was swollen and the current was very strong. I tried out a few pooh-
sticks, which overtook me at a fast walking pace. There was no way we
could cross it. We stopped for the night at a group of *gers*, nestled under tall
willows on the riverbank. Our host agreed with my judgement, impatiently
tapping his pipe on the toe of his boot as Baatar suggested that we borrow
a camel to take the baggage and swim the horses across. The detour to the
bridge would add three days to our journey. Baatsaihan was terribly upset;
he was missing his wife and children and was getting increasingly anxious
about his job.

The next day, we trailed despondently along the river towards the
bridge. At lunch, we came to Khovd Soum, a small village scattered among
the trees beside the river. We stopped for supplies and found a semblance of
a restaurant. The owner appeared and unlocked the premises – I am sure
we were his first customers for months. We dined on huge bowls of broth,
thick chunks of lamb, turnips, potatoes and a side platter of ribs. The
patron, a young entrepreneur called Donna, lifted our spirits by informing
us that the river, which splits into four tributaries at Khovd Soum, was
fordable.

After lunch, Donna led us along a tree-lined path on the riverbank.
Couples were out on afternoon strolls. We came to a dainty wrought-iron
footbridge. As we led our horses across, we looked back in horror to see
Jijig jumping into the deep water. The current carried her downriver for
about fifty metres as she swam across to a gently sloping bank where she
was able to hop out. Shaking herself out like a wet dog she trotted off
towards the most succulent grass she had seen in weeks. We wound our
way around large bushes, through knee-high grass until we came to the
next tributary. Donna knelt on his horse and coaxed it into the surging
water. The horse staggered across, submerged up to the middle of its saddle.
After finding the safest route, he came back. We hoisted up one of the enormous saddlebags into his lap and he headed back across the river.
Baatsaihan and I passed another bag up to Baatar, who followed.
Baatsaihan took the remaining baggage and I brought up the rear, leading
Peter and Jijig. With each step, the horses battled, forced into sidesteps by

Crossing the Khovd River. Jijig fighting the currents at the rear

the strong current. Despite the fact that we were kneeling, in places the water lapped at our feet and I was frightened we might become totally submerged. In the deepest parts, Jijig resorted to swimming. We had to repeat this three times. In between each of the three tributaries, we let the horses rest, and we feasted on huge branches of hawthorn berries. After exchanging addresses, Donna left us in the hands of our first Kazakh hosts. Many Mongolians *en route* had been horrified to find out that I was continuing into Kazakhstan, terrifying me with stories of the greedy, thuggish, inhospitable Kazakhs.

A man in a knee-high corduroy *del*, fastened with a thin leather belt embossed with silver studs, met us at the door of his *ger*. A small silver dagger hung at his side. He asked us inside. His *ger*, known throughout the rest of Central Asia as a *yurt*, was bigger than the Mongolian equivalent, finishing in a more triangular apex. The real difference was in the decoration. The inner walls were covered in carpets and lined with tall reeds, called *chiy*, which serve as protection against insects in the summer, allowing the air to circulate and providing an additional layer of insulation in winter. Two girls crouched on the floor, their heads covered in colourful scarves, weaving new brocade about five metres in length, which ran out from a spindle on to a long wooden frame. Brocades were threaded through the spokes of the *ger* and ran head to foot along the outside edge of the beds, as an indication that guests should sit on colourful cushions on the floor.

Baatsaihan and Baatar were fascinated, questioning everything and drawing comparisons with the Mongolian way. We dined on mutton stew, simmered for four hours as opposed to the Mongolian hour-long immersion. After dinner, our host's daughter serenaded us on a *dombra*, a two-stringed wooden instrument rather like a banjo and we spent a jolly evening learning Kazakh songs. Alcohol was conspicuous by its absence; the Kazakhs are Muslims. We were encountering a new face of Central Asia. Instead of photographs of the Dalai Lama we would see prayer mats turned west to Mecca. It was only when we entered a *ger* that we noticed these changes, for the surrounding steppe was unchanged.

Mongolia is host to about seventy thousand Kazakhs, the majority of whom live in Bayan Olgii province. Some emigrated there 300 years ago. Most fled to Mongolia to escape the genocide caused by Stalin's collectivization programme, in which over a million Kazakhs died of starvation. Others fled to China and Afghanistan. Those in China were forced to move again as the Han Chinese began to crack down on Kazakh refugees. A massive exodus spilled out of China down to Turkey and up into Mongolia. Those who went

Lunch. Feasting on hawthorn berries before wading across the Khovd River

south had a phenomenal struggle: escaping from the Red Army through the wastes of the thirsty mountains of the Gobi, over the inhospitable Tibetan plateau and down into India. Their epic struggle, in 1951, is described in a book called *Kazakh Exodus* by Godfrey Lias. One story sticks in my mind. The Chinese massacred many of the refugees as they crossed the Tibetan border. Abdul Mutalip, a young boy of nine orphaned by the ambush, laid blame on the shoulders of the leader, Ali Beg:

'Am I not now the head of my father's house ... and are not those beasts yonder mine?'

Ali Beg replied in the affirmative.

'Then speak to these men that they hinder me not to do what I will with mine own.'

Every day, the poor boy fell further and further behind the long caravan, which crested the staggering 6,000 metre passes on the 600-mile journey to Kashmir. Following the sheep droppings and tracks of the main party and feeding off the corpses of animals which failed to make the five-month journey, he staggered into the refugee camp several weeks after the bulk of the party, herding his horse and one surviving sheep before him.

We slept on piles of Kazakh carpets, covered with quilts. The old man lay in an exquisitely carved v-shaped wooden bed, belonging to his grandfather. Another heirloom hung above his bed: a carpet, thousands of knots coloured with traditional vegetable dyes, which would have made an antique dealer drool.

Leaving the river behind, we headed up through a valley like a barren moonscape. The guides herded the baggage horses, which proved to be considerably faster than leading them. It was too cold to stop for lunch. We were about 50 kilometres from Olgii. While the guides' thoughts were filled with home, I dreaded the next portion of the journey. How would I negotiate the border with my horses? Where would I find a guide? How would I know if I could trust him? I knew that winter was fast approaching and I needed to move south as quickly as possible to escape the coming snow. By late afternoon we were back in a grassy valley leading up to snowy ranges. Several miles below the summits, slate roofs of a distant settlement caught the early evening sun. The wind stirred an ocean of parched feather grasses. Streaky cirrus clouds wafted across an uncertain sky, sombre above the mountains, still blue overhead.

Our host that night was a Kazakh hunter. Dozens of trophies, caught by his prize eagle, adorned the spokes of his *yurt*: a golden owl, a couple of marmots and the pelts of a wolf and a lynx. His daughter modelled a fantastic fox fur coat for us, which made her look like a 1930s film star. He offered to kill a sheep; Kazakh tradition stipulates that any guest should be given fresh meat. We assured him that a little soup would do. While the soup was on the boil, he posed astride his horse. On his arm rested his fifteen-kilo eagle, with a monstrous wingspan, his elbow supported by a triangular wooden perch, balanced on the pommel of his saddle. We all took turns posing in full Kazakh dress, with the majestic and terrifying animal perched on a leather glove on our arms, insisting that he kept his hood on for the performance.

The Kazakhs bait the eagle chicks with pigeons, while they are too young to fly the nest, and catch them in nets. For forty days and nights, the eaglet is hooded and fed meat once a day. The hood is removed and meat put at ever-greater distances from the bird, which learns to respond to the voice of its master. Often meat is placed in the eye sockets of a carcass, to train it to go for the eyes first. Under the watchful eye of its mother, a week-old chick can kill a hare; at a month, it can catch a fox. An eagle can be a hunting companion for up to thirty years, often flying alongside grey-hounds. It can catch thirty foxes in a season, which runs from October to March, when its quarry is silhouetted against the snow. A good eagle can hold a wolf down with one of its talons, anchoring itself with the other foot, until the wolf exhausts itself in the struggle.

Our Kazakh host with his eagle, Khovd Province

*

Crossing three small ranges we rode in silence, heads down, determined to reach the conclusion. The horses were in a bad state, ribs pressing through flesh, weeks of bad grazing taking their toll. Even Baatsaihan, who ritually butchered animals for the winter, had taken to walking beside his horse Nazarbaev, our testy, iron-willed chestnut, who had shouldered our baggage for most of the journey from Ulaanbaatar. As evening set in, we clambered over large boulders in a dried riverbed, scanning the horizon for the town and saw the telegraph-mast of Olgii in the distance.

We arrived in the outskirts of Bayan Olgii late at night. Leaving the horses under the watchful guard of a shepherd, grazing by the river, we looked for a place to stay. I was afraid that the hotel would be closed but, after persistent banging, the door opened. Baatar greeted yet another college friend. We ate a feast by candlelight. There seemed to be no end to Baatar's economics class. The next morning, we met Azamat, 'very good', a tall Kazakh second-hand car salesman, with a long Turkish face, Roman nose, thick lips and a mop of brown curls. His baby face and charm belied the crooked interior. Azamat was worshipped in the local bazaar and quickly assumed Baatar's role as my fixer; the horses were to be moved to his mother's house, and Azamat arranged a dozen great bales of fresh grass. I began trying to persuade him to use his seedy underworld connections to smuggle me through the mountains into Kazakhstan but even he balked at this request; trigger-happy soldiers policed the border.

Baatsaihan was desperate to get home. We tried the market but there were no trucks heading east. We spent the afternoon playing pool and buying drinks for a group of Mongolian pilots but to no avail, the planes were full. The only seat going was lost because Baatar got the timetable confused. Baatsaihan finally lost his temper and both guides burst into tears. In an extraordinary gesture, Baatar asked for his salary – to buy Baatsaihan a second-hand motorbike on which he could get home. Despite my intention to keep a tight-fisted budget, the thought of the never-complaining Baatsaihan pulling up outside his family ger on a shiny blue motorbike, replete with sidecar, was too tempting for words. Azamat was only too happy to arrange a sale.

The following day started with a few rudimentary lessons for Baatsaihan. Next, we headed to the market, arming him with supplies for his 1,000 kilometre journey home. A fifty-litre barrel of petrol for the journey was secured in the footwell of the sidecar and we stuffed the seat with biscuits, Mars Bars, cans of sprats and several bottles of Coca-Cola. We drove in convoy to the edge of the town. Sitting on the side of the road, we cracked open the obligatory vodka bottles. For an hour we toasted and sang songs; 'Chinghing Mongol', 'Summertime', 'In Dublin's Fair City' and 'Edelweiss'.

While we said our goodbyes, Baatsaihan asked if there was any way that I might find him a job in England. I felt terrible saying no. He was a perfect 'Man Friday' and I would have loved to have been able to help. I tried to explain that it wasn't within my power to extend him a British visa. He looked offended and sad but soon the excitement of his imminent reunion with his family took over. Baatsaihan could no longer contain his excitement. He jumped up and with the briefest of goodbyes, threw his leg over the bike, donned his helmet and roared up the mountain. We watched the trail of dust until it disappeared.

Baatsaihan with his new motorbike

I spent the next week trying to persuade the Russians to let me cross the fifty-kilometre zone sandwiched between Mongolia and Kazakhstan but to no avail. The only way to get to Kazakhstan was to go back the way I had come and fly via Moscow. I left the horses in the care of Azamat's uncle grazing in pastureland above Olgii. With my tail between my legs, I flew back to Ulaanbaatar. Back in Ulaanbaatar, we telephoned the post office in Baatsaihan's village and arranged to call him the next day. Baatsaihan sounded exhausted. His journey home had been fraught with danger. For the first two days, the going had been good. On the second night, he had decided to keep going after dark. He swerved to avoid something that darted out into the road and fell off his bike, knocking himself out. He awoke after an hour to find that a large piece of his jacket was missing. He insisted to us that a ghost had visited him, which drained him of his energy. Luckily his bike wasn't badly damaged and none of the petrol had spilled. The following day as he began to climb a pass, heavy snow started to fall and snowdrifts soon blocked the road. He spent a freezing day wading through drifts pushing his bike. His food ran out and he was frightened that he would freeze to death. Luckily he came across a family who took him in and fed him. After two sleepless nights he was able to rest without worrying about freezing. The family showed him another pass which was still open. He got home after four days.

> Farewell forever,
> Cool mountain heights,
> Green carpet of grass.
> Never would we have left you,
> But the enemy is pressing us....
>
> Oh my native isles,
> Where with the stag and the wild ram
> Sheep herds were grazing.
> I must leave you forever to save myself,
> Oh my summer grazing ground.
>
> And the drowsy forest now
> Remains behind, like an orphan.
> My people, who live in these woods,
> Will now be tortured forever.'

> Dosqoza 1858.

10

KAZAKHSTAN – A BRUSH
WITH THE KGB

27 September, 1999

The customs man was lying in wait for me at Almaty airport.
'Thirty dollars. Is that all you have?'
'Yes.'
'There is a cash machine over there.' Luckily for me, while dollar signs lit his eyes, the machine flashed, 'out of order'.

I hitched a lift into the centre of town in a brand new BMW, driven by a 'heavy', protecting the owner of Almaty's hippest radio station. I booked into the rather worn Hotel Kazakhstan, the tallest building in Almaty, standing at a heady twenty-five floors. In the evening, I phoned Richard Lewington, the British Ambassador. He greeted my courtesy telephone call with an immediate invitation to dinner and genuine surprise that I hadn't asked myself to stay. Our man in Almaty was clearly the opposite of the ambassadorial cliché. Dressed in jeans, an open-necked shirt and no tie, he reminisced about Mongolia, his first posting, and regaled me with stories of official tours of Kazakhstan. Combining the detail of the conscientious Mandarin with infectious enthusiasm in delivery, he held the undivided attention of his dinner guests, two visiting Baronesses.

I spent a few days exploring Almaty and looking for a new guide. Alma Ata, 'father of apples', is said to be the genesis of the Cox's Orange Pippin and the tulip. Almaty began life as a small Russian fort named Vierney. After the destruction of Vierney in an earthquake in 1887, the city became home to many political exiles including Trotsky, before he was deported from the Soviet Union. By the early 1990s Kazakhstan was the 'Central Asian tiger', flavour of the month with investors looking for a share of the Caspian oil reserves. It is a city of tree-lined avenues, set on a grid-pattern dwarfed by the 6,000 metre peaks of the Zailisky Alatau Mountains. A smattering of international banking and insurance offices abut a dejected Russian opera house and tsarist buildings. Sentimental pastoral scenes in the art galleries are all that remain of Kazakhstan's nomadic past, scenes that have not been witnessed since the brutal collectivization of the thirties. Later art echoes Monet, idealized sturdy peasants, land armies, factory workers and heroic mothers.

In between sights, I interviewed prospective guides. The first, a mountain guide, prided himself on driving a hard bargain; he claimed that he received $100 per day in the summer and should be paid at least $25 a day in winter. He may have known about mountains but it soon became clear that he knew nothing about horses and not much about a possible route. When I spread a map out in front of him, he pointed at a patch of blue on my map and said, 'Alakol is a pretty lake.'

The next interviewee was an effete, Russian photographer swishing a blond ponytail and reeking of aftershave. Sipping his cappuccino, he produced album upon album of rather amateur photos, which included some soft-pornographic shots of his girlfriend. I showed the greatest restraint in pretending to take his candidacy seriously.

'Like horses, like photos,' he minced, showing off the fine command of the English language, which had given me cause to interview him.

I realized that it was pointless trying to get a guide in the city. I resolved to look for a herder or a farmer in the countryside and decided to get as near to the Mongolian border as possible, to continue my journey. On 7 October, I bade farewell to Richard and his wife and flew a 1,000 kilometres northeast over arid, empty, flat expanses, to Ust-Kamenogorsk. Described in one book as a 'dire uranium processing town' Ust-Kamenogorsk basks in a uranium glow and is a breeze away from Semipalatinsk, where the Russians thoughtfully detonated 450 atom bombs, 250 of which were tested above ground.

In Ust-Kamenogorsk, I contacted Yevgeny and Sergei, two jolly Russian brothers who ran a big-game hunting company called 'Ecosystems'. Emphasizing their 'green image', they both sported 'appropriate' battle fatigues. They came highly recommended by a British balloonist, whom I had the good fortune to meet at the Ambassador's Residence in Almaty. Sergei was not optimistic. The mountains were impassable and snow was creeping lower every day. I didn't have the correct paperwork to travel in the area and no time to wait for it to be processed. However, they introduced me to a young student, Rassul, who spoke excellent English and talked his parents into letting him travel with me for a while. Rassul was the perfect companion: enthusiastic, charming and always helpful.

We drove 300 kilometres east in torrential rain. Our transport was an army-issue 'summer of love' camper van, with Sergei, a grumpy ex-Russian navy seal with hands like plates, at the wheel. He hadn't slept for several days, having driven several thousand kilometres in the previous days. A Russian heavy-metal tape, his caffeine substitute, failed to do the trick. Rassul, his knuckles white from gripping the picnic table, suggested he take a catnap as we lurched off the road yet again. It was two in the morning when we arrived at the house of Katon-Karagay's hunting chief. After supper, I bunked down on a bearskin rug on the floor.

In the morning, I went out to explore our surroundings. It was raining and thick grey clouds hovered around the top of large hills, whose lower slopes were covered in trees which were beginning to lose their bright russet leaves. The streets surrounding the wooden houses of Katon-Karagay were deep in mud. The rain stopped briefly at noon, raising its curtain to reveal large white mountains, thick with snow.

Our host left us in the hands of a Kazakh version of 'Odd-Job', clad in a long blue raincoat and a trilby, who took us to his stud. After examining a ragbag collection of horses, we were told that they would normally retail at $600 apiece but that he was 'prepared to negotiate'. I tried out one horse, which seemed OK. Asking its age, they chorused in unison:

'Five.'

'Nine.'

These shenanigans continued for about twenty minutes.

'I have the number of the local governor.' I name-dropped as we skulked back to our van. 'He'll give us an honest deal.'

Sergei, who had rediscovered his sense of humour after a good night's sleep, roared with laughter.

'That *is* the local governor,' Rassul explained apologetically.

In a neighbouring settlement of small ramshackle wooden houses, word had already got around that there was a gullible English woman in town looking for horses. I was mobbed. We stood outside in the freezing, heavy rain, which poured down in rivulets through the deep potholes. Some tried to sell me nags, others stood there for sheer amusement, testing my hopeless equine knowledge. Rassul was too young, and perhaps a little naïve, to stand up to the men. I think he found it difficult to barter with them on my behalf.

'How old do you think this one is?' I pulled back the upper lip and stared into its mouth.

'Nine?' I queried, hopelessly feigning confidence. There was a titter all round.

'Twenty,' someone shouted in the back.

'Seven,' a drunk slurred in the front.

I examined the horses as best as I could, dismissing those with chipped hooves and any which looked, 'long in the tooth'. The crowd melted away. Sergei rescued me and we left to go and buy several dozen litres of honey to flog in Ust-Kamenogorsk. I hit on an idea.

'Let's incentivize the local honey man. If he's Sergei's friend, he must be all right.'

Rassul obliged, calling the man over and explaining the system.

'We will give you ten dollars for every good horse that we buy.'

Sixty dollars is two months' salary for a policeman. Proud of my system, Rassul and I spent the afternoon drinking beer and eating dumplings, waiting for results.

By evening I still hadn't heard from the honey man and learned with horror that he had been arrested for being in possession of stolen motorcycle parts. I reckoned he'd been framed by Odd-Job, the local governor, who was trying to corner the market in horses. The whole scenario reminded me of a chapter in Captain Frederick Burnaby's best-selling book, *A Ride to Khiva*. Burnaby was a swashbuckling hero of the nineteenth century who could lift a pony under each arm, was fluent in five languages and perished in hand-to-hand fighting in the Sudan, he and his seventy-three comrades, surrounded by the corpses of over a thousand of the enemy. It is with some relief that I read that even he had had great difficulties buying horses – the villagers tried to convince him that he should buy a one-eyed horse. When he refused it, they assumed he would feel fortunate if they offered him any old horse with two eyes.

I left Katon-Karagay and moved to a small village appropriately called Genghis Tai, a series of small wooden huts in a muddy valley. The village used to be on the old cattle trail, which ran from Mongolia into Kazakhstan. The villagers were proud of their association with Genghis Khan. As far as they were concerned, he was as much their hero as he was the Mongolians'. I managed to persuade our host, Chinibaev, to sell me a couple of horses for $175 apiece. His neighbour came over for dinner and offered his services as a guide. However, during the night, the neighbour had a change of heart; he was no longer interested in being my guide. By the end of the day, I had found enough horses but still no one wanted to be my guide. Although the money was tempting, I was repeatedly warned that the journey ahead was dangerous; there were too many bandits around.

Having bought the horses, I spent hours procuring papers, registering me as the new owner. Each seller had to sign over his horses to me. Chinibaev had already prepared his paperwork before disappearing to Ust-Kamenogorsk for a week. What should have been a simple and quite sensible process turned into a fiasco: there was no record of Chinibaev's dapple-grey.

'How can you register yourself as the owner of a horse, if it doesn't exist?' puzzled the chief, a soft-spoken, helpful man with a greying moustache.

'How about if he were to register the horse and then give it to me as a gift?' I suggested, pointing at a random individual in the police station. Our soft-spoken bureaucrat was horrified by my illegal suggestion. However, he quickly realized that it was the only way out of the mess, and luckily he obliged.

On my third day in Genghis Tai, two men in leather jackets drew up outside the door.

'I bet that's the KGB,' warned Rassul.

We handed over our passports to a short, balding, pudgy man with a moustache who did all the talking. We were in a border zone without the appropriate paperwork. Five minutes later, we were speeding along to the police station in a white Lada, the fat man driving. Rassul kept silent and I nattered on about the expedition, trying to get the policemen on our side. After taking down our passport details, they quizzed me at length. They wanted to know exactly what I did for a living. Banking might push the fine up, I thought.

'I am a computer operator,' I lied. This remark was followed by a flurry of orders.

'They are trying to find a computer to test you,' warned Rassul.

'What languages do you speak?'

'French and Italian.' The local English teacher had already been hauled in to serve as police interpreter; they didn't trust Rassul. Local resources didn't stretch to French and Italian.

To try to dispel the tension a little, I started to talk to the policemen in the room about England. They soon had me standing in front of a map of the world, explaining the major differences between Kazakhstan and England, leaving out sensitive things like democracy. I pointed out London, Oxford, Cambridge and Manchester (although I wasn't sure exactly where the football grounds were) with the aid of the chief's cane. In the end I got away with a signed admission of my guilt and a fine of $6 apiece. Rassul was terrified that he might receive a criminal record making it difficult for him to study abroad but in the end he got off with a warning.

Needless to say our patient host, Indira, guilty by association, wanted us out of her house. We saddled the horses and I arranged the bags as I had seen the guides do in Mongolia. We were just leaving when a Jeep pulled up outside the house and three soldiers jumped out.

'KGB is a different department. Now you must sign protocol,' explained a sandy-haired, freckled Russian officer, punctuating his

sentences with a crunch and spit of a pine kernel. His fellow Kazakh officers were also squirreling for nuts in a communal brown paper bag. The
protocol was a long laborious form. It took several hours to confess our
guilt, the officer crossing out Soviet Union in various places and writing
Kazakhstan in a neat hand. The officer warned us to stick to the roads
and to 'report' in every town to the police station. By the time the soldiers
left, Indira was a nervous wreck. We hurried away, the bags tipping off
the horses at 500 metre intervals, and camped in a field about five kilometres from the house.

I awoke in the night to the sound of something wading through the stream
behind us. We hurried around the horses to check that they were all there.
One was missing. We decided to guard the horses in shifts. I took the first
one. Wandering around the horses, I caught a pair of eyes in my torch
beam. Petrified that it was a wolf, I called for help. It was the missing horse,
which I decided to call Wolf. I am sure that the former owner tried to steal
it back and released it when he heard Rassul talking in loud tones about
fetching the police. I tethered it and went back to sleep.

In the morning, we had another drama; we noticed that one of the
horses was lame. It was the chestnut, which I'd bought from Chinibaev.
Rassul took it back to Indira. I managed to find a 10-year-old ex-racehorse
in the hippodrome, which I was assured would make a great baggage
horse. I named him Tom, which means big in Mongolian. I named the
other chestnut horse Three Socks, as three out of four of his legs were
white. The hippodrome owner persuaded his taciturn uncle, whom we
nicknamed 'Eddik the Silent', to come as a guide until Lake Zaysan.
Finally we were ready to leave. It was 11 October and I had been out of the
saddle for almost a month. Having ridden in a westerly direction for the
whole of the Mongolian stretch we now turned due south, following the
line of the Sino-Kazakh border for about 1,400 kilometres until we
reached the Kyrgyz border. It was a great relief; by riding south we might
escape the winter for another month. With any luck, we would reach
Kyrgyzstan before the snows came.

> But the real travellers are those alone who set out
> For the sake of setting out; their hearts are light, like balloons
> They never turn aside from their destiny,
> And without knowing why, are always saying, 'Let us go!'
>
>   Baudelaire

11

A TENTATIVE START

The rain clouds disappeared for our departure; the air was crisp and clear. We followed a small track along the edge of a wood, clambering up steep, snow-covered hills, dwarfed by the Altaic massif, several miles higher. The trees, a mixture of deciduous and pine, were in a blood-orange autumnal blaze. As we passed under the branches, the horses' hoofs made a dull thud on the ground stepping over roots, leaves and layers of pine needles coating the forest floor. It felt good to be listening to the rhythmic thud of horses' hoofs again.

It took a while to get used to them. My dapple-grey, which I named Jijig after my baby horse in Mongolia, was very nervous and shied at anything man-made. Rassul's horse which we named Black Hat, on account of a patch on his head, seemed very unsteady on his feet and kept tripping over roots and stones. Eddik rode far in front of us on the big horse, leaving Rassul and me to chat.

I passed the afternoon learning the Kazakh art of pine-kernel extraction. The only time the hand is used is to pop the nut into the mouth, the intact kernel is chewed and the shell rockets out of the mouth in two symmetrical halves. I worked out that the thinner end of the nut has to be bitten along the line of the wood but I kept splitting the kernel or ending up with hundred of bits of shell in my mouth, which I spat out in a splatter-gun fashion. It seemed, genetically, that only Kazakhs had the mouth for it. After sunset, the temperature plunged. A thick layer of frost encrusted my tent overnight and my hands burned as I rolled it up in the morning.

As we descended into the valley, families were gathering the winter hay and loading it on to large trucks; at the end of the day, they perched precariously on top of the hay and swayed home. Young women in printed dresses and bright floral headscarves waved to us as we rode past. The chill, bright evening sunshine covered fields of stubble in a golden glow. Huge crops of sunflowers were wilting at the start of winter but we found a few containing seeds that weren't rotting. In the distance, I could make out the strange metal skeletons of *yurts* with no covers. Rassul explained that they were graveyards and the *yurts* were individual graves. As we drew near I could make out crescent moons atop the *yurt* frames. Both guides respectfully passed their hands over their faces in an *amin*.

As we set up camp for the evening, a shepherd rode up to warn us that we were camped in the territory of four wolves which had been creating havoc among the local flocks. Wolves hunt in packs in the winter. We built a big fire but I was still scared. Even the taciturn Eddik had something to say about wolves:

Shepherd with flock

'A man from our village was driving through the mountains with his family. He stopped in the woods to relieve himself and didn't come back. His wife went looking for him and she disappeared too. The terrified children were found huddled in the car several days later. Jackals are also bad. A lady in a neighbouring village was attacked by a pack of jackals at the bus stop. She managed to put her children on a wall, the poor things watched them tear her apart.'

The wolf population in Kazakhstan is multiplying at a frightening rate. A handsome bounty used to encourage the local farmers to shoot them but the money isn't there any more. Our shepherd complained that he was no longer able to protect his sheep; he didn't have a gun licence and could not afford to buy one.

Gradually, we left the mountains behind and headed down towards the monotonous flatness of the Kazakh steppe. After several days' ride, we made it to Zaysan, an enormous man-made lake, fed by the Irtysh river, which transformed the barren land into a fertile environment for rows of brilliant sunflowers, fields of watermelon and, of course, wheat.

The Virgin Lands Campaign was the culmination of a brutal century in which the nomadic traditions of Kazakhstan were harrowed into the ground, buried and sown over with wheat. The Kazakhs were driven out from their fertile pasturelands, on which generations had herded their animals. In the 1890s, 3 million Russians were resettled in Kazakhstan, a 'promised land'. By 1916, forty-two per cent of the available land in Kazakhstan was in the hands of foreigners. The nomads' herds were driven on to marginal ground. A severe winter followed by a drought halved the herd count. The First World War drove the Kazakhs into a state of heightened nationalism and Islamic militancy ran wild. The nomads were taxed, their animals requisitioned for the war effort and their labour demanded for the draft. By 1922, the herd had shrunk to a third of what it had been six years before.

Stalin decided that this would be a good moment to collectivize the Kazakhs. Between 1928 and 1932 the Kazakh population declined by 1.5 million through starvation, emigration and violence. The size of the herd plunged a further eighty per cent. Under Khrushchev, Kazakhstan was transformed from open steppe to a patchwork of arable fields. In his famous Virgin Lands Campaign, crop acreage grew from 7 million hectares to 23 million in a five-year period. The soil was worked to exhaustion. I have read that a high wind can remove nine tonnes of topsoil from a two-and-a-half-acre plot in thirty minutes.[13] The rivers filled with agricultural chemicals and productivity see-sawed from 20 million tonnes one year to 5 million tonnes the next. Such was the inefficiency of the communist government that in bumper years, grain rotted in the barns and in famine years, people starved.

The loss of their herds devastated Kazakh nomadic culture. The Kazakh author, Abai Kunanbaev, summed up the importance of a nomad's herds:

> Honour, reason, science, all for them is less than livestock. They think that by the gift of livestock they may receive the good opinion even of god. For them religion is livestock, the people are livestock, knowledge is livestock and influence is livestock.

In Kazakh nomadic vocabulary, derogatory terms existed for sedentary people: *balykshi*, meaning 'fishermen', *eginshi*, 'grain-growers', and *jatak* for a man who has lost all his animals. It was sadly ironic that Genghis Khan's descendants had become farmers like the Chinese whom he so despised, scratching at the ground for a living, like chickens.

Several days' later as we rode along a wide track, cut into the rock above the lake, one of Wolf's shoes came loose and we rode to the sound of clip, clop, clip, clink. There were no blacksmiths nearby so we stopped at what looked like a factory to ask for a nail. It was a low-security prison. We sat down to tea with one of the convicts, who had been there for six years and had a year to go. Our horses and bags stood outside in the courtyard under the watchful eye of another criminal.

'Be careful they don't see our vodka. People kill for a bottle,' warned Rassul. They furnished us with a rusty nail for which they demanded a dollar.

In just over a week we had covered 250 kilometres and I had seen little evidence of Kazakh hospitality. The local people hadn't been friendly and were only hospitable at a price. It didn't bode well for the future. Rassul and Eddik were both leaving soon and I would be on my own. I had to find a new guide. So far, I hadn't met anyone whom I could trust. As on so many occasions on the trip, I could feel fear and anticipation knotting in my gut. But I was determined to continue whether or not I found a guide.

Fields of long grass break the monotony of the steppe

As luck would have it, the day before Rassul was due to leave, we ran out of bread and I stopped at a farm to buy a couple of loaves. A slim young man in his early twenties, with a small moustache covering a slight hare-lip, came to the gate. His name was Ruslan. His face was scarred in several places and I wondered whether he'd earned the scars in a fight.

'Buy a loaf of bread?' he asked incredulously. 'You can have one. Please come in; have some potatoes and melon.' We sat in the farmyard, flies swarming on every surface, and Ruslan made lunch. Women were conspicuously absent. Despite his small build, Ruslan didn't look like a man to cross; however, he seemed very down-to-earth and a good person to have on my side.

I watched him as he fried the potatoes, wondering if he could be my guide. He didn't know that I was looking for a guide. He had nothing to gain from me. He had offered us lunch because he was a decent, hospitable man. He looked as if he could look after himself, and me: someone I could do with in bandit country.

'Rassul, we have found our man.' Gut instinct is all you can rely on when picking a guide. 'Tell him I'm prepared to pay him ten dollars a day if he takes me to the Kyrgyz border.'

I knew that $10 a day was a fortune for anyone, even someone from Almaty, where a good monthly wage was a $100. I had to make the package highly attractive; it was harvest season and he would be travelling far from home and taking large risks. Besides, I thought, how much is my life worth? I wanted him to protect me like a national treasure. My insurance policy was that he would receive the money when we got there; the money was in a bank in Almaty. The last part was a lie but I didn't want to run the risk of being mugged *en route*.

'Kyrgyzstan? That is more than a thousand kilometres away!' He was already doing his sums. 'I don't know the way, I can't read a map.'

'That doesn't matter. I'll do it,' I reassured him. He talked the matter over with his brothers.

'OK. I'll do it.' We decided to leave the next day.

That night, I saw another side to Ruslan's family. A couple of the village's drunks sat around knocking back vodka in the kitchen. Soon Ruslan's brothers were all smashed, his father was blotto, even his mother was legless. Ruslan, slightly worse for wear, was trying to maintain a respectable face for his guests. I retired to a bed in a backroom. As I was dropping off, a scuffle broke out and a man fell through the flimsy curtain separating my room from the kitchen. Ruslan staggered through the curtain and dragged his father up and out of the room.

I lay in bed, flinching every time I heard any movement near my room. It was dangerous to trust Ruslan; every member of his family seemed to be an alcoholic. I was petrified about what he would do when we were alone. But what other options did I have? I didn't want to give up. I didn't want to go home. I had grown to love the privations of the trail and living off my wits. I loved the hunger which made every mouthful taste like a gourmet meal and the exertion one day which made me fitter the next. I revelled in the sense of achievement for each kilometre that I covered. I felt inextricably bound to the course I had chosen and I decided to abandon myself to fate.

> Transparent air
> Icy rocks
> The sun was setting – rose colours appeared
> Impenetrable curtain of rain
> Night was howling
> Wild choir of the geese and ducks
> I drink the air as if it were wine
> I bloom like the steppe
> The firmament reflected in the waves is like a school of little fish
> Snowy heights
> Aromatic and thick grass
> Grey mist, transparent smoke
> Tent-dwellers
> Yellow steppes
>
> Wide lakes, flowering valleys,
> Free nomadic wandering, free pastures,
> All of these you would not even dream of today.
> Today one does not even know
> What kind of freedom there once was in the steppes.
> Now there is only the sand storm,
> And on that sand
> Pushed close together
> Are now the auls.

Qarasev 1876–1921

12

THE STEPPE

In the morning, Ruslan's father was still drunk and his mother was delirious.

'Who are all these people, Ruslan? Get them out.'

The fact that I was her son's new employer, offering to pay him an inconceivably large sum of money, didn't register. Ruslan hustled her out of the room as he packed. He found an old sack, which he stuffed with clothes. He slipped a monstrously large knife down his boot and announced that he was ready. I asked him to give his identity papers to Rassul, who took down the numbers. He said he would email them to my parents. I said goodbye to Rassul and Eddik. Suddenly I was alone.

Ruslan brandishing a knife. This was the knife Ruslan smuggled into his boot on the first day

Five minutes after they'd left, Ruslan's father staggered towards me, his blotchy face overgrown with run-away hair, his clothes smelling as though he had wet himself on multiple occasions. He was pointing and grinning at a nag that he had substituted in the place of my large baggage horse, Tom. Its ribs strained at skin covered in sores and bare patches. Ruslan told his father to leave us alone. My baggage horse was retrieved from its hiding place behind some outbuildings. I could tell that Ruslan shared my sense of desperation to get out of there as quickly as possible. His father kept trying to help us load the horses, slurring orders at his son, which were ignored.

We rode in awkward silence to the ferry. I spoke almost no Russian and Ruslan spoke no English. The horseshoes slipped and skidded on the metal gangplank on to a ferry, which we shared with cars and lorries. The landscape on the other side of Lake Zaysan was semi-desert, dunes covered with a smattering of feather-grasses and small tamarisk bushes. We rode along a road in the dark for several hours. My horse, the dappled grey, kept shying at passing headlights. Ruslan and I each led two horses, tied head to tail, caravan-style. Flipping through my Russian dictionary, I found the words for water, grass and wood, *vada, trava* and *drava*, the three necessities for a campsite. Finally we stopped underneath a bridge in an old riverbed, out of sight from the road. I set up the tents while Ruslan hobbled the horses. We dined in silence on potatoes and soup.

That night I slept with my hunting knife at the ready in a pouch above my head. Next to it I placed a rape alarm and a torch. If Ruslan or anyone else came into my tent, the shock of the rape alarm would buy me a few seconds in which to use the knife, if I had to. I slept fitfully. Ruslan kept getting up in the night to check on the horses. I kept thinking he was heading for my tent.

We packed up and loaded the horses together, Ruslan quickly learning the system for tying the baggage, which we had refined in Mongolia. It felt good to be more involved with the horses and heaving the heavy saddlebags soon made me incredibly strong. I showed him how to thread the doubled-up rope under the saddle, how to loop the loose ends through the rope, under the saddle and lash the rope tightly around the bags in a T-shape. A canvas girth knotted to the ropes ensured that the baggage was immovable; this was essential to prevent saddle sores. Heading for a nearby village, we stocked up on rice, tinned meat, tomato purée, onions, potatoes, Russian bay-leaves, Kazakh cigarettes (for Ruslan) and all the chocolate bars we could find. I decided to follow a series of tracks marked on the map which linked small tree-lined settlements, the only feature in an otherwise barren, flat steppe.

*

Our journey through the steppe, much of which was bleak and monotonous, was punctuated by reinvigorating stops in small farms, consisting of simple wattle and daub houses; *yurts* are no longer a common feature in Kazakhstan. Ruslan's background as a farmer opened doors and I began to see a different side of Kazakhstan. Outside the settlements, the farmers were hospitable, helpful and supremely generous. Unlike Mongolia, herd numbers in Kazakhstan were fairly pathetic and many of the families with whom we stayed were living on the breadline.

Whenever we arrived at a farmhouse, the farmer's wife would immediately warm the kettle on a simple mud stove, with four holes on the top and a small iron door into which she shovelled dung. The holes were filled with a series of inter-slotting concentric iron circles, which were added or subtracted depending on the size of the saucepan. The granular tea was made up as a concentrate in a small metal teapot. A small trickle of concentrate was poured into each cup, followed by boiling water and a ladle of milk. I usually asked for black tea or *chorni chay* and spooned delicious home-made blackcurrant jam into my cup. While Kazakhstan is the economically more advanced nation, every day I saw echoes of Mongolian culture. The food was very similar: rancid butter, cream, fried pastries and hard curd, to which the Kazakhs add a huge dose of salt. There were also smatterings of Mongolian within the Kazakh vocabulary such as the word *myangga* meaning 'one thousand' (a vestige of Genghis Khan's time when his Central Asian armies were divided into decimal units).

By contrast, many people in the settlements, which were characterized by almost universal unemployment, were hostile and I felt very uncomfortable. Ruslan, anxious to avoid detection, insisted that we set up the tents after dark, where possible behind a line of trees. He was always careful to make sure that our campfire never gave us away. We never camped within five kilometres of a settlement, which often meant riding for several hours in the dark. I felt like a criminal on the run but Ruslan was right to be scared. We were a walking goldmine; even our six horses were worth more than the average annual salary, a tempting quarry for unemployed villagers many of whom were looking to finance a drinking habit.

One settlement that sticks in my mind is Bolshevik, a town we came to after two weeks' ride, which was racked by economic ruin. The horses skirted pot-holes like craters, past ruined houses, torn yellowed plastic-sheeting flapping in factory windows, a broken pedestal where once an iron-cast Lenin would have harangued the passer-by, waving his Manifesto. Outside the village our track was punctuated by solitary, unconnected wooden pylons, which once powered the surrounding farms into the twentieth century and brought communist propaganda to prized televisions that now gather dust in candle-lit rooms.

However, our experiences of settlements weren't always bad. One morning we were riding along the pot-holed streets of a small settlement called Tossai. Gingerbread houses with peeling paint stood alongside ramshackle wooden huts and wattle and daub cottages. A middle-aged, respectable man in a worn suit stopped our horses and invited us into a large house with a corrugated iron roof. About thirty guests were milling around outside. Three trestle tables, covered with a piece of orange cloth, dominated the main reception room. A woman in a dark-green velvet dress, her head covered in a bright floral scarf, hurriedly removed the cloth. The tables were piled high with sweets, cakes, biscuits and pastries. Bowls of steaming stew were brought to us and we sat in someone else's place in a party on our own.

'What are you celebrating?' I asked. Our host, Tokian, shook his head as I suggested a birthday, wedding or an anniversary and pointed at a photo of an old couple, which graced the white wall above the dining tables. An embarrassed flush spread over my face as it dawned on me that we were attending a wake.

Later that week, we stayed with a farmer, wealthy by local standards, owning one hundred sheep, fifty cattle, twenty horses and plenty of fodder for our mounts. Three small houses and a few solitary outbuildings made up the farm. His young wife prepared us a huge dish of fried potatoes on the wooden table; her husband sat at the head, ceremonially chopping pieces of boiled lamb over the potatoes. We ate in the flickering light of a gas lamp while their daughter, a young toddler, played with a well-loved doll with one arm. After dinner, we gave them colour leaflets about the journey, which I had printed for potential sponsors. Tracing my route on the map and flipping frantically through my dictionary, I managed to explain what we were doing to our hosts and a couple of young farmhands from next-door. This was the first explanation that Ruslan had been given. Henceforth, he took up the role of chief spokesman and as my Russian got better, I would chip in.

The farmhands rode with us for much of the next morning singing traditional Kazakh ballads and their western favourites 'Yesterday' and 'I just called to say I love you'. As we bade them farewell, one gave me his whip; the handle was made from an old bicycle pump, with a small piece of leather attached. Two hours later, the farmer caught us up, his horse lathered in sweat. I thought we must have left something behind. Instead he thrust a letter into my hand; he wanted me to sign it. It transpired that the letter was addressed to the Akim, or local governor, of Bolshevik, begging him to reconnect the electricity, which had been cut off for the last three years. Once I had signed it, he contentedly folded up the signed letter with one of the leaflets, in the firm belief that my endorsement would invest his request with the requisite authority. Ruslan spent the afternoon communicating the problem to me through my pocket dictionary.

'Wires kaput. Aluminium expensive. Imported from China. No electricity.'

I had visions of the Akim of Bolshevik, his measly budget squandered elsewhere, squatting in his thunderbox, clutching a new source of loo roll in his stubby fingers.

That night we camped near an enormous rock which looked like an asteroid in the interminable flatness. Despite the cold, Ruslan had dispensed with his tent.

'It takes too long to set it up and slows us down in the morning,' he pronounced dismissively, the novelty of sleeping under canvas having worn off. He had taken to sleeping outside my tent door, rolled up in his sleeping-bag and a couple of horse blankets; his thick cotton-padded army-issue jacket and matching dusky rose dungarees, made him look like John Boy from *The Waltons*. Each morning his 'bed' was coated with a thick layer of frost.

Ruslan on his horse

At daybreak, we spent several hours frantically searching for water. My maps were accurate but at least half of the farms marked on the map were kaput and we couldn't rely on the blue dots, indicating wells. Ruslan finally spotted a couple of men on horseback in the distance and they led us to a farm. Our host, a retired academic in a well-worn grey suit, instructed his son to water our horses and invited us inside for lunch. His wife, a taciturn but friendly woman in her mid sixties, opened several jars of vegetables, which she had pickled for the winter and found a piece of meat. You cannot get fresh vegetables in the countryside during the winter; they are too expensive. We sat on simple wooden benches around a wooden table in their small, but impeccably clean, house.

'*Piay chay, piay; cushi, cushi.*' 'Drink tea, drink; eat, eat,' they encouraged, watching me and barely eating anything themselves. Our host's son was studying genetics in Semipalatinsk. It seemed extraordinary that he should choose to retire in a dusty barren patch of nowhere, a few days' ride from Bolshevik, with only an asteroid for company. He explained that he used to be a history teacher. He proudly took me through his stack of history books piled under his bed, which traced the history of the Kazakh nation back to Genghis Khan's oldest son, Jochi.

Genghis Khan's wife, Borte, was kidnapped on her wedding day. When she was wrested back from the enemy she was already pregnant. On Genghis Khan's death, his empire was divided amongst his sons. In accordance with Mongol tradition, the oldest son, Jochi, received the lands furthest away from home. Jochi predeceased his father by six months and his Khanate was divided between his sons; Orda received the White Horde, modern Kazakhstan, while Batu was given the Qipchaq Khanate, known as such because of the Qipchaq Turks who inhabited the area before the arrival of the Mongols.

During Ogedei's reign (1229-41), Batu Khan spread the Mongol rule of terror into Europe. The Russian princes were trounced; Kiev was destroyed as a centre of commerce, much to the glee of the Doges of rival Venice; Kozelski was renamed 'the city of woe' and only the Cathedral of St Sophia was left standing in Dmitri. As the Mongols advanced towards Poland, the rulers enlisted the help of the Teutonic knights of St Mary's. The knights, weighed down by forty-five kilos of chain mail, couldn't compete with Mongolia's featherweight mounted archers. Herded and outmanoeuvred like animals in the hunt, they were showered with volleys of arrows and rarely had a chance to demonstrate their superior abilities in hand to hand combat; nine sacks of ears were sent to Batu in tribute. An arrow through the throat silenced the trumpeter in Cracow before he could finish sounding the alarm; the city was razed to the ground. Ogedei warned King Bela IV of Hungary to surrender Mongolia's old rivals, the Cumanian horsemen, or suffer. He paid the consequences.[14] The famous chronicler, Matthew Paris, described the carnage:

> For touching upon the cruelty and cunning of these people, there can be no infamy (great enough); and, in briefly informing you of their wicked habits, I will recount nothing of which I hold either a doubt or a mere opinion, but what I have with certainty proved and what I know … the Tartar chief, with his dinner guests and other lotus-eaters (cannibals), fed upon the carcasses as if they were bread and left nothing but the bones for the vultures … The old and ugly women were given to the cannibals … as their daily allowance of food; those women who were beautiful were not eaten, but were suffocated by mobs of ravishers in spite of all their cries and lamentations. Virgins were raped until they died of exhaustion. Then their breasts were cut off to be kept as dainties for their chiefs, and their bodies furnished an entertaining banquet for the savages.

In Wiener Neustadt, the Duke of Dalmatia captured a party of Mongols. Amongst the prisoners was an Englishman, possibly the chaplain of the parish of Little Dunmow in Essex. Banished from England during the Barons' Revolt, he joined the Knights Templar. Unfortunately, he lost everything he had at dice in Acre, a vice greatly frowned upon by the Knights, who had expelled him. His knowledge of English, Latin, German, Saracen and Hungarian, which he had picked up fraternizing with troops in Acre, made him the perfect ambassador for the Mongols. Father Yvo took down the man's famous testimony:

> This fellow, on the behalf of the most tyrannical King of the Tartars, had been twice, as an Envoy and Interpreter, with the King of Hungary, menacingly and plainly foretelling the mischiefs which happened afterwards, unless the King would submit himself and his kingdom unto the Tartar yoke.

He was executed in July 1242 near Wiener Neustadt and buried in an unmarked grave.[15]

As suddenly as the gates of Tartarus had opened up, the Mongols retreated back home. Ogedei died and a succession crisis ensued, the throne disputed between Ogedei's family and Tolui's line. While Genghis Khan had nominated Ogedei as Great Khan, should the succession now continue through Ogedei's line? Tolui's family, who had the advantage of being closer to home, thought not. The enthronement of a new khan required a *kuriltai*, a meeting of all the other khans, to endorse the new leader.

Ogedei's son Guyuk was the natural choice. But he had made enemies. Batu Khan resented the princeling's supercilious attitude to his illegitimate uncle. He backed Mongke, the heir to the rival Tolui line, but did not attend the *kuriltai*. Guyuk was victorious; he reversed many of Genghis Khan's policies and put many of his advisers to death. Batu was next on his list but Guyuk died on a murderous mission to Batu's court. Guyuk's mother, Oghul Ghaimish, assumed the regency and hoped to get another son sworn in as Great Khan. Emboldened by his successes in Europe, Batu managed to get Mongke, head of the Tolui line, sworn in as the new Great Khan. Oghul Ghaimish was punished; all her orifices were sewn up and she was cast into the nearest river. Not long after Mongke was installed as great Khan, attempts were made to overthrow him. Seventy generals had their mouths stuffed with stones until they died.[16]

Perhaps Genghis Khan's mistake was to divide his empire between his sons. Internecine disputes ultimately destroyed his legacy, which split along the boundaries marked out for his sons. Gradually these smaller fiefdoms collapsed. Batu's Golden Horde and the White Horde were briefly reunited with Tamerlane's help under the leadership of Toqtamish, a distant cousin of Batu. However, the Timurid dynasty, which lacked a secure succession, was also short-lived. When the Shaybanids destroyed the Timurid Empire in 1428, the Kazakhs had to look elsewhere for protection. The Golden Horde had by now split into three: Astrakhan, Kazan and the Crimea. Ivan the Terrible ultimately destroyed Kazan and Astrakhan; the Crimea fell to Catherine the Great. The Tartars continued to exist as a community until Stalin had them deported in the Second World War. When the Shaybanids were in turn weakened by defeats inflicted by the eastern Mongolian Kalmucks, the Kazakhs deserted the Uzbeks and sought refuge with the Chaghataihid khanate. The name Kazakh probably comes from the Arabic *qazac*, meaning 'rebel'. In time Kazakhstan itself split into three 'hordes', tribal groups, reflecting natural geographic areas containing summer and winter pasture. The Great Horde occupied eastern Turkestan, the Middle Horde lived in the central Steppe region and the Little Horde, the west bordering the Urals. As time went on, the fissures between the three hordes widened, fissures with which families still identify today and this made the Kazakh nation unable to deal with outside threats, most notably from the Russians.[17]

A Kazakh herder. The mountains behind him mark the Kyrgyz border

After an evening and half the next day leafing through our generous host's history books, we bade them farewell. The eternal flatness was broken by a band of hills on the horizon, the foothills of the Altai Mountains. Our route, 1,400 kilometres south through Kazakhstan, often took us close to the Chinese border, delineated by the mountains. I was always nervous on these occasions, as I worried that I would have another brush with the KGB because we would once again be venturing into the border area without a permit. We headed towards a gap in the hills, which never seemed to get any closer, stopping for 'lunch' – five minutes for bread, paté and chocolate, crouched behind the horses. In the afternoon, I noticed pus oozing from underneath my saddle. Ruslan admitted that he'd noticed a small sore, the width of a pencil, that morning but hadn't thought anything of it. It was too cold to take the saddle off. We came to a river as the evening sun touched distant pearly mountains. Two men, whose tractor had broken down, were rolling up their trousers to wade across the icy water. We gave Amangeld and his friend a lift on our spare horses; he invited us to stay. As we rode into Kesilgesik, young boys were driving the flocks off the surrounding hills towards the village. A hundred metres from the settlement, a member of each household was waiting to claim his animals. Scampering sheep bleated in all directions chased by husbands, wives, daughters and sons. Others, more disciplined, trotted to their relevant pens. Mountains of grass were heaped on all rooftops; stacks of firewood and little piles of dung stood against every available wall.

Amangeld's wife Laura, a stunning girl with a mass of medusa-like black hair, greeted us in the yard of one of the larger houses. She was the local maths teacher. Her mother, a jovial, rotund woman, served us welcome bowls of soup and the usual bread, cream and jam. After tea, I was just about ready for bed when a huge black sheep was dragged struggling to the doorway. Initially, 'cooking' was done outside with a blowtorch. The par-charred mutton was then boiled for several hours. A neighbour enter- tained us, singing and strumming on a *dombra*, which sounded a little like an Indian sitar. The women sang, wailing guttural trills, interspersed with nervous laughter. Ballads are a very important part of Kazakh culture, which relies heavily on an oral tradition passed down through generations in poetry and music.

Laura's father was very interested in our journey. He quizzed Ruslan and me at length about where we had been and why we had undertaken this expedition. I tried to tell him I was a traveller, a *putichestva*, but that wasn't good enough.

'Is your government paying you to do this expedition?'

'No.'

'Are you a geologist? Maybe your heavy bags are filled with rock samples.'

'No.'

'So who is paying you to do this journey?'

'No one.'

'So why are you doing it?'

My fifty words of Russian didn't stretch to 'an escapade'. Such an expla- nation seemed self-indulgent and frivolous, even in present company, a family more comfortable than most. I found that the easiest justification was to say that I was *pisatylnitsa*, 'a writer'.

Our supper was ready at midnight. Amangeld, head of the family at twenty-eight, had changed into a three-piece suit. His thick, black, wavy hair had been neatly brushed into a side-parting and he looked like an adult cherub. With *gravitas* beyond his years, he presided over the charred sheep's head, which graced the centre of a huge platter of boiled mutton. First he cut the cheek, handing pieces around on a small dish. Next he sliced the meat over quadrants of home-made pasta. The mother ladled a couple of bowls of broth containing blanched, crisp onions on to the pasta. We each were given a bowl of the delicious broth, to which we added yoghurt and curd.

We ate in a state of exhaustion; I sat next to Amangeld's cheerful three-toothed grandmother, who was wearing a velvet burgundy cardigan with embroidered gold facing and a turquoise headscarf dappled with pink roses and shot with silver thread. Her 81-year-old husband in a red velvet skull-cap sat on my right, his eyes blank and glazed. As I got ready for bed, Laura insisted on measuring me up for inner soles for my boots, which she cut out from pieces of felt. Her mother insisted on giving me another woollen hat; one was no longer enough. Each day on horseback had become like a perpetual chairlift ride in a wintry ski-resort. Despite the broken springs, the wrought-iron bed was a welcome luxury, which a member of the family had kindly given up for me to enjoy.

Breakfast consisted of the remainder of the previous night's lamb, potatoes, bread, cream and tea. As we got ready to leave, a policeman appeared. He leafed through my passport, not quite sure what he was looking for but keen to convey his sense of self-importance. I stood beside him anxiously diverting his attention from my Kazakh visa, which expired the next day, and showing him visas from Guatemala, Hong Kong, China, Japan, Mongolia, Burma, Nepal and Thailand. I hadn't given any thought to my visa: here in the middle of Kazakhstan, such details seemed irrelevant. Finding no fault with my passport, he decided to take Ruslan down to the police station. Ruslan insisted on going alone. While Ruslan was being interrogated, the household was bustling with activity as all members carried out their daily tasks. I found a small corner of the room and sat down with my well-worn copy of Grousset's *Empire of the Steppe*, keen to discover what befell the Mongolian Empire.

By Khubilai Khan's reign, the Mongol Empire had passed its zenith. Internecine feuds had split the empire into warring strongholds. Tutored by Uighurs and having spent much time in China, Khubilai Khan was regarded by the Mongolian tribal chiefs with suspicion. When Mongke died, the leaders of the Golden Horde and the Chaghadai khanate cast their lots with his younger brother, Ariq Boke. Khubilai Khan's only support came from the Ilkhanate of Persia. Khubilai Khan succeeded in defeating Ariq Boke but remained largely a Chinese leader. Recognizing the need for legitimacy in China, he invested himself with the title of Emperor of his newly created Yuan dynasty.

Khubilai's most notable achievement was the consolidation of the Chinese Empire. With the help of Persian siege engineers, he smashed through the defences of Hsian-yang, the last stronghold of the southern Chinese Sung dynasty and united the north with the south. A lesser-known aspect of his rule is the transformation of his empire into a significant naval power. With the help of the Koreans, the Mongolians invaded Japan, inflicting severe losses on the Japanese. The Japanese were saved by a timely *kamikaze* or 'divine wind'. Faced with the possibility of losing all their ships on the rocks, the Mongols made a speedy departure; 13,000 sailors perished. Five years later the Mongolians returned to Japan, which had increased its fortifications. After six months' fighting, the *kamikaze* wind returned and a further 60,000 sailors in the Mongol navy perished.

In south-east Asia, Khubilai's army overcame 2,000 elephants fielded by the fearsome Burmese King Narathihapate, who was reputedly able to put away 300 curries in a day. Khubilai's success was short-lived and he went on to incur major defeats in Java and Vietnam, his army ill-suited to jungle warfare. His wife, Chabi, died in 1281 and his chief heir, five years later. Khubilai lost interest, lapsing into huge eating and drinking binges. His gout worsened and he became extremely fat. He died in 1294 and is supposedly buried in the Khentei Mountains near the tomb of Genghis Khan.[18]

The streams remained iced up all the next day. By evening, Ruslan and I were snapping at each other. It was cold, neither of us felt like camping and cooking but we were stuck in a range of hills out of sight of human habitation. Just as we were beginning to give up, we spotted a huge herd of horses. A lone herder directed us to a nearby farm. We rode in pitch black for an hour; my eyes were leaden and unable to focus, my backside was raw and calloused. Finally I heard dogs barking and knew we were near our target.

A wizened *babushka* hurried us inside. She sent her son off to tend to our horses while we ate stew. Before retirement, she had been the local biochemistry teacher; her husband worked for the local communist mouthpiece. They lived in a dingy two-roomed adobe hut and looked after the family herd of about forty sheep; the rest of the family lived in a nearby village. Her daughter, a doctor in her thirties, was visiting with her 5-year-old daughter. Her hair was scraped back under a bright red scarf, which clashed with her purple cardigan. Once, her bold Turkic features must have been striking, now her face sagged, brightening occasionally in a metallic smile. As we ate, the *babushka* and her granddaughter sang Kazakh ballads. Despite her drab appearance – a shabby grey cardigan, woollen leggings underneath a skirt – her profound, etched, handsome face lent dignity to her pathetic surroundings. She sang tunefully, her voice wavering, age having robbed her of the ability to hold her notes steadily.

About thirty kilometres further on, we came up against a range of precipitous, rocky hills which we needed to cross. Ruslan kept asking to take a look at my map. Although I had explained to him various features such as contour lines, he was beginning to see through his teacher. A precipitous rocky range ahead spelled trouble. I was not sure how we would find a path through them; nothing was marked on my map. To make matters worse, it bucketed down and we were later bombarded by hail. Ruslan had no waterproofs so I gave him my cape. My down jacket held off the rain for a while but within a few hours, freezing rain had passed through five layers of clothing. We soldiered on. My face burned, I couldn't feel my hands but I hadn't the heart to ask Ruslan for my cape. If we camped, there would be no chance of drying out my clothes. Just as I was giving up, we spotted a collection of buildings in the distance.

At teatime we reached a small collective. My teeth were chattering like those in a comedy skeleton. A young man hurried out and invited us in for tea. His wife, a neat, professorial woman, dragged me off into a side room, stripped me naked and brought me a tub of piping-hot water. Motioning me to a stool, she proceeded to wash my hair for me. I have never been so grateful for a tub of hot water and a bit of privacy. For the previous three weeks, I had had to make do with wiping myself with Wet Ones doused in antibacterial gel. At night, it had been too cold to undress and I hadn't been able to wash my clothes, they would have frozen. I emerged from the bedroom dressed in a Kazakh velvet gown, flushed from the hot scrub. My knickers, bra, socks, long johns, jodhpurs, woolly trousers and three sweaters were dangling above the stove, already washed.

My new friend, Aynura, was a Russian teacher. She spoke a few words of English and was thrilled to be able to try them out. While we chatted, her sister made noodles topped with intestines and stomach. It's amazing what you enjoy when you are hungry. After dinner, we heard conspiratorial giggling in the next room. Her two young daughters aged six and eight, dressed in long velvet shifts, shuffled bashfully into the room. One adjusted her wonky headgear, a gold embroidered box-hat topped with a feather, the other was hiding under a fur hat with a large fake diamond in the centre, which looked as if it belonged to one of the three wise men. Both had small butterfly clips in their hair, which fluttered as they moved. We clapped to the music as they swirled, hands outstretched to the fingertips, snaking their arms, twirling their wrists, palms up, down, out to the wall. As they ducked and swooped, their mother's bangles jingled up to the elbow and tinkled down again.

Overnight, thick snow cloaked the surrounding hills. I was worried; it was 2 November and we would soon be fighting a running battle with the winter. The journey had been beset with delays. Difficulties with my guides in Mongolia, delays at the border, the detour to Moscow, negotiations for new horses and guides had set me back several months. If the heavy snows came, I would have to stop for the winter.

Once again I find myself in front of the small painting in a simple frame. Tomorrow morning I leave for the village, and I gaze long and intently at the canvas, as if it can give me a word of advice for the journey ahead.

Aitmatov

13

APPROACHING WINTER

After negotiating for a waterproof for Ruslan, we set off with Aynura's husband, Marat, who kindly offered to guide us over the hills into the next village. Weaving around trees, fighting through undergrowth and clambering over rocks, we made our way to the top of the hill. The mountain-tops were veiled in thick cloud. Thick snowflakes blew into our faces and the visibility dropped to twenty metres. I couldn't see anything; my glasses kept steaming up beneath the huge hood of my cape. I kept my eye trained on Marat's fox-fur bonnet. Four hours later, we reached Zhanat, frozen to our saddles and highly grateful to an old couple for their timely invitation for bread, jam and tea. Marat bade us a speedy farewell and rode home.

We asked local villagers for directions to the shops; our provisions were low and Ruslan needed cigarettes. That afternoon we saw the menacing side of the settlements. A group of drunken villagers sent us off on a wild-goose chase, a gathering crowd following behind shouting out new directions and mocking us when we came to another dead end. Forgetting the supplies, and anxious to get some distance between Zhanat and us, we rode on. The snow drifted down gently, enveloping the surrounding countryside in a blanket of silence. The moon reflected off the snow, making it easy to see our way. Ruslan and I kept looking back, hoping that we weren't being followed, praying that the thick snow would cover our tracks.

A number of farms were marked on the map but each time we rode expectantly towards one, we found another ruin. We decided to stop at midnight and camped in a deserted barn. Ruslan didn't want the horses to graze out in the open in case they gave away our position. We tethered them to pillars running the length of the barn and fed them some old straw we found on the roof. I slept badly; the horses restlessly pawed the ground, searching for wisps of straw that they'd left behind. Each time they moved, I was convinced we had company.

*

Throughout the following morning, the horses stumbled around, clods of snow sticking to the bottom of their shoes. We kept stopping to bang their shoes clean, but by mid-morning, the snow had melted. Crossing the river, past another abandoned farm, we headed along the main street in Taskesku. The village, formerly several hundred strong, was deserted, visited by an economic pestilence, which had sent every inhabitant scurrying for the next town. Behind a crumbling cemetery wall, topped by crescent moons, one or two graves were still tended in a surrounding sea of weeds.

Ten kilometres past the village, we followed a tiny track through well-tended fields of potatoes and wheat and climbed steeply up a ravine, greenery giving way to scree. I prayed that for the sake of face, my map-reading would do me justice this once. At the top of the mountain, we found ourselves looking down on the glinting roof-tops of Taskeskin, a large river slithering between us and the town. Several hundred kilometres through the haze, the celestial peaks of the Tien Shan erupted out of the bleak monotony, the mountain water soaked up by the Sary Ishikotrau Desert, which stood in our way. I hoped that a couple of blue circles on the map, marking wells, would enable us to cross with horses. Only local know-how would tell me whether the wells would be dried up and derelict like the rest of rural Kazakhstan.

Ruslan insisted that I photograph him, standing in his stirrups clutching the silver jaguar hilt of his long knife, which he thrust heavenwards looking as though he would massacre the townsmen below. We hurried beyond Taskeskin, riding along broken irrigation channels in the pitch black for several hours until Ruslan said it was safe to camp. Neither of us could be bothered to cook; we each ate a Metro, the Turkish equivalent of a Mars Bar, and turned in.

Saddling the horse in the morning, I noticed that Three Socks and Black Hat were both getting saddle sores. The other horse, which Ruslan sarcastically nicknamed 'Champion', was tiring. Only Tom and Wolf were holding up with no problems. At lunch, the wind picked up. We got lost in swells of giant feather-grasses, standing up in our saddles to catch our bearings by the Tien Shan. We didn't stop for lunch; we were short on snack food. Ruslan said he was hungry enough to eat a sheep. Ruslan asked me to describe a pizza, my craving. I said it was like unleavened bread covered in cheese and tomato. Once he heard that some had meat toppings, he agreed that pizza sounded good and asked me to take him out for a pizza when we got to Almaty.

We began crossing the Sary Ishikotrau Desert. It wasn't a typical desert, few sand dunes, no fiery rockfaces, just dried-up earth and desert scrubland. I was hoping that we could cut out a day's ride and some of the desert by taking the ferry across Lake Sassykol. There was no fuel for the ferry. Despondent, we rode in silence. Ruslan was no longer afraid of snapping at me. I sulked in the saddle and kept to myself. Each day we were covering less and less ground. The days were short; it was dark by 5.30. The horses were tiring easily; the brown winter grass contained a fraction of the nutrients of summer grass. On a good day we were managing twenty-five kilometres; I'd been doing forty in Mongolia. Dragging ourselves out of bed, loading the horses and sitting all day, freezing in the saddle, was sucking my resolve away. I was starved of real conversation. My pidgin Russian didn't stretch to long conversations. I could hold simple conversations but there was no way I could explain in Russian how lonely I felt and how I wished I could turn to someone else occasionally for moral support. Ruslan was lucky. He could confide in the local Kazakhs whenever we stopped for the night. Every day, I had a silent fight inside me and I fought to suppress a voice willing me to give up. Every day, I thought about cheating. Who would know if we took a lorry for a few hundred kilometres?

Trekking across salt flats we reached the edge of Lake Sassykol, home to many birds, whose tranquillity is disrupted by the relentless shudders of great juggernauts plying the A350, the main arterial road between Semipalatinsk and Almaty. That evening, we came across a young man standing by a washing line weighed down by half a dozen fish. A crude cardboard sign, balanced on a wooden chair, encouraged passing lorry drivers to stop for a snack. I asked him if our horses could drink from his well and whether he dealt in hay and we were soon sitting at a long wooden table in his house, dining on fish. They did a good trade there, selling fish for one to three dollars apiece, depending on the size. While we were eating our supper, the son came in with a huge bag of onions, which he had bartered for the rest of the day's catch.

I awoke at dawn to a bustle of activity. The men were off to inspect their nets. A *babushka* was sitting on an upturned bucket in a corner turning the handle of the 'separator', a big mixing bowl full of boiled milk. As the mixture whirled round, the cream floated to the top, filtering out through the upper spout into a plastic red washing bowl; the milk sank to the bottom and poured out through another spout into a milk churn.

Our host, a fat unshaven Turkic man with small Asiatic eyes and an uneven fringe of brown hair protruding from a fake fur hat, confirmed that in about twenty kilometres, we would find a small settlement of railway workers where there was water. At sundown, we found the railway line crossing the desolate plain. A train piled high with coal chugged past. Ruslan gazed at it in wonder, counting the carriages.

'Forty-six,' he exclaimed, awe-struck. 'I've been on a train before, when I did my military service in the rocket station in Semipalatinsk.'

'Have you been to Almaty before?'

'Yes, many times. I have an uncle in Almaty, he drives airport buses.'

'Maybe you could fly home?'

'I flew many times when I was in the army,' he swaggered. After a long measured pause Ruslan continued:

'Achak. When we get to Almaty, will you take me to the zoo?'

A group of workers were heading home on a wooden wagon, which glided along the rail tracks, an exhausted worker pumping away at a lever to keep the momentum going. We called out for directions. 'Saikam is eight kilometres that way.' We heaved a collective sigh and trudged alongside the railway. We rode for several hours in the dark. I couldn't see the ground and relied entirely on Three Socks's night vision. Finally we heard dogs barking and Ruslan was soon tethering our horses to a white picket-fence by the railway station. He went inside, seeking an invitation. A dozen friendly eyes looked up at us as we walked in. We were standing over a low table, piled high with local delicacies. I washed my hands in a small basin and sat down to join the party.

One guest identified the birthday boy among the other railwaymen: a moustachioed man named Altai with a hedgehog hairstyle and deep, jolly crows' feet. He was thirty-three. His generously proportioned wife sat beside him, her hair pinned back in a loose bun, folds of flab ballooning over a loose-cut pair of trousers and a leopard-print shirt straining at an ample bosom. For several hours we sang, each taking turns to toast.

'To *druzheba* (friendship). May the next year bring your family happiness, health and wealth.'

I sang 'Happy Birthday' to make up for a lousy toast and slugged back yet another vodka.

'Safe journey!'

'To Tony Blair.'

'Down with Nazarbaev,' I roared.

'*Druzheba*', slurred Ruslan, breaking the embarrassed silence I had caused around the table. We crested a drunken wave, singing, dancing and toasting; the crescendo eventually descended into a hazy silence and deep sleep.

I woke at six, my mouth was parched and my head was throbbing. I found Ruslan cradling his head on the steps outside; the party had wound up a couple of hours beforehand. I fed some grain to the horses and was rewarded with an exceedingly painful nip on my left breast from Black Hat as I tried to share some of his food with the other horses.

All morning, Champion tripped and stumbled.

Ruslan kept mocking, 'How much did you pay for this horse? Two hundred dollars? Congratulations! They told you this was Katon Karagay's Champion?'

'Shut up, Ruslan.'

At midday Champion sat down. Ruslan whipped him hard, knowing that we had to get him on his feet fast.

'Get me Tom,' he ordered. He attached Champion's bridle to Tom's tail. 'OK, go.'

I led Tom forward, tugging on Champion's bridle while Ruslan pulled Champion up by his tail. Back on his feet again, he walked shakily towards a clump of long grasses. Champion was exhausted. We decided to rest up for a few days. In the night, we could hear barking and decided to track down the source the next morning. The barking emanated from a pig farm. Russians, who make up over 30 per cent of the population, purchase the majority of the meat, but the Kazakhs are not adverse to a bit of pork once in a while. They seem to wear their Islam rather loosely. I never heard the call to prayer there, or saw anyone praying and they drank hard liquor in obscene quantities.

Our hosts at the farm were a young couple. The wife, a stout young girl, her hair hidden by a pink headscarf shot with silver, sat at a table rolling out dough with great precision. She pulled the flattened dough towards her, folded it in half before rolling it out again. She repeated this several times before finally chopping it into noodles, all the while bouncing a baby on her knee and singing like a cherub. The infant, demonstrating all the early signs of perfect pitch, gurgled in unison. As we waited for our noodle stew, I took the baby on my knee and sang 'Old Macdonald Had a Farm', which had the baby burping joyous bubbles every time I got to the chorus. While the men smoked, I snacked on teaspoons of cracked wheat, rolled in butter.

After dinner, we played cards with half the pack, six and above. The young girl threw herself headlong into the game, her thin veneer of femininity cast aside as she slapped her winning cards on the table, thrashing the men in every game. They didn't notice me sneaking off to the nearest bed. I was soon fast asleep.

A couple of days' ride from the pig farm, we hit a patch of rolling dunes, hard work for the already exhausted horses. Wolf tracks dotted the sand. As we led the horses, Ruslan and I had a long conversation using my dictionary and mime. He asked me if I would consider buying his farm. I tried to explain that I know nothing of farming but he ignored me. I wondered if it was a put-up job by his father. He kept insisting that it was a good farm; it had six tractors, three houses on a plot of ten hectares. His father paid $3,500 for it when the Soviet Union collapsed. They made enough money to purchase it by fishing on Lake Zaysan. Even in the winter, they would fish. In fact, this was the time of year when he could make money. He could make $40–$50 on a good day. Holding on to one end of the family fishing net, Ruslan would drill a large hole into the ice through which he would feed a four-metre pole attached to the other end of the net. Four meters further on, his brother would be waiting over another hole to retrieve the net and feed the next length of four metres under the ice. And so on, until the net stretched seventy-five metres. In the summer they farmed watermelons. Part of the surrounding land was still owned by a large landlord from Ust-Kamenogorsk. They leased the land from him, paying him from the proceeds they made from selling grass.

I wanted to help Ruslan. He was a sound individual surrounded by alco-holics (but I couldn't broach this with him). He needed to get out of the house and set up on his own. Couldn't he use the salary, which he would earn in the course of the next month, to contribute towards the purchase of a house? Of course, came the reply, in his village, $300 would buy him four cows or two houses!

After his rest, Champion seemed to be much better. Ruslan rode Black Hat and I rode Three Socks; Tom and Wolf carried the baggage. We tied Champion to the back of the caravan. An hour before nightfall, we came to a river. It was quite deep, but nothing that we hadn't already encountered and the current was not strong. Ruslan led the way with the baggage horses; I was meant to follow behind leading Jijig, with Champion at the back of my caravan. Carelessly, I rode alongside Ruslan's horses and got too close to a clump of snagged driftwood. I'm not quite sure what happened next, but something startled Jijig who dragged Champion towards the driftwood and broke loose from the caravan.

I looked back to see Ruslan wading back into the water. Champion was floundering in deep water, his hoof stuck in the branches. I waded in to help, holding Champion's head up to keep him from drowning. I stood waist deep for half an hour, while Ruslan found a length of rope and tied one half around Champion's neck and the other half to Tom's tail. Tom sensed something was wrong; he became skittish, shying and prancing nervously. Ruslan steadied him and encouraged him forward. Suddenly Champion was pulled free and dragged half-way up the bank where he lay shivering, staring up at me in resignation. The ropes had chaffed his neck and he had gashes on his back where he'd been cut by pieces of driftwood.

Ruslan warned me that if we didn't get the horse back on its feet, it would die. Like before, we tried to tie his halter to Tom, Ruslan pulling him up by his tail. Champion thrust out his front feet and was almost upright again when he keeled over and his legs folded beneath him. Again and again, we pulled his front legs out from underneath him and tried to drag him up; each time he tottered and fell like a newborn foal. We left him to rest while Ruslan collected the other horses. Ruslan insisted that we move on; we were wet and cold and our clothes would soon start to freeze.

Ruslan went over to Champion and gave him a last brutal whack of his whip. He staggered to his feet. In broken Russian I tried to explain that we should leave Champion. He would be fine there; he had grass and water. We set off again and I looked round to see Champion at the back of the caravan. I was too tired and cold to bother trying to explain again that he should leave the horse behind. In less than an hour, we would be at a farm and we could leave him there. After twenty minutes fighting through a thicket we realized that we wouldn't be able to get through to the farm marked on the map. Ruslan insisted that we cross the river again; he would find a safe place for us to cross. He slowly picked his way across the river and I followed, petrified that we would re-live our earlier ordeal. We made it safely to the other side. His horses scaled the muddy bank and I followed. Champion slipped on the mud, wet from Ruslan's dripping horses, and collapsed half-way down the muddy bank. We tried to get him to stand again but he kept slipping on the mud and sliding further down the bank.

For several hours, we tried to get him back on his feet again; I held Tom's reins, pulling Champion by the head while Ruslan tried to lift him by the tail. At each attempt, Ruslan barked directions at me, some of which I misinterpreted, unleashing torrents of abuse. Several times, we came close and then Champion teetered and fell over again, groaning. Ruslan stretched out Champion's front hooves again and we kept trying. My head was swimming with orders and words that I'd never heard before. We scrambled around in the dark, oblivious of the fact that our clothes had frozen our backs. We tried pulling him up with both horses. The directions became more complicated and difficult to communicate and Champion became more exhausted with each attempt.

Finally, Ruslan threw down his whip and sat down. I looked at my watch. It was midnight; seven hours had passed since we waded across the river. Ruslan built a fire next to Champion. I took my knife out of my boot and cut grass. I found a couple of packets of Muesli and poured them in front him. Gathering together all of the horse felts, and the groundsheets, I lay them on top of Champion. He was slumped half on his side, not quite sitting up, in a puddle of his own urine and shitting where he lay. All night,

I lay in my tent shivering, unable to sleep as I listened to slow moans from Champion as he shifted his weight around and made feeble efforts to stand.

He was no better in the morning. We tried to get him on his feet, but he had given up the fight. We couldn't just leave him there; the wolves would get him in no time. I drew my forefinger across my throat and pointed to Champion. Ruslan, a farmer, used to the ritual slaughter of animals, checked himself. Swallowing nervously, he withdrew his knife from down his boot. I cursed the Kazakhs. Why wouldn't they allow us to have a gun? I didn't turn away when he slit the jugular; it was my fault and I wasn't going to run away. Champion, seemingly resigned to death beforehand, thrashed around as the blade went in. As the blood seeped away into the earth below, he lay rasping, blood caught in his windpipe which hung out of the hole in his throat. I wish I could say it was quick, but it wasn't and Ruslan had to break his neck. He moved the head back to where it should have been, took off the bridle, threw it into the bushes and went down to the river to wash.

The other horses kept their distance. We packed up quickly, walking up and down the bank past the body as we moved the bags and loaded the horses out of sight of Champion. We didn't talk about it; I think we were both disgusted with what we had had to do. I shivered on my horse turning the events over and over in my mind. Ruslan rode ahead wearing half of my spare clothes; none of his had dried. All day we negotiated irrigation channels hidden by huge elephant-grasses. Several times we were forced back, the banks too steep. Wolf balked at every crossing, repeatedly breaking his bridle, which we had to mend with makeshift knots. Each of these obstacles was a welcome relief which interrupted the voices in my head which kept repeating that it was my fault. We stopped for a rest in the late afternoon, neither of us felt like eating.

We soldiered on but the ride was no longer enjoyable. Every day we were simply going through our paces, trying to get mileage under our belts. Ruslan and I frequently snapped at each other, tired of trying to make ourselves understood. The horses were tiring and despite the meticulous care we took in saddling the horses, Three Socks and Black Hat's sores were getting worse. Even the village vet shrugged his shoulders in resignation; he didn't have enough money to buy medicine. The nearest supplies were in Taldy Kurgan, 200 kilometres away.

'I trained at university in Almaty,' he told us. 'It was very expensive. I had a good position on a Kolkhoz. Now it is kaput. I have no clients. If an animal is sick, the farmer kills it. Vets are too expensive.'

His house was littered with memories of better times: the playroom was scattered with broken toys, a redundant television in the corner – all day we'd walked underneath electricity poles with no wires between them. A tape recorder stood on the shelf, the back open, powerless gadgetry if you cannot afford the batteries to run it. Visiting the thunderbox was even more depressing. A neat stack of torn up textbooks sat within reach on a shelf. Curiosity got the better of me as I squatted and I reached for a piece. It was covered in complicated mathematical equations. Further down the pile, I found colour biology books neatly torn in four. Nothing was wasted in Kazakhstan, except a good education.

Learning to ride when they are young. Our host's 2-year-old daughter in the saddle

Winter arrived on 13 November. We stopped on a farm for two days and waited for a blizzard to blow itself out. Ruslan befriended Kairat, formerly the local schoolteacher, a skeletal figure with mousy brown hair, who fancied himself as a Kazakh Bob Dylan insisting on serenading us for hours on his guitar. By extraordinary coincidence, his family had once lived twenty kilometres from Ruslan's farm, now 600 kilometres away. Kairat invited us to his house for dinner, a drinking orgy which started with Kazakh cognac, moving on to vodka and finished after a few toasts of moonshine, which caused Kairat to rush from the room heaving. Finally we were allowed to sleep! The next morning, he was back on his guitar, strumming away for an interminable afternoon. When he wasn't playing, his 2-year-old daughter screamed the house down with her temper tantrums.

Farewell to Kairat. His neighbour is holding Jilda, my new puppy

At least the snow stopped. As we saddled the horses to leave, a mangy 2-month-old puppy was thrust into my arms. Ruslan had informed the villagers that I was on the look-out for a guard dog. I didn't know anything about dogs; my father's peripatetic career had never allowed us pets but I decided that buying a young puppy would be the best way of assuring that our future guard dog only owed its loyalty to me. I was told the puppy would balloon into a monster of a dog. She looked cute: off-white, with a black brindle, big brown eyes and floppy golden velvet ears. Her fur was matted and dirty and she looked like the runt of the litter. She wouldn't have been my choice, but now that she had been given to me, I felt responsible; it wouldn't be right to give her back. Who else would want her? I knew that she would have a good life with me and would not have to suffer the privations of the other dogs in the village. Earlier that morning, as I squatted in the thunderbox, another dog, possibly one of her relatives had scrambled underneath me and feasted on the contents. Reluctantly, I stuffed the puppy down the front of my jacket and handed a dollar to its owner. Despite the freezing wind and the deep snow, we set off again; I was desperate to get away from Kairat and his guitar.

As I rode, the puppy remained motionless, save for the occasional whimpering; I kept thinking she must have suffocated. Once in a while, I reassured myself that this was not the case, popping a lump of curd or a piece of bread down my front. The puppy shuffled around in my midriff, found the food, snuffled and chewed contentedly. As she gained confidence, she began popping her head out through the top of my jacket, looking around, sniffing the air, deciding it was rather chilly and snuggling back down again. She particularly liked nestling her head up my armpit and into my sleeve. I can't imagine why. Getting up and down from my horse for loo stops was rather difficult with my new addition. As I squatted, I would point at her and encourage her to do the same. She seemed to get the message. On one occasion, having done her business, she trotted underneath me in mid-session; it was with great reluctance that I put her back into my jacket. Several days later, I realized to my horror that she had brought with her a whole host of hangers-on, who were hopping around in my hair; I began to itch all over.

For the next few days, we trudged through the snow, which had bleached the steppe into a pastel glare. One evening, at dusk, we stopped at an isolated farmhouse. The foothills of the Tien Shan were powdered pink in the evening sun and the steppe had lost the brightness of sun on snow. I had barely swung my leg out of the saddle when a tubby lady, Aigul, the caricature of a farmer's wife, with pin-prick eyes creased into nothingness by a chubby grin, charged out of the house waving a cardboard coupon from a tea-packet in my face.

'What is the English word for *slon*?' Aigul kept asking in Russian. As I stepped through the doorway, she followed, flapping the coupon and persisting in scattergun staccato, 'English word for *slon*?' She began waving an arm frantically in front of her nose as I leafed through my dictionary; I still hadn't got used to the order of a Russian dictionary and I couldn't find 's' which is written like a 'c' in Cyrillic.

'How do you spell *slon*?' By this stage she was apoplectic with curiosity. At last I found the word. Elephant. Write it, she demanded. I filled in the blanks in the tea coupon and she hurried into a room for an envelope.

'I will post it to Moscow tomorrow and win a big prize.' Her tiny eyes beamed with excitement. I was now an honoured guest. She hurried around the room, plumping up cushions for us to sit on, clattering around the stove as she put on the kettle and prepared dinner. All the while she hummed contentedly, already convinced she'd won. Her excitement soon set off the shrill shrieking of a newborn baby. She bustled next-door and came back, carrying the screaming bundle, continuing at her chores and bouncing the baby in one arm, cooing 'Johnny, Johnny'.

Later her husband tumbled in, the door slamming in the wind as he stamped the snow off his feet. As he hung up his sheepskin coat and fox-fur

Aigul with Jilda as a puppy

hat, his wife excitedly twittered away in Kazakh; the only word I understood cropped up regularly:

'*Slon ... slon ... slon*.' She rushed into the other room and picked up the
packet. 'Elerhant,' she explained to him authoritatively.

He looked imploring in Ruslan's direction as if to say, 'Save me from this
ceaseless twittering.' He wouldn't dare say it out loud. The inane, useless
grin plastered on a whiskered, weathered but youthful face, said it all; she
wore the trousers.

After breakfast, I watched Aigul milking the cows, dressed in a bright
pink raincoat with a white scarf wound around her head like a turban. She
shouted and growled at the cows as they trotted around the cow shed,
avoiding her sky blue bucket. Finally she caught one, which was scratching
its behind on a pillar. I was in no hurry to leave. Particularly when Aigul
offered me the chance to wash in the family sauna. It took three hours to
heat it up. The baby cried all morning and she soothed it, still singing
'Johnny, Johnny'. I don't know which was more grating. I felt sorry for the
farmer's wife, stuck inside all winter in a one-roomed house with a screaming infant. Every now and then, she checked to see if he had wet himself
and replaced his tights with a dry pair, which hung along with half a dozen
others on a small washing line inside. Without even rinsing them, she hung
the wet pair up to dry.

Sunset on Lake Issyk-kul in bright, crisp light

Jilda and I were ravenous in the morning after our long slog the previous night. Heading for the dining area, I was told it was closed for 'the president's visit'. Akaev liked to hunt big game from the lodge on weekends. The corridor to my room was also closed, I wasn't allowed back inside. I was likewise banned from walking outside. It soon transpired that we were not allowed anywhere and that I was also not allowed to leave. Not only did the idea of banning me from everywhere defy all logic but it also seemed an unreasonable way to treat one's guests.

Sensing my disappointment, the hotelier, Ignait, sought to make amends. Accompanied by his children, we drove up into the mountains until the Lada's wheels spun into exhaustion. We got out, lifted the car up, turned it around and found a suitable place to park. Trudging up through the snow, we found the resort, a few button lifts but no guests, no skis and no power. Not one to be defeated, Ignait tied a couple of plastic bags around his boots and armed with a couple of sticks as poles, he whizzed precariously down the slopes. Jilda found the experience terribly exciting, yapping furiously and chasing us up and down the slopes as we slid down on anoraks fastened around our bottoms, our very own polyester toboggans.

Back from the mountains, I embarked on another adventure in late January and flew down to Osh, secreting Jilda, who now weighed eleven kilos, in a roly-poly. She wasn't too happy about her confinement and squirmed around in the bag. Luckily she didn't make much noise and few noticed her until after take-off, when I took her out and put her on the seat next to me, much to the shock of the airline crew.

On the plane, I met a young out-of-work lawyer named Kursan. His face looked slightly Egyptian and his young features frequently relaxed into a smile, revealing rows of gold teeth. He was travelling with his sister and an unshaven man with a pale white chubby face called Talent, an 'entrepreneurial friend', clad in a full-length grey flasher-mac. They invited me to stay with them.

Osh is a predominantly Uzbek city, from which one travels east into the Fergana valley or south along the Pamir highway into Tajikistan. Unfortunately the area was caught up in a web of political intrigue. Kyrgyzstan's weak defences served as a useful conduit for the IMU, the Islamic Militants' Union, to foment Islamic extremism in the Fergana valley. Russian estimates at the time reckoned that outside aid to Islamic extremist organizations in Central Asia was more than a billion dollars per annum. The previous year, crack terrorist units, trained in Afghanistan and funded by Osama bin Laden and his al-Qa'eda organization, breached the Kyrgyz border and kidnapped four Japanese geologists, panning for gold near Batken. The Kyrgyz Minister of Interior Security was sent down to negotiate their release; he was also kidnapped. Hundreds of terrorists swarmed in the famous rice-producing area, initially paying locals for produce and eventually requisitioning vast numbers of animals. According to a friend, the Kyrgyz could not afford their part of the ransom and had to pay part in cash and part in livestock. The Japanese supposedly paid the $2 million ransom and the geologists were released.

Kursan's brother-in-law, a border guard on the Kyrgyz-Tajik border, was a man of wrestling proportions: a fraction under six feet and at least seventeen stone. I couldn't believe that I was staying under the roof of a type whom I had grown to distrust. He had no qualms about fleecing me under his own roof, doling out his hospitality with largesse and chumminess and leaving it to Kursan to ask for a succession of 'contributions' towards the *plov* which added up to more than the cost of a couple of sheep. All night, we knocked back glass after glass of vodka amid meaningless toasts to *druzheba*, health, wealth, world peace, family: any excuse to allow our hosts to sink another shot.

I felt like death as we climbed Suleiman, a large rock in the centre of Osh, on which Babur, the famous founder of the Moghul dynasty, built a retreat. Mohammad himself is supposed to have prayed there. Behind the temple stood a large slab of rock set at a forty-five-degree angle, smoothed from years of rubbing by the locals. A collection of country folk sat gossiping around the rock, taking turns to slide down it and pray to Allah. An old lady was orchestrating the ritual. I asked if she was a shaman, the Central Asian equivalent of a witch doctor.

'No, we are only interested in the light side, not the dark side.'

One lady lay on her back at the bottom of the rock chute, praying. She stood up and started coughing, choking and retching violently, trying to rid herself of the evil spirits responsible for her backache. Such hybrid practices, which combine Islam and Animism, are common throughout Central Asia.

The view of Osh from Suleiman

Not long after Mohammed's death, the Arabs of the Umayyad dynasty invaded Central Asia. By AD 713, they had conquered Samarkand and Bukhara, destroying the Zoroastrian fire temples and building mosques. By the beginning of the second millennium, Bukhara was second only to Mecca in the Arab world, flourishing with poets, mathematicians and physicians, such as Ibn Sina.

The nomadic peoples embraced Islam much later. Mongke Khan, installed by Batu, sent his brother Hulegu to destroy the power of the Ismailis, known as the Assassins, whose murderous missions had not only made it as far as the Mongol courts but also into the bedchamber of England's

Edward I. Having exterminated the cut-throat Ismaelis, Hulegu set out to fulfil the second part of his mission, the submission of the Abbasid Caliph in Iraq. Estimates of the carnage in Baghdad vary between two hundred and eight hundred thousand. The Caliph and his family, in accordance with Mongol tradition that forbids the spilling of royal blood, were sewn up inside a carpet and trampled to death. Prince Kamil Muhammad, one of the Caliph's commanders, was trussed up like a chicken and forced to eat his own flesh in slices until he died.

Hulegus's chief wife and his chief commander were Nestorian Christians; this had helped unite many Georgian Christians under Hulegu's banner. Fresh from his success in Baghdad, Hulegu's holocaust rampaged through Aleppo and Damascus, creating the Ilkhanate of Persia. The crusaders debated joining the savage Mongols, despite their atrocities against orthodox Christians, and conquering the Mamelukes in Syria thereby eradicating Islam for good. But Islam was saved; the Great Khan Mongke died of dysentery contracted on a campaign against the Sung dynasty and was supposedly buried along with 20,000 witnesses, despatched to serve their master in the after life. Another kuriltai was called. Hulegu withdrew from Syria, leaving a small detachment to guard Damascus. The Mamelukes wasted no time. Within the Mameluke ranks were many Cumanians, formidable steppe horsemen captured by the Mongols and sold into slavery to the Caliph of Egypt. The small Mongol detachment was easily massacred by their fellow nomads and with it, the Mongol myth of invincibility perished.

Batu Khan was succeeded by his brother Berke, who became the first important Muslim Khan. The massacre of the Caliph of Persia offended Berke, the recent convert to Islam, and created a further schism in the Genghissid line. In 1262, Berke's Golden Horde, allied with the Mamelukes, declared war on Hulegu, head of the newly created Ilkhanate of Persia. Berke later sided with the Chaghadai Khanate, supporting the young pretender to the imperial mantle, Ariq Boke, against his older brother, Khubilai, who sided with Hulegu.[19]

As we strolled back into the centre of town, our host caught sight of a brand new BMW 5 series and flagged it down. The driver got out and greeted him like an old friend. It came as no surprise when later we found out that he was a kingpin in the local drugs trade. Apparently fifty per cent of customs officials cooperate with the drugs trade. A customs official in Central Asia is a privileged position reserved for family and friends. Recruits pay for the entitlement to a stream of bribes, which are tantamount to an annuity. Some don't even bother to collect their $20 monthly salary.

The drugs were coming from Afghanistan and at that time accounted for over eighty per cent of the world heroin market. The trade is inextricably linked to factional rivalries of Afghan warlords. In 1997, Tajik authorities seized eight tonnes of heroin belonging to the drug baron, Hadj Gulyam Balosh, who had been financing the Afghan war. Osama bin Laden was supposed to have had sixty heroin laboratories, which funded his terrorist activities. In October 1998, officials in Osh stopped a supposedly humanitarian shipment from Iran containing seven hundred tonnes of weapons destined for Ahmad Shah Masoud. Some of Afghanistan's heroin was exported via Osh, although the Turkmen border was said to be the most porous.

Not satisfied with the preceding evening's drinking binge, our hosts went 'larger' on the vodka, slugging down toast after toast amidst numerous games of backgammon. My counterpart was a Russian, who had returned from a 'business trip' in Tajikistan. A former handball champion of the USSR, he was built like a brick privy and a perfect operator in the trade. The chips flooded into his hands as I floundered, my mind befuddled by vodka. His shining grin showed his ability, like so many Russians, to 'put his money where his mouth was'.

The next morning, I escaped to the bazaar, determined to nurse my hangover on my own. I sat in a *chaikhana* alongside bearded Afghans, blue-eyed Tajiks, Uzbeks in their trademark skullcaps, local women in flowered headscarves shot with silver, and Kyrgyz in their conical felt hats. I tried to rehydrate on threepenny pots of tea, served from a 250 litre cauldron, and braved a few of the greasy signature dumplings while I watched the world go by.

When Kursan seemed to have had all the drinking he could take, he suggested we travel to his parents' house, sixty kilometres south of Osh; I happily obliged. His mother was a shaman, one of a dying breed in Central Asia. Shamanism, the common animistic heritage in Central Asia goes back before the Mongols and Tibetans chose Buddhism and the rest of Central Asia opted for Islam. A shaman embodies many roles – priest, mystic, doctor, magician. Blessed with powers inherited from birth, shamans can travel between heaven and earth and in different time zones. The shaman accompanies the dead to the underworld and tries to bring the sick back into this world. They can recover lost objects and are even said to be blessed with the ability to wrest happiness from the souls of animals and give it back to humans.[20] She greeted us from where she sat, enveloped in the folds of her woollen cardigan, skirt, leggings and fat. Her head was covered in a large grey woollen *babushka* shawl, which masked much of her face. Her overpowering stare unnerved me. Was it calculated or was she invading my thoughts and mapping my future? One moment she radiated formidable strength and the next she seemed on the verge of tears. Her movements were all made with deliberate weariness, reminding her family constantly of her heavy divining burden made worse by high blood pressure. Her daughters milled around her, plumping up cushions and bringing her fresh ferns, which she burned in a metal bowl, like incense, to alleviate her symptoms and to ward off evil spirits. Occasionally she passed the bowl over our heads with great ceremony, wafting clouds of smoke around the room. Often a shaman's powers are inherited; her grandmother was a shaman. She found out that she had the powers when she dreamed of her cousin's impending death.

Kursan's mother, a shamaness – one of a dying breed in Central Asia

All weekend, the house was under siege from villagers seeking the healing powers of the shaman. One woman sought help for a cold, which had plagued her for a month. A couple arrived seeking marital advice. She reached under a cushion beneath her ample bottom and produced her divining necklace, a long strand of multi-coloured stones and beads, which she cast down on a piece of red silk with a flourish, as though it were winning dice. A couple of kittens scurried on to the window-sill and gazed down at the beads. Each time, the necklace fell in a different way and she read the snaking length of stones to the young couple, combining the roles of witch-doctor with curate. She interspersed her sentences with Muslim prayers and finished off with an *amin*, covering her face and closing her eyes in prayer. The young man slipped some money under the cushion underneath him and the couple bowed and left. Another couple sought advice on the auspicious moment for childbirth. She produced a length of black cotton, which she knotted with deliberation and used to scrape his tongue. She then knitted the slobbery length into a small charm, gave them a few words of counsel, said another prayer and they left.

After her 'surgery,' we trekked up to a sacred, frozen fount head, a mass of deadly cascading icy daggers bursting out of the side of a rockface. Votive rags were tied in the bushes. The old lady headed into a cave and began to light pieces of sheep's felt, which she placed in various recesses, all the while muttering prayers and chanting. She sat on a rock in the flickering light, swaying slightly with her eyes shut, singing her prayers. At some point, she seemingly made the transition between Muslim and shaman. After several minutes, her eyes flew open; her face twitched and contorted and she began to cry. I comforted her as her shoulders convulsed. After a minute, she ran her hands over her face and got up and started walking down the mountain.

We stopped at another witch's house, now a ruin. A long staff bearing a black yak's tail fluttered above our heads in a corner. A huge ram's horn, covered in ribbons, sat on a piece of crumbling masonry. A series of triangular windows, one of which was heavily charred, conducted the sunlight into the roofless ruin, allowing the witch to use the sun as another divining tool. In the middle of the house lay the stone sarcophagus of the witch.

After a couple of days, playing cards and drinking vodka, I returned to Bishkek. Talent explained that he was staying on 'to do business'. Although he was apparently in the business of textiles, he had decided to branch out into the car trade. He was taking dollars into Uzbekistan, which he planned to swap on the black market at a rate far exceeding the official exchange rate. He planned to buy a car and smuggle it back to Bishkek, avoiding the Kyrgyz import tariffs, making himself a small fortune in the process.

After all the alcohol consumed in Osh, I decided to recover from the previous week's binge in a sanatorium on the shores of Issyk-kul. The waters of the lake were pale turquoise and the mountains were enveloped in a freezing mist. My hotel was nicknamed the Aurora; the enormous concrete eyesore supposedly looked like the battleship which launched the October Revolution. The hotel was a cavernous, chintzy, sixties-built, rabbit warren, with dozens of small chilly rooms offering massages, mud baths, aromatic herbal treatments, water and steam treatments. Most of the more bizarre treatments required a consultation with the doctor so I opted for a sauna and a massage.

Fully expecting the Russian equivalent of carrot and dandelion soup, I was shocked, and somewhat relieved, that the set menu started with a beet-root and fish salad drowned in mayonnaise, followed by a greasy stew with creamed potatoes and overcooked carrots. The meal finished with a gener-ous portion of rice pudding, with a huge blob of butter floating in the centre. The bar in the corner was doing a roaring trade in vodka. A recent survey in Newsweek ranked the Russians as the most obese nation in Europe, putting them on a pinch-an-inch par with the wobbling bellies of the USA; I now understood why.[21]

Up on the mountain behind the spa, hundreds of large stones littered the grass adorned with images of long-horned ibex, horses, hunters, deer, dancers and wolves: petroglyphs executed over two thousand years before. Small green dots on the rocks, the only semblance of conservation, indicated authenticity in a sea of well-executed imitations by bored shepherds, appealing to their Scythian artistic ancestry.

I got back to Bishkek. Kursan telephoned to let me know that Talent had been arrested and was languishing in jail in Uzbekistan, his car-smuggling racket blown open by the authorities. Kursan wanted to meet up; I knew he was going to try to ask me to post bail and I wasn't in a position to do so. We met in a local restaurant. Needless to say, he wasn't interested in eating, rapidly downing several beers before moving on to vodka shots. He walked me home and asked if he could have one more vodka. I had a cheap bottle in the fridge, which I opened with my hunting knife. It was late and I was tired and I asked him to leave. As I got up to motion him to the door, he pushed me down roughly on the floor and started trying to kiss me. I kept shouting 'stop' and tried to wrestle him off but he was too strong. As he continued to slobber on me, I kept thinking: he is not going to get away with this. I fumbled around for the hunting knife, sitting beside the vodka bottle on the low-slung coffee table behind my head. Grabbing the knife, I pressed the blade hard against his throat.

'Get out of my house now,' I screamed.

It was like turning the lights on. He sobered up immediately, jumped up and ran for the door. As I pulled the metal gate across, he tried to apologize. I slammed the door in his face.

I got up late, wincing at the pain in my shoulder, a reminder of how roughly I had been forced to the ground the previous night. I'd promised

Ira that I would meet up with a couple who lived on the next floor, who wanted to practice their English, for a museum tour. I couldn't cancel our date; they had been looking forward to it for days; besides, there was no point sitting at home dwelling on the events of the night before. As we walked to the museum, I was oblivious of Sveta's nervous excited chatter as I thought about how stupid I had been the previous night: was I wrong to have offered to take him out to dinner in repayment for his family's hospitability? Perhaps I shouldn't have let him walk me home – but the streets of Bishkek were dangerous. I knew that I should have turned down his request for a drink; I was stupid and lucky to have got off so lightly.

The English class was waiting for us in the entrance: builders, accountants, physicians, students, geologists, all were there in the hope that a smattering of English would give them the leverage to break out of their penniless condition. Natalia, their teacher, was a petite woman, more like a retired Russian ballet teacher than a would-be archaeologist turned English teacher. Severe, elegant and expansive, her pupils reverted to cowering schoolchildren as we wandered past glass cases containing ancient Kyrgyz saddles, whips, a full-sized model *yurt*, and Scythian tools. We stopped in front of a large glass cabinet.

'Now. Who is going to tell our guest, Claire, what is in this case?' All were momentarily tongue-tied. 'It is a traditional Kyrgyz gown, repeat after me, it is a traditional Kyrgyz gown.'

I looked around at the faces. Half were Russian and half Kyrgyz. I wondered whether the Russians also regarded this as their cultural heritage.

'You see her white headress? This woman is a walking pharmacy; all the family medicines are stored in her forty-foot turban. When she dies, she will be wrapped in it, how do you say in English?'

'A shroud.'

A life-size model of a woman sitting on a stool, spinning wool was the next focus of attention.

'This woman has forty plaits in her hair. The plaits represent the forty daughters of a hunter who went out into the forest. When they returned to their village, there wasn't a soul left; the Uzbeks had massacred their families. So they returned to the forest and mated with wolves; their offspring became the forty tribes of Kyrgyzstan.'

Historically, the Kyrgyz originated in the Yenisei Basin. First references to a people known as the 'Kyrgyz' appeared in Huan Tsang's chronicle in AD 629. In AD 840, the Kyrgyz overthrew the Uighurs in Mongolia and by

AD 1000, they had overthrown the Uighur Empire. Moving south-west, they eventually established themselves in the Tien Shan.[22]

We stopped at a model of the eleventh century Burana Tower, a huge minaret, now only a small stump.

'There is a beautiful story about this tower. A wicked father locked a young maiden in the tower. Every day, her lover would visit her and she would let down her long raven hair....'

Natalia wouldn't allow us to visit the two floors devoted to Lenin. Its existence is testament to the phlegmatic approach that the Kyrgyz have to politics. A colossal iron Lenin still lectures in the main square, Manifesto in hand gesticulating towards the Tien Shan, whose peaks were also converted: Peak Communism, Peak Lenin and even The Academy of Sciences Range. Now he points out the view to passing tourists who pose beneath the pedestal for a photo opportunity.

Despite Gorbachev's popularity in the west, his movement for *glasnost* and *perestroika* hold a different meaning for the Central Asians. Gorbachev has been accused of failing to understand the rising tide of nationalism, treating the 'stans' as mere colonies rather than members of the Union. His presidency coincided with the demise of most of the old guard who had governed Central Asia for twenty years. He insisted on Russian replacements. In Kazakhstan, he replaced Kunayev, a Kazakh, with Kolbin, an ethnic Chuvash from Russia, causing riots, seventeen deaths and the declaration of martial law.

Throughout Soviet Central Asia, ethnic tensions reached boiling point. Despite rising anti-Russian sentiments, most of the unrest was between ethnic minorities, the culmination of Stalin's policy of divide and rule. Since the mid-nineteenth century, the fertile land in Kazakhstan and Kyrgyzstan had been reallocated to Cossacks and Ukrainians. Then, during the Second World War, Central Asia became Stalin's human garbage dump: Volga Germans and Koreans from the Soviet Far-East were deported along with Chechens, Tartars and anyone else who might be construed as traitors to the war effort.

Stalin recognized the potent and potentially dangerous force of Islam as a unifying factor in Central Asia. To prevent the call for a pan-Turkic union, he invented nations and created nationalism. Each 'stan' was given a flag, a president, a parliament; competitions were organized to compose a national anthem and the history books were rewritten. None of the Central Asian borders was drawn up along purely ethnic lines. Patchwork borders were plotted. Despite being predominantly Tajik, Bukhara was deemed too (religiously) sensitive to give to the Tajiks, who were given a little piece of the Fergana Valley, populated by Uzbeks, to make up numbers. Some

Kyrgyz nomads found themselves in Tajikistan, while Kyrgyzstan was given Osh, a large Uzbek city at the head of the Fergana Valley, to reach their population quota. Such social manipulation was bound to set the groups off against each other, perhaps intentionally, for that would deflect anti-Russian sentiment.

Ethnic tension finally exploded throughout Central Asia in the 1980s, set off by a combination of economic deprivation and nationalism. In Uzbekistan, dozens died in gun battles in the Fergana Valley between ethnic Uzbeks and Meskhetian Turks. In Osh, when land from an Uzbek state farm was given to Kyrgyz for housing, the Kyrgyz and Uzbeks massacred one another; seventy five per cent of the local houses were burned down and it was said that dead babies were hung from butchers' hooks. Riots also broke out in Ashkabad and Dushanbe.

However, when independence came, it was not wrestled from Moscow. In Russia, a strong intellectual movement, led by the likes of Solzhenitsyn, encouraged the leaders to dump their Central Asian colonies:

> We don't have the strength for the peripheries either economically or morally. We don't have the strength for sustaining an empire – and it is just as well. Let this burden fall from our shoulders, it is crushing us, sapping our energy and hastening our demise.

On 8 of December 1991, the presidents of Russia, the Ukraine and Belarus signed a treaty in Brest, disbanding the Soviet Union and creating the Central Independent States. None of the Central Asian leaders was ever consulted.

Central Asia was cruelly torn from Mother Russia's breast. Overnight, Kyrgyzstan, once part of a superpower, became a third-world backwater. Subsidies, amounting to as much as forty-five per cent of local budgets, were stopped overnight. Tens of thousands of Soviet troops were demobbed. The army was no longer obliged to buy Uzbek cotton and Kyrgyz wool for uniforms. The Kazakhs lacked the 'donkeys' to pump their vast oil slick and the drilling equipment to extract their iron, coal, gold and uranium. Overnight, Kazakhstan found herself a space power and the first Muslim nuclear power, armed with Intercontinental Ballistic Missiles. The Uzbeks were left with seventy-five per cent of Soviet cotton but only five per cent of her textile factories. Factories were abandoned, their workers laid off; one of the largest factories in Bishkek, making machine gun parts, was doomed. And how could the Kyrgyz sustain a factory that processed Cuban sugar?

Like an enormous retreating high tide, the seas of Russia drew back leaving environmental detritus on their former colonies' shores, which some say will cost $800 billion to clean up, and economic chaos. By 1993, inflation was running at 1,500 per cent. In the decade since independence, Tajikistan has lost two-thirds of its GDP, Turkmenistan just short of half, Kazakhstan and Kyrgyzstan two-fifths. Even the Russians, who had been sent to build the empire, were left high and dry. Now the bulk of working people earn between $3–9 per month: $15 is considered a good salary and $30 well above average.[23]

The communist leaders who were confronted by this crisis still remain in power, each choosing a different future. Nazarbaev, in Kazakhstan, combined economic liberalism with authoritarianism, attracting foreign investment, while repressing his people. Dubbed 'Mr Ten Per Cent', he is said to have creamed off enough money into escrow accounts to make him the seventh richest man in the world. The country is governed from top to bottom by a corrupt web of patronage and clan loyalties. One floor in Almaty's central state museum is devoted to the glorification of Nazarbaev.

Askar Akaev, a Kyrgyz mathematician, surrounded himself with former pupils from the Academy of Sciences. Initially a darling of the West, who aimed to transform Kyrgyzstan into a liberal democracy, he had begun to develop a taste for power, preferring a one-party democracy which consistently returned him to office. He hadn't stolen Lenin's two floors in the museum yet....

After our visit to the museum, Boris and Sveta invited me to dinner in their apartment. Boris's forehead was a series of deeply trenched frown-lines, receding to a sparse, greying hairline; he was only thirty-five. Whenever I saw him, he had a cigarette dangling below a grey blond moustache and he was wired on caffeine. He spent the evening toing and froing from his workshop, a small room constructed on the balcony. He repaired televisions for a living and was working on one which needed to be ready by the next morning. He claimed to work best at night, slaving until five in the morning, sleeping four or five hours, before starting work again. The vast quantities of coffee he drank to keep awake, often shook the steady hand needed to solder the minuscule electronic circuitry and his eyesight was beginning to suffer.

Sveta, his wife, was a dark-haired, blue-eyed mousy woman, who oozed serenity and offset the frenetic staccato pace of her husband. She helped her mother in the children's computer club, while managing the unpredictable household budget, which ran, or ran out, on a day-to-day basis. Whatever happened, Boris had his coffee and fags to get him through another television set. In short coffee breaks between jobs, he would tell me about his life.

'I was born in Tashkent. I met my wife in Chelabinsk in Siberia. Her mother was not happy about Sveta coming to live in Kyrgyzstan. But life was very difficult in Chelabinsk. All you could find in the shops was vodka and salt. In Bishkek, things were much easier.'

'But were things better under communism?'

'Claire, many people will say life is better under communism, but they remember only the good things. In principle it was good system; I had a good job as a technician in the computer factory, working on Russian-made computers like IBM main-frames. But it was a police state; I could be arrested for having a video recorder because I might watch western propaganda. I remember my uncle was always singing 'Delilah' by Tom Jones. We were very frightened that someone might hear him and report him to the KGB. At least we have some freedom now but life is very difficult. Our new capitalist, democratic political system is not at fault; the problem is corruption. In the beginning I was an optimist; Kyrgyzstan was a free, democratic and independent country. Now I have no idea what the future holds. I am scared for my children. They could get on a bus one day, and the driver may rip up a valid student pass and ask for money or beat them up. You hear stories like this every day.

'I would like to borrow enough to expand my business repairing televisions. But the bank manager wants ten per cent for himself and twenty per cent on top for interest. How can I repay this sum of money? Only the family and friends of ministers can afford to borrow. If you start any business here, it is impossible to compete against contraband trade. The government charges huge duties on raw materials while allowing relatives to smuggle finished goods through customs for nothing. A businessman here is like a fish caught in the ice, you cannot move for bureaucracy and corruption.

'Every spring, the government announces a budget in the newspaper for machines to mend the roads. In summer, the papers say the machines have been purchased and will arrive in the autumn. We wait and wait and in November, the headlines confirm that the money has disappeared. My road tax this year has risen by eightfold to eight hundred som; that is two weeks' wage. Kyrgyzstan borrows so much money from the World Bank and the IMF and yet we see nothing. Russian people always ask *pochemou*, "why?" The answer is always the same: *pochemoushto* – "because"....'

'So I make do with my business at home. I repair televisions for five dollars and videos and video cameras for ten. Sometimes the work is simple, other times it takes several days. If I have money to spare, I buy old televisions, which I repair and sell.' He showed me a hybrid television he was working on. The controls were Grundig, the speaker made by Sony, the screen by Panasonic. 'I bought this for twenty-five dollars and I hope to sell it for a hundred,' he said proudly.

'I am trying to emigrate to Canada but it is a very difficult process. I need at least ten thousand dollars to pay the embassy, the agent and lawyers. If my application is unsuccessful, they don't return the money. So I am selling this flat. Last year, my neighbour sold his flat for nineteen thousand dollars. After the problems with fundamentalism in Osh, many people returned to Russia; now I cannot get ten thousand. In this block alone, about fifty per cent of the occupants have emigrated to Germany and Russia but I don't want to go to there. When a Russian looks at me, he doesn't see a Russian, he sees a Kyrgyz immigrant. Now I am also a foreigner here too. There is no hope here for my children.'

'It will be sad to leave; I built this apartment. It was the first "Molodoy Specialist" building. We used to live in barracks, huge buildings housing one hundred families. Each family had one room. There was only one kitchen in the building and one bathroom on each floor. Then young specialists were allowed to build their own apartments. When we weren't working in the computer factory, we were building this block and we guarded it every night.'

That night Boris and Sveta invited me to a heavy metal concert, given by one of Boris's friends. We drove down a seedy side-street and stopped outside a nondescript doorway. A rough Kyrgyz bouncer waved us down a flight of cellar steps and through a thick round metal door, similar to the portal in a submarine pressure chamber; it had once been a nuclear shelter. We entered a dark cavernous room, which looked like a Comintern wine cellar, transformed into a Hell's Angel biker's paradise with black netting cascading from the ceiling and obscene psychedelic paintings on the walls. A group of bikers was thrashing out a sequence of screeching cadences on electronic guitars, while the lead singer bawled out what sounded like a series of Russian expletives. We sat around a table next to a group of leather-clad, middle-aged revellers, whose table was littered with empty vodka bottles. Luckily, Boris's friend's band was closer to Meat Loaf than the Sex Pistols and we jived on the dance floor. Boris tried to pair me off for every dance with his best friend Sergei, a denim-clad Russian version of a Luke Duke with a handlebar moustache.

The other figure in my life in Bishkek was my Russian teacher, Elena, a middle-aged divorcée. Her smooth, luminous skin, neat black bob, and simple but elegant appearance contradicted the image of a mother single-handedly supporting three children. Her lessons had been refined through years of teaching Russian at the airbase. Pilots throughout the communist world, from Algeria to Cuba, were sent to Bishkek to train on Migs in some of the most hazardous and mountainous terrain in the world. In my first lesson, she produced dozens of picture cards, simple pieces of cardboard on to which she had stuck pictures of fruit, vegetables, animals, transport and fictional restaurant conversations. Throwing me back to schooldays, she laid a small table in the corner of my sitting-room and I was forced to act out little ordering scenes, somehow more embarrassing when there are only two of you in the room. The next time we had a lesson in directions, which seemed more like an aerobics class.

'*Peredee*,' she said, jumping around and thrusting her arms forward like a female cop on a shoot out. '*Vzadee*', she hopped again, throwing her thumbs behind her head. 'Left, right,' we hopped around some more, thumbing lifts in each direction. By the time she left, I was exhausted.

She invited me to dinner at her house the following night. I had expected that Elena would live in a more salubrious area. Half an hour out of the centre, past the second-hand car dump, the taxi turned into a litter-strewn wasteland, at the end of which was a group of low-rise flats. Her first-floor flat was dingy and damp.

'I bought this new metal door last year. Sometimes I am alone here at night and get frightened. The neighbours were jealous; someone poured varnish into the lock and now it does not work.'

One didn't have to scratch far beneath the carefully manicured exterior, to see the real Elena.

'I left my husband three years ago. By that time, I hoped Dmitri would be old enough to understand. I tried to make it work, Claire, but he was drinking very heavily and was always unfaithful. Now he is clever with Dmitri, taking him to the park, giving him presents to try to buy his love. But he does not pay for Dmitri's clothes, his school and he doesn't pay for the bills. This house is in my husband's name but he refuses to sign it over to me; I could lose it at any time.'

As she talked, lines I hadn't noticed before tightened around her mouth, she looked fragile, jaded and her energy evaporated.

'I was young when I met him. He was older than me, a handsome offi-cer in the air force. Once I had a good job; I worked in the university, I taught the pilots and I always had food on the table. I used to take my holidays in the Crimea. Now I have foreign students. Sometimes I have a few, sometimes none. Two years ago, my bank collapsed and I lost one thousand five hundred dollars; it was everything I had saved from my students.'

'My daughter Natasha is a teacher. She gets twenty dollars a month, if they pay at all. Sergei cannot find a job, after all the money I spent on university. I am sorry, I have talked too much and it is too late for you to travel home on your own. You will have to stay here. I am sorry you cannot have a bath; we have no hot water. Maybe we will have hot water in the morning. This summer we had no hot water or gas for several months. One week, we didn't even have electricity. People were cooking on open fires on their balconies.'

Despite its vast potential for hydroelectric power, Kyrgyzstan only produces a quarter of its energy requirements; its gas needs are being met by the Uzbeks, when the Kyrgyz can afford to pay. The current system of barters and swaps leads to frequent and sometimes lengthy disruption of gas supplies and bolsters Uzbekistan's leverage over its neighbour. However, Kyrgyzstan has one trump card, which it has yet to play. If Kyrgyzstan's reservoirs were to switch to the water collection regime, Uzbekistan's water supply would dry up and its cotton fields would be ruined. The water card may be too big a gamble for a weak Kyrgyzstan to risk playing on a stronger neighbour.

As I sat on the loo, I glanced at a large piece of white paper, which was stuck on the back of the door. Elena had been working her way methodically through the English dictionary, scribbling words down with a thick felt-tip pen. She was on the letter F: Fearful, Fearless, Feasible, Feast, Feat, Feather, Feature, Feckless, Fecund, Federal. Under the shopping list of words one phrase was underlined: 'I am fed up!'

Returning her hospitality, I took Elena and her son Dmitri to the ski resort, Kashka-Suu, in the mountains just outside Bishkek. We drove up there with a cabbie called Sergei, a well-educated Russian with a bushy fisherman's beard. Sergei said he couldn't afford to be a poet any more.

'I used to write for a living; there was a market for my articles and I published many of my poems. Now, when there is nothing to eat, I get in my car and drive around looking for customers. By the time I have earned enough to eat, I'm too tired to write. Whatever I write languishes in my drawer; no one can afford to buy books any more and the publishers return my work.'

As we drove up through small villages of well-tended cottages, he explained that they used to be populated by Germans. Anyone with a German grandparent had a passport out of Kyrgyzstan; they left in droves. We skidded along a partially-frozen stream bed, and up a track covered in fresh snow, revving up the hill until we hit a patch of ice and slithered down again. Sergei was quite determined to get us to the top. Again and again we reversed and attempted the steep climb but ten metres from the top, the wheels went into a spin. I got out and dug around in the opposite bank for grit, earth and twigs. We lined the road and I pushed. The wheels whirled, earth and slush splattered my face; the car skidded as we negotiated the icy spot that had foiled us on our previous attempts. Finally, I felt the car surge forward. Our joint efforts had formed a bond. Sergei was only a phone call away when I wanted to go somewhere.

Kashka-Suu possessed the only chairlift in Kyrgyzstan, a primitive wooden contraption. Unfortunately, the lifts were only operational on weekends. However, I was able to hire the drag-lift for $5 an hour. It consisted of a thin piece of rope attached to a piece of sawn-off plank which was hard to keep between my legs as the narrow end kept slipping out. On the other end of the rope, the lift operator pointed to a hook, which he explained I had to attach to the waist-high moving wire when I was ready to go. Jilda, who was now five months old, struggled through the deep snow to keep up behind me, only to have to chase me down again. When she tired, she would sit in the snow and howl, her enormous white ears, with pink centres, added to the hilarity of others on the slopes as she could only keep one up.

By the weekend, a heavy snowfall had dumped a thick layer of powder on Kashka-Suu's only run. Elena had to leave to teach one of her students. The crowds began to arrive and the money, which wasn't supposed to exist in Bishkek, revealed itself with the appearance of flashy Japanese Jeeps, full of designer-clad Kyrgyz in Salomon boots, with matching skis slung over their shoulders. Within a few runs the slopes were an obstacle course of bare rock and sheet ice.

At lunch, a handsome, blue-eyed young lawyer invited me to have lunch with him and his friend, a rough, unshaven man who looked as if he'd taken a break from combat in Chechnya. Were they Russian? I could have spat at them and got the same reaction.

'We are Kafkaz,' came the stern reply from the swarthy Georgian. 'Stalin was a Kafkaz,' he added proudly.

'Wasn't Stalin a murderer...?' I started.

'Stalin didn't murder anyone,' he stated definitively, his friend casting me a warning look, suggesting that it would be foolish to disagree.

Both were lawyers on a skiing weekend with their girlfriends. Half a dozen shots later, we returned to the ski slope. I spent the afternoon skiing with the blue-eyed man. The lunchtime drinking was a warm-up for the evening. Before we sat down to dinner, we had already worked our way through a bottle of rum and a couple of bottles of vodka. After dinner, we drank several more bottles of vodka in the sauna, occasionally sobering up and risking cardiac arrest by diving into the freezing plunge-pool. A fumbling, steamy kiss with the blue-eyed man, followed by an admission that his girlfriend was waiting for him in his hotel room, drew the evening to a close.

At breakfast I could barely speak. The swarthy one was as rumbustious as before, either unaffected by the previous night's binge or still under the influence. He spent the whole of breakfast prodding me under the table and casting knowing looks in the direction of his friend, whose girlfriend was sitting next to me. I was relieved when Sergei turned up early.

'Don't get on the wrong side of the Georgians,' he warned. 'They are a dangerous bunch.'

'They are a lethal cocktail,' I groaned, feeling another rush of nausea and trying to cover my mouth to stop him detecting my boozy breath.

After my coarse weekend, I needed culture and respectability, so I took my neighbours to see *Swan Lake*. The Opera House on Sovietskaya still wore a shabby grandeur; its imperial proportions deflected attention from peeling paintwork and a set that would be more fitting in a school nativity play.

'Last time I came to the Opera, it was a disaster,' joked Dinara. 'One ballerina lost her tutu and another fell into the stalls!'

Second-row tickets were a tidy $2. The performance was patchy, unsurprising given the lack of funding, but the leading lady restored the dignity of the company. She was cheered at every turn by a gaggle of students from the ballet school who rushed up on to the stage with endless bouquets at the curtain call. We went back to the Opera House the following week to see Leoncavallo's *Pagliacci*. There were some strong voices in the company but the thwarted husband let the side down. Notes stuck in his throat as he reached the crescendo in the aria about broken love, possibly overwhelmed by the emotion but, more likely, simply too old for the part; he lost the tune completely.

Later that week I heard that there had been terrible snows in Mongolia. Hundreds of thousands of animals had died. Without their animals, I knew that the Mongolians had nothing: no milk, no meat, no dung and no felt for their boots, clothes or *gers*. The previous summer's drought, which I witnessed in the west, had been the worst in sixty years. It had destroyed the grass cover and in several areas, plagues of Brandtii voles destroyed the roots. The animals failed to fatten up sufficiently. Heavy snowfalls, the worst winter for thirty years, had left most of the country under a metre of snow. Estimates reckoned that by the end of the winter, at least 3 million animals would die.

There was a report about the *dzud* on Kyrgyz television. The idyllic green hills had been transformed into lifeless tundra, pounded by a relentless cutting wind. The steppe was littered with carcasses, butchered by cold and famine, rigid limbs outstretched. Open, distorted mouths were frozen in their last gasp. One reporter had found a dead lamb curled up inside the carcass of a cow. Hundreds of skins were piled up against the sides of a *ger* and a herder lamented that for every animal he skinned, there were two more waiting in his yard. He couldn't keep up, there was no meat left on any of his animals whose bellies were filled with dirt and grit. All he had to feed his animals was marmot oil mixed with tea, which helped the animals to pass the grit. The only animals which were well fed were dogs and wolves. The report showed ragged animals, ribs protruding through papery skin, trying to stand up to the buffeting wind. A horse was lying on its side, its only movement the slight rise and fall of weak, shallow breaths. A couple of mangy horses kept a nervous distance, one had a stumpy tail, the rest chewed off by a hungry mate. A few early spring lambs tottered around their starving mother's legs, tugging at dry udders.

I called Baatar in Ulaanbaatar who told me that many herders had lost all of their animals. Baatsaihan had lost thirty-nine out of his forty cows. The Mongolians have a saying, 'Help comes from help.' I thought of all the Mongolians who had looked after me and shown me kindness; I had to do something in return. I spent weeks sending begging letters and contacting all the journalists I knew to report the story. The enormous generosity of family and friends enabled me to send US$16,000 to Mongolia, which helped a thousand families in Zavkhan province in the west of Mongolia to buy emergency supplies.

While Mongolia was still under a metre of snow, Kyrgyzstan was having a thaw. Soon the foothills of the Tien Shan were brilliant green and the meadows were full of daffodils, snowdrops, narcissus and wild iris. Icy brooks chattered and the snow receded further towards the frozen permanence of the glaciers. I helped Elena in the garden of her *dacha*, a small hut in the foothills; her orchards were dusted with the petals of plums, apricots, peach, pear and cherry blossom in full bloom.

As the temperature rose, Bishkek became a hotbed of political intrigue. Bazakov, the head of Patipak, the Uighur association in Kyrgyzstan, was shot outside his house. Uighurs pointed the finger at the Chinese. China had been putting increasing political and economic pressure on Central Asia republics, to arrest and deport 'ethnic separatists' fleeing from Xinjiang, who were seeking independence from China. The Uighur issue threatened to become as much of an embarrassment as Tibet. Some Uighurs were being recruited into Al Qa'eda's ranks. The Chinese were negotiating with the Taliban; Uighurs should be sent to the disputed territory of Kashmir to fight the Indians and should not return to China. A few months after Bazakov's murder, several Chinese diplomats were murdered in Bishkek and I wondered at the time whether this was a quid pro quo. Uzbekistan was also putting pressure on Kyrgyzstan to do something about its Islamic militants, cutting off the Kyrgyz gas supply in 1999 and 2000.

Kyrgyz domestic politics were also in turmoil. Akaev, the Kyrgyz president, had arrested his chief opponent, Felix Kulov and charged him with selling arms for personal profit after the collapse of the Union. It was sad to see that Akaev had finally gone the way of the rest of the leaders in Central Asia, preferring the certainty of a one-horse race. Ancient clan rivalry was also important: Akaev's power base was Naryn, in the east while Kulov's was from Talas, in the west. Traditionally the Naryn block had always won out. Policemen had cordoned off the main square after rowdy demonstrations from Kulov's supporters. Romantic strollers in the park had to contend with Dzerzhinsky as well as an army of soldiers, who had been posted in all public places. The police insisted on using my garden as a lavatory and Jilda frequently came home with human excrement fresh on her breath.

Dinara had the latest gossip on the election. She claimed that people were not demonstrating to support Kulov. He used to be the head of the KGB in Bishkek and was as bad as the rest of them. They were protesting at the loss of freedom of speech and because his arrest signalled the end of democracy. I asked her if she would vote but she said that there was no point.

'Even before Kulov's arrest, my vote was meaningless. I may wander down to the polling booth at the end of the day to see if my vote has been stolen – an hour or so before polling finishes, crooked officials mop up the votes which haven't been cast. When only twenty-five per cent of the population bothers to vote, they need the extra votes to pretend that turnout was good. What is the use of getting ninety per cent of the vote if only a handful of people voted? Even if I were to vote, I'd need to take my own pencil – that's one of the best tricks. How can you tick a box with a pencil which has no lead in it?'

April finally came and I knew that the impenetrable icy maze and snowfields of the Tien Shan would soon be clearing. It was time to leave Bishkek. I was terribly sad saying goodbye to my neighbours who had become like family. Ira, Sveta and Elena allowed their children to take the morning off school to see me off. Ira had stayed up all night sewing me a smart olive corduroy shirt. Dinara gave me a traditional Kyrgyz silver bracelet; Boris and Sveta had made a video of our times together and their daughter, Masha, had picked me fresh daffodils. Sergei, the taxi driver who drove me into the mountains, hurried over to my flat and handed me a

A spring picnic with Ira, Yelena and Dinara

letter, instructing me to read it when he had gone. As I headed back to Kazakhstan, I opened it:

Farewell Claire. I'll always remember our drives together, those hours with you were a wonderful escape from the monotony my life has become. You made me feel young again; your energy and optimism illuminated my dull life. I am too old to write to you as a lover, but I hope that you will accept the love that I feel towards you as that of a friend. I will never forget you.

When the goose honks once, spring is on the way.
The crows caw incessantly, but spring is still far off.

Mongolian proverb

15

REBIRTH

I managed to get a message to Ruslan via his uncle in Almaty airport. Apparently, after I had left for Bishkek, his mother had turned up in Almaty insisting he showed her the bright lights, and he'd returned home empty-handed. I was determined not to let Ruslan make this mistake again and spent the next two months convincing him that he should buy animals and build up a herd. In two months he could earn $600. If he started with twenty calves, within two years they would be worth $3,000. He could sell a few cows and buy more calves.

It was evening on 20 April when we found the farm where we'd left the horses. The sun, a sinking yellow orb in a blood red sky, silhouetted distant hills. Aigul was surprisingly pleased to see us, given the fact that I was there to take the horses away. She said that she had been looking out for me every day since the beginning of April. Her husband, Usen, looked slightly shocked and embarrassed to see us but his eyes lit up when he saw the two bottles of cognac, which he had requested from Almaty. For some reason, he wouldn't let me see my horses until the morning. Aigul made dinner: the home-made pasta with sauce, made from slices of old fat and tomato paste, was so high that it was fizzing. But the evening was not about eating; Usen wouldn't let us sleep until we had finished both bottles of cognac.

In the morning Aigul admitted that Black Hat had been attacked by a wolf. I resigned myself to the news, wondering if they'd eaten him. I couldn't make a fuss as I was staying in their house. The other horses looked in good condition and fit for the difficult ride ahead, although Three Socks had a small sore on his back, which could pose problems later on. We decided we should try to find a replacement for Black Hat so that we would have a horse in reserve.

My largest horse, Tom, was harnessed on to the family cart and we bumped along a small track across the steppe to a neighbouring farm where we had a delicious lunch of freshly-shot quail, eggs and noodles. Only one of the horses was remotely suitable but he was a little young and too expensive. Dejected, we went home. Ruslan and Usen disappeared behind some outbuildings for most of the following day. When I asked if we could go to the village in search of horses, Usen claimed that a man was bringing a horse to the house and we needed to wait. I sat inside with Aigul and bad-mouthed them for their drunkenness. Expecting meek compliance, I was surprised by the strength of her reaction.

'I am stuck with Usen. I don't even like him, but what can I do, I have three children. Someone has to milk the cows. Occasionally he comes back with a bird that he's shot but most of the time he is a useless idiot. You are lucky to be seeing the world. I spend all day in the house with a screaming baby. My young sons are at school in the village, they only come home on weekends and in the holidays.'

The highlight of her day was tea with her only neighbours. The man with the horse never appeared. Sensing my irritation, Usen and Ruslan sobered up. In the evening, we saddled the horses and galloped to the near-est village, eight kilometres away. Jilda was surprisingly good with the horses. After an initial bout of barking as I mounted my horse, she scam-pered dutifully behind us, keeping up and relishing her new freedom. By the time we reached the village, it was getting dark. We stopped at a rela-tive's house. He agreed to put the word around that we were looking for a horse. Needless to say, for the favour we had to join him for a few hours of toasting. Pie-eyed, we galloped back home by moonlight. I fell off Jijig three times, losing my glasses in the process. Miraculously, Ruslan and Usen found them the next day.

After inspecting a number of manky, mangy animals the following after-noon, we rode to a family of Chechens. In February 1944, Stalin deported 500,000 Chechens to Siberia and Central Asia; thirty per cent died in the upheaval. The family had a magnificent stallion for sale. A frisky chestnut, he was branded by a slit in the top of his ear.

'We must call him Aykulak,' whispered Ruslan. 'Crescent Moon Ear.'

'Sshh. Pretend you don't like it very much. We need to get a good price.'

Undecided, we paced up and down. Ruslan rode him and I shook my head, watching our hosts fidget through the corner of my eye. When asked if I wanted to buy the horse, I said that I was worried that it was rather jumpy. They resorted to emotional blackmail saying that they needed the money to pay for a kidney operation and I began to buckle. After haggling weakly for a while, we settled for $250, my most expensive purchase of the trip.

Having agreed to the sale, we sat down for tea in their house, an old Russian train-carriage. As we were getting up to leave, they announced that they no longer wanted to sell the horse as they were not sure if the doctor, who would be performing the operation, would prefer the horse or the money. Couldn't we ask him? That wasn't possible, he lived in Almaty. What use was a horse in Almaty? That didn't sway them. How many people are prepared to pay that much for a horse? If the doctor takes the horse instead of the money, he is effectively buying the horse. Do you think he would be prepared to spend $250 on a horse? They were nonplussed. I asked Ruslan to explain that the doctor would effectively be buying the horse for $250. Would he mind? The horse was ours.

Aigul was very happy with the money she received for looking after the horses and slaughtered a turkey in our honour. We left in the late afternoon. Usen joined us; he wanted to experience a night under canvas.

The steppe, once depressing, desolate and lifeless, was reborn. The fresh spring grass was splattered with the yellow and purple bloom of primroses, primulas and plumbago. We had barely covered ten kilometres, when we startled a couple of saiga antelope, which bolted into the cover of long reeds. A large flock of sheep huddled in the shade of a tall tree. Jilda ran at them, scattering the sheep, splitting lambs from their mothers and enraging the shepherd. At dusk, we left the steppe and followed a rugged path, winding up into the hills, littered with rock shards and boulders. We camped in the middle of the track, feasting on the remains of the turkey, while Usen regaled us with stories of wolves and bears in the surrounding hills.

It was good to be under canvas again and somehow I felt comforted by the feeling of the hard ground underneath me. I lay awake, listening to the wind buffeting the tent and drawing a mental plan of our route. We needed to navigate through a chain of foothills, which stood in our path to the Kyrgyz border, 400 kilometres to the south. They were not particularly high, but the snowline started at roughly 2,000 metres and we would frequently find ourselves above that altitude.

As we picked our way over a dry stream-bed the following morning, Ruslan called out and pointed at the ground. A small trickle was creeping along the dry cracks underneath the horses' feet, flowing its first familiar spring passage.

That week, the hills proved tricky to negotiate. No paths were marked on the map and we occasionally found ourselves peering over precipices or struggling down impassable gullies, ridden with boulders. Much time was lost retracing our steps and picking the best way down. Our other problem was Aykulak's libido. On one occasion, Ruslan asked me to hold him, while he adjusted the baggage. Momentarily, I let his halter drop. He bolted off after a herd of mares, leaving Ruslan's saddlebags strewn around in his wake. It took Ruslan several hours to catch him.

We continued on, picking our way around a patchwork of wheat fields over undulating green downs. We didn't bother leading Three Socks, whose sore was healing well, with the aid of antibiotics. He kept stopping in enticing patches of wild lucerne and munching until we were almost out of sight when he would canter to catch up. He and Jilda had an interesting rapport. She would bark at him and run perilously close to him until he was suitably irritated. Then he would canter behind her, his head hanging low as if he planned to hoover her up. She would scamper off and bide her time for a while before returning to her bossy attempts at shepherding him. By then, her floppy ear had answered its call of the wild and both enormous ears permanently stood to attention, taking in the sounds of the steppe. As I got to know her better, I realized that her ears, far from being a source of amusement, were often the antennae of her emotions.

Finally we spotted the smokestacks of Taldy Kurgan below us in the distance. There was no path down the mountain and we had to lead the horses down a precipitous slope of shale and boulders to the valley below. The horses' shoes were beginning to chip and we were in desperate need of a blacksmith. We plodded along a road for an hour in the dark before we met 'Johnny', a wiry individual with wispy, unruly grey hair and a squint. He was thrilled to be able to talk to a foreigner, showing off a smattering of French and showing me well-loved translations of Dumas and Balzac.

Over a fine dinner of fried eggs and chives, I asked him what he thought of Putin as the new President of Russia. Perhaps Putin had ambitions to rebuild the union? But politics no longer bore any relevance for Johnny; he didn't have a television; he could hardly afford to buy newspapers and his eyesight was so bad that he could barely read any more. He used to be an architect; he designed a neighbouring phosphorous factory but now he was a farmer with twenty cows to his name. He kept apologizing that he could only offer us eggs; he couldn't afford to eat meat. As the evening wore on, Johnny became drunk, morose and tearful. He told us that he had recently lost his 13-year-old son. He had been playing with a shotgun when it went off.

'I didn't cry. My wife was pregnant at the time but I cried when the baby was born.'

Johnny introduced us to Max, a coarse but affable blacksmith, whose heavily scarred face spoke of violence when the situation warranted it. For most of the following day, we camped under a tree on a large collective farm. I thought that Aykulak would prove difficult but Ruslan wound a rope around each fetlock and held the upturned hoof between his knees, while Max drove the nails in. In fact it was Three Socks who proved to be too difficult for them. He dealt a sharp kick to Max's hand, which provoked a torrent of obscenities, and a hard clout on his nose. Three Socks was forced on to his side by a group of farmhands, who bound all his hooves together like a pig on a spit. Max calculated his price in litres of vodka. I think we agreed on half a dozen.

We wove along a dusty track, cutting through the hills past a shabby brown *yurt*. It was the first one that I'd seen since Mongolia; I wanted to go inside but a couple of menacing dogs charged out on to the track and wouldn't let us close. Further up the path they went for Jilda; I let off a couple of warning shots from my starter pistol and they bounded away. As we wound along the track, Ruslan and I practised 'Moscovsky Vechera', a famous Russian ballad; Elena had scribbled the words down before I left Bishkek. Ruslan wasn't doing much justice to the song; he couldn't remember the words and couldn't hold a tune. We were stopped in mid-phrase by a huge herd of heifers charging down the track towards us, kicking up the dust until they were hidden in a cloud. They seemed to have an unstoppable momentum and even Ruslan couldn't disguise his fear. As they approached, we steeled ourselves for the inevitable crush. But Jilda was having none of it. She stepped out cautiously and then bounded towards them, barking menacingly as only her instinct for self-preservation could teach her how. I called her repeatedly, unable to bear the thought of rescuing her trampled body after the charge. They continued their beeline for us, until we could feel the ground vibrate. Suddenly they veered off to one side, Jilda in hot pursuit, until dog, herd and dust cloud disappeared. She came back alone, panting furiously but unharmed.

That night one side of the valley was incandescent as huge fires licked up the side of the mountain, burning the winter stubble to make way for the spring grass. I remember it well, as the next day was my birthday. On my big day, Ruslan turned into a village and said he would catch me up. As I rode on, a white Lada pulled up ahead of me. The driver, a young, gangly man with a wispy moustache and dressed in a pair of slacks and a T-shirt got out and flashed an official pass at me. I was fifty kilometres inside the Chinese border area without the proper pass; he was convinced that I was going to cross illegally into China. I tried to explain that I was riding to Kyrgyzstan, not China, and pointed to the visa in my passport. He took my passport and refused to give it back he would have to take me into custody.

'But it's my birthday. I am having a party. I have biscuits and vodka. Perhaps you'd like to come?' He took another look at my passport and smiled.

'Happy Birthday! Twenty-nine years old! Are you married?' He couldn't come to my 'party' so I cheekily offered him a bottle of vodka; perhaps he could celebrate the occasion later with his friends? As he handed me back my passport, Ruslan rode up bearing a Grieg's tulip and some fresh butter and cream for my birthday. The policeman turned his attention to Ruslan.

'Where is his passport? You can go but he must come with me. I'll keep this,' he said, waving Ruslan's passport.

'But how can I celebrate my birthday on my own?'

By this stage, I was tugging gently on one corner of Ruslan's passport, smiling sweetly, while he held on to the other. I reached into my saddlebag and produced the bottle of Stolichnaya. Pulling a little more firmly on the passport, I coaxed it out of his hand and replaced it with the bottle. He looked down at the label and his eyes lit up. He advised us to go quickly; the best way to get away was over the bridge and through the mountains, before the other border guards caught us. Raising the bottle in thanks, he drove off.

We hurried down to the river. Aykulak refused to cross the rickety cable-bridge, prancing nervously near the first plank, trotting backwards and rearing. I led the other horses across, the bridge swaying above the deafening river. Ruslan cantered off to look for another crossing point but there was none. I led Tom back across, hoping that he might set an example to Aykulak. Ruslan led Aykulak a few feet behind. As we reached the other side, the rest of the horses took fright and bolted, scattering baggage in their wake.

The celebrations took place in a small shack in the hills owned by potato farmers. It wasn't a night of revelry. Our hosts, an old man, his son and a surly Russian hired hand, were nonplussed when I produced another bottle of vodka and a few packets of biscuits. After a couple of shots and a few biscuits, they laid out their mattresses and went to sleep. We stayed up chatting with Alexei, the Russian. He was an educated man, but belonged to a homeless class of men, which Ruslan said were known as *bidtjch*, who took what work they could in exchange for a bed. He spoke of a wife and two grown children. Ruslan reckoned that he had fabricated a family for 'face'.

Before we left the farm, Ruslan decided that Aykulak might calm down if he 'got laid'. A petite filly was presented to him in the yard. The poor creature was half his size and she clearly wasn't 'up for it'. Whinnying and bucking, she threw up her hind legs, kicked him hard and cantered away. Aykulak was clearly aroused by her 'hard to get' act and gave chase; she wasn't to be caught so a halter was placed around her head and she was tied to a post. Aykulak repeatedly tried to mount her, oblivious to her protesting kicks, but nothing would break her icy reserve. After an hour of trying, we gave up.

We rode on through a broad, green valley, splashing through gushing streams fed by the melting snow. A light dusting of snow still covered the upper slopes of the hills. Jilda spent most of the day chasing butterflies and birds. After a long chase, she would sit down, indicating that she had had her fun and wanted us to stop for the day. Within a few weeks, I could see tight sinewy knots forming in her legs and she soon learned to pace herself. Although I had bought her as a guard dog, I couldn't bear to think of a confrontation with a wolf and insisted that Jilda slept in the doorway of my tent curled up on a piece of felt. That month, the ticks were terrible. Every night, before I let her near the tent, I would comb through her hair and find half a dozen bulbous passengers, slightly bigger than a thumbnail, which I would gently twist off, trying to ensure that the head didn't remain burrowed under the skin. While I felt sorry for Jilda, I must admit a certain sense of satisfaction as I burst the swollen animals between thumb and fore-finger and watched the blood splatter out!

They soon spread; each night I would feel the back of my head near the bottom of my skull where I invariably found a posse, beginning to 'dig in'. Frequently there would be a piece of my scalp in their proboscis but thank-fully they never swelled up with my blood. This made them impossible to squash so they had to be incinerated. This often meant passing the squirm-ing vermin to our hosts, who chucked them in the stove.

One afternoon that week, we rode through a barren and rocky valley, known as Altyn Emel, the Mongolian for 'golden saddle'. According to local legend, one of Genghis Khan's sons (nobody seemed to know which one) lost a golden horseshoe while riding through the valley. Convinced that it had been stolen, he decimated his army. An old man with a hoary beard and Biggles goggles who directed us to the valley claimed that Genghis Khan's son had been mortally wounded when his horse kicked him and he'd died there. We stopped at a small spring; the surrounding bushes were blossoming with tiny ribbons and offerings from passers-by. I cut some strips from my Mongolian saddlebags and knotted them into the branches.

We descended into a stony wasteland where three huge golden eagles were gliding on updraughts from the baking ground and a small herd of kulan, or Asiatic wild asses, nibbled at the sparse vegetation. The northern side of this mountain range, from whence we'd come, robbed the south of all the water from the melting snow. It was a scorching day. The faded blue sky was clear save for one giant, mushrooming cloud. Mirages glimmered on the horizon like huge lakes and lizards scurried away from the horses' hoofs over the brown scree. Jilda spent the afternoon trapping them under her claws and toying with them like a cat with a bird. Frequently, only her bottom remained in sight as she burrowed into minefields of suslik holes. When she came up for air, her muzzle was thick with dust and she kept sneezing. Chasing around in the desert was thirsty work. That day she learned how to place her front paws on the side of my saddle and drink from my water bottle, which I tipped above her muzzle.

The following morning, as we were saddling up, I bent down to pick up a piece of rope to tie the baggage and recoiled in horror upon discovering that it was a snake. Ruslan nonchalantly reached down and picked up the squirming creature by its head.

'I was bitten by one of these once; my leg swelled up to almost double its size and I couldn't walk for a week.'

The heat broke; ominous black clouds rolled over the mountains towards us from the north. Golden pools of sunlight broke through the storm clouds, bathing the valley in chiaroscuro. Soon we were peering through a curtain of rain at the mountains ahead. We found a shortcut through a series of rocky outcrops, partially eclipsed by low cloud. On many of the taller rocks, votive stones had been piled up into ovoos. I wondered whether any old tombs lay hidden among the lofty rock faces. It was Jilda's first taste of heavy rain and she kept hiding under bushes, determined not to get wet.

That afternoon, I managed to turn my horse's hoof on to Jilda's paw. She had a deep gash in one of her pads, which bled profusely. She lay on her back obediently, whining as I cleaned the wound and stuck on some butterfly stitches. After bandaging up the paw, we covered it in a green, woollen sock. She was limping badly and kept sitting down. I draped her over my saddle and we rode on.

In the early evening, we came across a camel farm. An old couple lived there with their six children, one of whom had an impressive portfolio of pencil portraits. The family looked after sixty camels owned by various people in the neighbourhood. Looking east from the farm we could make out black mountains, streaked with snow, against a lavender sunset.

After supper, Dalikan, a corpulent 60-something-year-old sagging in all the right places, suggested a sauna and insisted on coming in with me to oversee the cleaning process. She lathered me with soap and scrubbed for almost an hour with what looked like the white string-bags you get for free with detergent tablets. Occasionally she passed it to me with instructions to clean my 'nethers'. When she had removed the filth and no doubt several layers of skin, I was allowed to dress.

Ruslan kept me amused the next day regaling me with tall tales from his village, Kurchum. It started when I asked him where he got the scars on his face. Pointing to a deep groove below his right eyebrow:

'I got this one when I was kicked in the face by a horse. If the horse had been shod I would have lost the eye. This one, I got in a fight.'

'What was the fight about?'

'The men in Kurchum don't like us villagers from Slovenka. We are always fighting. They won that time. We were fighting on their turf and we were outnumbered.'

'What do you fight with?'

'Knives usually.'

'Does any one get killed?'

'Of course. My brother almost killed one of them. The guy was in hospital for weeks. My brother was sentenced to eight years. He got out in November.'

'And women?' I asked, rather cheekily.

'Yeah. I have a girl. She is sixteen but she's a virgin. I have slept with thirteen women.' He looked to me for reassurance that this was a manly sum and I shrugged my shoulders. Sensing my disbelief, he counted out loud: 'In the army, there were one, two, three, four. The year I came back from the army, I had three and,' he switched from Russian to Kazakh, muttering an assortment of women's names, 'six since then.'

At dusk, we followed a boulder-strewn track up through a narrow ravine. The horses kept slipping on the rocks which were damp from the persistent drizzle. When the path finally opened up, the top of the mountain was blanketed in thick, freezing fog and it was too dangerous to go any further. We camped in high-altitude meadowland. It was raining hard. The horses disappeared into the fog before we had a chance to unsaddle them.

At first light, it was snowing as we packed up to leave, the hillside powdered white. We set off down the mountain in terrible visibility, navigating by compass. Gradually the sun burned through the cloud revealing a virtually unbroken line of ice-blue peaks, which delineated the border between Kazakhstan and Kyrgyzstan. Thick white clouds hung in the valley like large felts. In the distance, we could see the V-shape of the 2500-metre pass which we needed to cross. Our immediate obstacle was Kalgan, the Kazakh border town. I didn't want to run the risk of meeting any police or border officials who would have questioned the legitimacy of taking five horses and a dog over the border; only the dog had the necessary veterinary paperwork.

We dropped down the side of the mountain and into a small village on the outskirts of Kalgan. Ignoring attempts to engage us in conversation, we hurried through communal meadowland and waded across a river rather than risk using the bridge. At dusk, an old man with a big smile, boasting three teeth, rode out to us on a white horse and invited us to stay. He was dressed in a worn grey blazer, blue shirt and a woollen sailing cap. Ruslan stayed up late chatting with him and playing chess, their faces bathed in the warm orange light of a gas lamp. In the middle of the night, his son tiptoed across the room, supporting a large wife, who was leaning heavily on his shoulder.

Ruslan playing chess with one of our Kazakh hosts

In the morning, I asked what was wrong with her. I thought she might be pregnant. Thinking I might be able to help, they escorted me into her bedroom. She turned over on her front, pulled down her pants, revealing an ample bottom. An enormous pus-filled boil was erupting out of the centre of the left cheek. It looked ready to lance, but I couldn't face the prospect of performing surgery. I poured over leaflets on my various antibiotics and found one, which claimed success with boils. I gave her some iodine, cotton wool and antibiotic cream with instructions to keep it clean. After we had prescribed the old man's wife Tiger Balm, for her rheumatic wrist, our old friend was only too happy to help us with our route planning.

*

Poring over the maps, we finally decided to head up the Ir Soo valley. This unpopulated valley ran parallel to the checkpoint in the Karkara valley and we were assured that it was deserted. We crossed a deep river, Ruslan balancing Jilda over the front of his saddle while the sun played on ripples in the river. As we climbed through the wide, gently sloping valley, we met many shepherds, taking advantage of the first signs of the spring pasture. The grass was just turning green. If we had arrived much sooner, we would have been wading through snow. Further up the valley, the ground squelched under foot and Jilda whirled around munching snow in cold patches hidden in the shadows. The sounds of lambs bleating to their mothers, and whistling shepherds, faded into the distance. Five hundred metres above us, above the denuded tree-line, the mountains were still enveloped in a thick wintry silence.

We were both edgy. At one point, we came across a group of houses. I thought I had led us straight into the checkpoint. We rode close to an escarpment, trying to keep out of sight; at any moment, I expected someone to come rushing out demanding our papers, but the village was deserted. An hour further up the valley, when we were sure we were clear of the border, we stole across the main road and hurried out of sight along a small track, which disappeared into the hills.

Our earlier fears were forgotten. Everything was suddenly better; we were free. The same mountains were taller, the pasture greener, the wild flowers more beautiful.

'What do you think of Kyrgyzstan, Ruslan?'

'It's all right, it looks the same as Kazakhstan.' He shrugged, trying to appear flippant and jaded by international travel.

I hoped that we would happen upon a *yurt* and looked forward to some Kyrgyz hospitality but all we saw were empty, abandoned farmhouses. It was getting dark; we had just decided to set up camp when we noticed that Jilda was missing. I began to panic: it was dark; she could be anywhere, maybe she had followed our scent back into Kazakhstan. I jumped on my horse and rode back the way we'd come, whistling frantically for an hour until the lump in my throat and my quivering mouth made the action impossible. I blew on the whistle around my neck, calling out her name, tears streaming down my face. Finally I heard her whimpering but I couldn't see her. I got off my horse and she trotted up to me, her head hanging mournfully low, panting hard and exhausted. She whined and howled for several minutes, nipping my hand in admonition. As we rode back, she kept sitting down. I got off my horse, wound a stirrup through her collar and led her back to our camp. We didn't have many supplies left and made do with rice boiled in ham and chickpea soup, most of which we gave to Jilda. She was soon curled up next to me in the tent, fast asleep.

Carrying Jilda across a river, Kazakhstan

Maybe you'll all agree with me,
And with what I have to say—let's see!
To the west there lies Issyk-Kul,
Beautiful land, and lake brim-full!
If your steeds by Ili you chase,
There you will find a place for the race.
All is convenient for us there—
Rivers and pastures everywhere,
Trees on every side there are—
That wide space is called Karkira.
There is salt to evaporate,
And no sediment will it make.
Firs and birches and poplars are there,
You have your logs, and some to spare,
If you cut down some of those trees.
Places for races you'd find with ease.
That's a good place for holding the feast!
All the tribe-leaders gathered there
Eager agreement began to declare.
They decided this matter first,
They thanked everyone, then dispersed.

Time for the feast was decided too—
When summer's hottest days were through,
When the cattle well-fed were found,
When the autumn gold falls around,
When the peasants winnow again,
When they pour out and take early grain.
To Samarkand and Kokand, not far—
Then they'd migrate to Karkira
With old white-beard Koshoi at their head.
Now, just see, it is as we said:
All the bogatirs who had met
Went off home, all ready and set.
When the sultry heat declined,
When the autumn days were more kind,
They decided their people to call.
In Karkira they would gather all.

Manas

16

THE CELESTIAL MOUNTAINS

A couple of Kyrgyz teenagers, sharing a horse, fell in with us as we followed a wide track through Tien Shan spruce into open pasture-land towards a knot of majestic white summits. The ground was a riot of primulas, fox-tailed lilies and the smell of wild onions wafted up from under the horses' hooves. Ruslan was struggling to converse in Kyrgyz. Despite the fact that the language is almost identical to Kazakh, his ear wasn't attuned to the accent and frequently he had to resort to Russian to make himself understood. The elder boy sat in front steering the horse and sharing one of Ruslan's cigarettes with the younger one who was balanced precariously on a cushion on the back. Both dragged frequently on the cigarette, expelling the smoke in quick puffs and occasionally exhaling it through the nose.

In the early evening I got chatting with a young cattle-herder with friendly eyes creased in a permanent smile. I asked him if he knew where we could hold a party; it was Ruslan's twenty-fourth birthday the following day, 9 May. He offered to host a party and find us a sheep and we were soon ensconced in 'barracks' along with thirty families, on a collective farm. Each family had a one-roomed house and a small terrace in a long bunga-low building. Perched half-way up a hill, we were staying in a stubborn fragment of the past, appropriately called 'Communism'. I can still picture the view from the farm. A herd of cows congregated under the red flag, flapping in the breeze. Further back, two green arêtes plunged down the valley in a 'V', framing the soaring white snowfields, skirted by low cloud hanging in the valley floor.

Each family owned between seventeen and twenty-five cows, depending on years of service. Herding was done collectively but each family milked its own cows. Once the milk had been rationed between the workers, the rest was poured into a huge refrigerated vat. Milk from the surrounding farms arrived by horse-drawn cart. Altogether they produced a tonne of milk per day, which was sold to a cheese-making factory; much was bartered for flour and tea. Despite the fact that the milking machines still worked, most preferred to milk by hand – their lightning fingers were faster, they claimed.

I was impressed by how well the cooperative system worked: the farm had electricity and each family had meat drying on a line on the terrace; everyone had flour and tea. After the collapse of the Soviet Union most Kyrgyz abandoned collective agriculture for private ownership, in the hope that the West would fund the transformation. However, although the West was happy to oversee the dismantling of the Soviet apparatus, they have not succeeded in replacing it with anything better. One of the great mistakes was that, in the interests of private enterprise, the national herd was divided into tiny flocks; many people received a couple of dozen sheep, not enough to sustain a family. Within a few years the families had eaten their sheep and, within ten years, Kyrgyzstan's herd numbers had plunged from around 10 million to 1.5 million.

On Ruslan's birthday, we went shopping for the party in a poorly stocked kiosk in the local village, Sovietskoe. We found stale snacks, biscuits, some dubious sweets and ten litres of moonshine, sold in recycled glass bottles sealed with an old plastic bag and a rubber band. Ruslan singled out a fat black sheep, for which we paid $40. Having trussed its legs together, it was strapped on to a precarious ledge on the side of the milk truck. Back on the farm, the party was in full swing; an empty five-litre vat of what could have been mistaken for paint stripper sat outside our host's house. The sheep was dispatched in traditional halal style, its throat slit over a basin. I gave Ruslan a camera so that he could record the journey; he spent the day taking pictures with scattergun frequency.

The meat boiled for four hours and we had to pass the time with a toast in every home. We numbered a dozen at the table, with a crowd loitering in the doorway. Several large joints had been distributed amongst the neighbours. The first course was innards, followed by the Kyrgyz speciality, *beeshbarmak*, which means, 'with five fingers', which is how it should be eaten. It arrived in a metal washing-basin; noodles topped with a greasy but tasty stock filled with partially cooked onions. Our host fished around in the bowl, scooped up some noodles, clasping them between four fingers and thumb, and popped them neatly in his mouth. His lips were soon glossed with fat, which hung in globules from his moustache. The second course was the same as the first, only without the onions, the same meat and noodles, chopped finely. All the while, we sipped delicious broth from a separate bowl, into which our hostess, a pretty woman with a long angular face framed by a yellow floral headscarf, ladled several teaspoons of curd.

*

The weather turned from spring to winter. We loaded the horses in a flurry of snow and two women from the collective chased us all the way down the road wishing us a safe journey. We followed a gentle track, down the valley towards Lake Issyk-kul, past a herd of goats standing in pillar formation on the ruins of an adobe house, which lay among bright green weeds. Angry black clouds shadowed us and an icy wind sent chills down my spine. Snow at less than two thousand metres didn't augur well for the first pass we had to cross, which was a fraction over four thousand metres. Our pathway took us through a patchwork of fields of daisies and dandelions, flanked by poplar trees.

In the early evening, we hurried through Karakol, a town with a population of almost seventy thousand living in white-washed houses with slanting wooden roofs and carefully-tended plots and gardens. Zigzagging to avoid irrigation channels, we passed the chunky, neckless bronzes of sculptured sentinels guarding the war memorial, skirted the hippodrome and wandered through a deserted power station. Eventually we found a small track climbing a hill behind the town and looked for a farm that would afford our animals some security from thieves.

Our hosts that evening were Torghuts, a family with Mongoloid features: small black eyes set in ruddy faces with high cheekbones and flat noses. They were thrilled to find that I had been to Mongolia and spoke a little Mongolian. The Torghuts are a Mongol tribe that settled in Xinjiang, which was known as Dzungaria meaning 'left hand', representing the protective left flank of the Mongols. In 1618, 25,000 members of the tribe left Xinjiang in search of better pastureland. Twenty-five years later, they settled on the banks of the River Volga, 3,000 miles away from their homeland. At first they lived in peace, taking orders from the Dalai Lama in Tibet but, over time, Russia sought to exert more influence and attempts were made to convert them and to break up their nomadic lifestyle, settling them in fixed abodes. Their leaders decided to return to Xinjiang. The escape plan was hatched in secret. All except the senior leaders of the Torghuts believed that they were escaping an attack from the Kyrgyz. Four hundred thousand Torghuts, 5 million livestock, 1 million beasts of burden and 100,000 dogs began the perilous journey home. The Russian army pursued them, the Kyrgyz hounded them and the wells *en route* were poisoned. Overcome by hunger, exhaustion and thirst, almost three hundred thousand died. All the cattle died. One hundred and twenty thousand Torghuts made it back to Xinjiang.

A small group remained stranded on the west bank of the Volga; they were unable to join their fellow tribesman in flight. A violent storm the night before broke the ice on the Volga and they could not cross. These people became known as Kalmyk, which means 'the remnant'. By 1930, they numbered one hundred and thirty thousand people, enough to warrant the creation of the Kalmyk Autonomous Soviet Socialist Republic. Like the Koreans and the Volga Germans, Stalin exiled the Kalmyks to Central Asia, accusing them of Nazi collaboration; they were allowed to return in 1957.

His forefathers were lucky, explained our host, they made it back to Xinjiang. But in the 1930s, the Uighurs rose up in revolt against the Chinese and the Chinese governor murdered many Torghut leaders; the tribe fell into disarray. His grandfather escaped to Kyrgyzstan.

'I speak a little Mongolian but my children don't speak a word; they are Kyrgyz.' He uttered the word Kyrgyz with contempt. The Torghuts and Kyrgyz have been at daggers-drawn for centuries. Over time, the Torghuts have woven an evil ancestry for their enemy, claiming that the Kyrgyz are descended from a Mongolian villain who violated his own mother. Genghis Khan punished him by circumcising him and cutting off his heels. This accounts for the Kyrgyz heeled riding-boots and their eagerness to embrace Islam.[24]

I had read about the rivalry between Kalmyks and the Kyrgyz in Manas, the ancient Kyrgyz epic poem written over 1,000 years ago, the story of the legendary man who unified the forty tribes of the nomadic Kyrgyz. Containing more than half a million lines it was first translated in the 1850s. Throughout the centuries, the poem was kept alive by the Manaschi, talented story-tellers, many of whom received divine inspiration for their vocation. Each Manaschi had his own version of the poem. Manas was born late to a rich elderly father who foresaw the arrival of the new leader of the Kyrgyz in a dream about an eagle:

> How he gleamed from head to tail,
> Swan-white pinions spread as well.
> How when he glanced with gaze severe,
> Alpkarakush seemed standing there.
> Golden plumes on his tail there grew,
> Golden-feathered his legs were too,
> Golden fluffiness, soft to feel,
> But his talons were hard as steel.
> Fierce he was, and struck what he sought.
> Mighty Allah gave him support.

Here is a hawk, with a beak of steel,
Talons as sharp as a dagger to feel.
Feathered friends which in heaven flew,
Fluttered in fear when he came into view.
All the beasts which ran on the earth
Scarcely dare stir when he flew forth.

After the child was conceived, the Chinese heard rumours of the emergence of a dangerous enemy and ordered all newborns called Manas in the Altai to be killed. Meanwhile, Manas's mother realized that she would be giving birth to a special boy, when her only craving was for tiger's heart. When the big day came, her labour pains lasted seven or eight days and all the women who helped with the delivery ended up flat on their faces. His elderly mother's skirts were ripped in five places during childbirth. We are told that the infant weighed as much as a 15-year-old and tugged so hard on his mother's nipple that it almost killed her!

As Manas grew up, he failed to show any signs of leadership, he was mischievous and unruly, a 'good-for-nothing, with riches drunk, unbeliever, a self-willed skunk'. His father, Jakib, sent him to a shepherd called Oshpur to learn how to look after the flock. Instead of looking after the sheep, Manas killed many of the old shepherd's lambs, cooked his friends *shashlik* and kept hiding his host's pipe. Oshpur despaired and asked Jakib to take his son away. When Jakib arrived to collect Manas, a band of Kalmyks appeared from nowhere and beat up Oshpur and Jakib. Manas killed the leader and the rest took flight. Despite the fact that Manas was only in his early teens, he was elected leader of the tribe along with his father. In accordance with tribal traditions, he was tossed in a white felt blanket and crowned with bronze. Ninety mares were killed in his honour and a nine-day celebration was held. The elders hoped that Manas would lead the Kyrgyz forces against the Kalmyks and the Chinese.

At this stage, the Kyrgyz didn't occupy the area now called Kyrgyzstan but lived in the Yenesei basin. Manas united the forty disparate Kyrgyz tribes with the help of his forty companions-at-arms and moved his people to the Altai. Forty holy spirits called *chiltans* assisted him, appearing in the form of vicious animals and vanquishing his enemies, particularly those who were not of the Muslim faith. The Altai Kyrgyz migrated again to other valleys in the Altai Mountains and into the Fergana valley. Here they intermarried with the local inhabitants of Andijan, Samarkand and Bukhara, and tried to stave off attacks from the Kalmyks. Manas married Kanikei, the daughter of the ruler of Bukhara. The bride price was steep: thirty females camels with black heads and white bodies, thirty male camels with black bodies and white heads, 500 pure white steeds with black tails, fifty black cows with white offspring and fifty white bulls with black offspring. However, the bride was worth the effort:

> Her waist is like young of camel's
> Her eyebrows are curved like chi
> She has a large forehead, black eyes
> Her speech is sweet
> Her back is sloping, her bosom is
> like that of a wild ram's.
> She is white-faced and her eyes are
> like a young camel's.
> Her rosy face shines
> Her slender waist sways.

The marriage strengthened Manas's hand as Kanikei actively encouraged her husband in his struggle for independence for the Kyrgyz people. The early part of the poem is taken up with clashes with the Kalmyks; later he defeats the Chinese. There are also many illustrations of Kyrgyz culture: weddings, christenings and funerals at which there are numerous contests, wrestling matches, horse racing and *ulak*, a game of polo played with a headless goat. Eventually Manas succumbed in a conflict with his enemy, Konurbai, in which he received a heavy blow to his head and an arrow in his right cheek. His forty companions carried his corpse to an isolated place and buried it. His son, Semete, succeeded him and Semete's exploits dominate the final part of the trilogy.

In the morning, I left my horses grazing on the hillside and paid a visit to the Przhevalsky tomb outside Karakol. Having read many of his books and shadowed some of his routes, I was glad to be able to pay my respects. Przhevalsky was one of the greatest explorers of Central Asia in the nineteenth century and every Russian schoolboy's hero. Some fans even claimed he was the biological father of Stalin. Covering 19,000 miles through Siberia, Mongolia, Tibet and Xinjiang, he spent nine years mapping out some of the most remote and inhospitable areas in the world. An army officer by training, he was invaluable to the army, tracing the Amur valley along the border with China, bringing back invaluable information on Yakub Beg, the Khotanese leader of formerly Chinese Kashgar. Crossing the Taklamakan from Khotan to Aksu, he located the wandering lake of Lop Nor and went on to visit the 'Caves of a Thousand Buddhas', long before the Hungarian archaeologist, Aurel Stein, plundered them in the early twentieth century. He was also a contender in the race for Lhasa but, unfortunately, he was turned back 145 miles from the Tibetan capital.

Sponsored by the Imperial Geographical Society, he was well versed in botany and zoology, meticulously noting down details of all the flora and fauna which he found *en route* and transporting specimens to mother Russia. One such specimen was the Przhevalsky horse, believed to be extinct in the wild and known only from Palaeolithic cave paintings in France and Spain. The Przhevalsky horse is the earliest species of horse still extant and only living ancestor of today's domestic horse. After Przhevalsky's discovery, every zoo in the Soviet Union had to have one, and soon there was none left in the wild. Only recently, an extensive breeding programme has resulted in the re-introduction of the small, stocky, dun-coloured pony into the wild.

The memorial museum was a taxidermist's paradise, with exhibits ranging from stuffed elks to Marco Polo sheep, balding like over-loved teddy bears. Alongside Przhevalsky's furry and feathered discoveries were hundreds of his letters, diaries, sketches, maps, surrounded by a curious *trompe-l'oeil* mural. His tomb is located outside the museum, at the end of an avenue of pines: a stone plinth underneath the wings of a large golden eagle. Gravely ill from typhus, contracted on a hunting expedition in the Ili River valley, Przhevalsky died beside Lake Issyk-kul in 1888. The golden eagle now presides over the remnants of the Russian torpedo base, part of an arsenal of deadly toys discarded all over Central Asia as the great powers tired of the Great Game.

In the evening, I wandered down to the lakeside and sat on the golden sand sheltered by tall reeds and tall grass with fiery crimson plumes and watched a family watering their two horses, still attached to a simple wooden cart. The green foothills were covered in small rivulets, fed by the surrounding peaks. Clouds cast long white reflections in the deep blue water – a still, magnetic mirror. Soon the setting sun transformed the lake into a blazing oil slick before it died behind the jagged silhouette of the Kyrgyz Alatau.

For the next few days, we circled Lake Issyk-kul, skirting waterlogged pasture and fields of bright green shoots of newly sown wheat. The Tien Shan were hooded in wintry clouds and the waters of the lake were a deep sapphire. Issyk-kul, 'Warm Lake', is one of the many large, high-altitude lakes found in Central Asia, the product of massive landslips during the last Ice Age. Underwater excavations have revealed human remains, pottery and many dinosaur bones. This fact may explain Hsuang-Tsang's belief

A family watering their horses in Lake Issyk-kul

that 'Dragons dwell in the waters of the lake'. Local legend about the lake is more exciting. Once upon a time, the Kyrgyz had a good king whose only fault was that every day he would request a different barber. Eventually there was only one left in the country. After visiting the king, the barber harboured a terrible secret. A holy man suggested a remedy for his burden.

'You must whisper the secret down a well, when the sun has sunk to rest, but remember to shut the lid afterwards.'

The barber hurried to the nearest well and whispered, 'The king has ass's ears.' Paranoid that he had been overheard, he fled the scene, forgetting to replace the lid. The water spilled over the sides of the well and continued to rise until the whole plain was flooded. Parallels must surely be drawn with Midas, another donkey-eared king. Maybe the story originated with Alexander's armies. The magic well theory is a popular one. The more bawdy will say that the holy man gave a young girl the keys to the well. While she was drawing water, she met a young man and became so caught up in the throes of passion, she forgot to close the lid and an almighty flood ensued.

Such legends have since spread far. One of the largest lakes in Mongolia, Khovsgol, has a similar legend. It had once been dry; a huge ogre had drunk every last drop from the lake. Many years later, a tiny boy, no bigger than a thumb, discovered a spring with his adoptive mother. One day he also forgot to close the well's lid; the lake reappeared; once again the ogre drained the lake. The plucky little fellow killed the ogre and cut off the top of a mountain to bury him. The waters didn't stop rising and so his adoptive mother dived into the lake and replaced the lid of the well. This drained all her energy and she drowned; the lake was named 'Mother Lake'.

Recently, a group of Kyrgyz archaeologists launched an expedition near Lake Issyk-kul to look for the burial site of Saint Matthew, one of the twelve apostles. While no trace has been found yet, excavations in two cemeteries have revealed over six hundred tombstones with Syriac inscriptions and crosses on them, dating between the ninth and fourteenth centuries. The lake is also said to have been a favourite camping spot for Tamerlane, who built a large castle on its shores. Six centuries later, Issyk-kul became a spa centre, hosting many Soviet leaders, such as Brezhnev. Despite its crystal clear waters, its purity was in some doubt; recently, a massive cyanide spill by a global mining giant into one of the principal feed rivers has not done much for its bathing appeal.

As we circled the lake, our chief concern was the security of the horses. Near villages, we found it was best to try to stay with local families rather than camp, as Ruslan quite rightly assumed that people would be less willing to steal from their neighbours' guests. That night, we turned on to a small track up the valley. The stillness of the night was broken by the sound of dogs answering the calling of other dogs. We followed the sound of barking and stopped outside the gates of a small cottage. Two enormous Kafghaz dogs were leaping up and down, tearing wildly at their chains. A Russian man appeared at the door with a gun and asked what we wanted. I'm sure it helped that he saw a girl at the door. He lowered the gun and invited us inside.

The cottage was very basic; it had a small gas stove with an oven in which his wife, Lena, made *piroshki*, small bread buns stuffed with egg and chives. While we were waiting for supper, Vasili offered us vodka and delicious dried fish. Vasili used to be director of a large state farm, which had since collapsed. He had managed to find a job as director of a smaller establishment.

'Did anyone see you come up here? It's not safe to keep your horses here. I bought the dogs last year to try to deter rustlers. They used to come at night and steal five sheep at a time. During the course of a year, they took a hundred sheep and ten cows. One night they stole six horses, one from me and one from each of the neighbours. The animal would have been in the meat-market at first light and impossible to trace, not that anyone would bother; the police are also in on the racket.'

Lena's family moved to Kyrgyzstan in the mid-nineteenth century. To control the region, the Russians resettled the area with Russian and Cossack farmers. The conduct of the Russians left a bitter taste with the Kyrgyz. During the First World War, the Cossacks ransacked Kyrgyz villages, slaughtering herds and burning villages. The repression continued for ten years and twenty-five per cent of the Kyrgyz population died. Many Kyrgyz fled to Xinjiang; some still remain there today. A European explorer, Gustav Krist witnessed the exodus:

> To an enormous distance I could see camel train after camel train; the entire horde was on trek, flying from the officials of the Soviets.... I little suspected at the time that I had been the witness of the last march of the free Kyrgyz.

It was a joy to sleep in clean sheets in a proper bed. In the morning Lena made us a rice salad with fish. She sent us on our way with more *piroshki*, fresh fruit and dried fish. She refused to take any money so I hid some under the pillow in my room. As we left, I noticed that Jijig's sore from the previous year had returned. I injected him in his flank with antibiotics. It was a tricky task as I could see him steeling himself to kick. I moved my saddle on to Three Socks. Ruslan was riding Aykulak while Tom and Wolf continued to carry the baggage.

Following a track above the lake, turquoise in the crisp sunshine, we met a man on a feisty dapple-grey horse. He was sitting astride an ornate, traditional Kyrgyz saddle: fine leather, fastened to a wooden frame with an array of small silver studs, the high pommel finished with a small curved grip shaped like a horse's head. Under his saddle the embroidered saddle-blanket boasted great success at the racetrack. Ruslan was impressed. The horse was an Akhal Teke which the man had ridden from Turkmenistan. The journey had taken twenty-seven days. One hundred Kyrgyz had made the journey a month before; each had two horses and covered ninety kilometres a day. As we rode away, we calculated that, at our pace, it would take at least three months.

The following day, we headed up the Barskoon valley. The black denuded mountains were streaked with snow. Our grey track snaked up the valley above us, leading to a gold mine, situated at 4,000 metres owned by Kumtor, a Canadian-Kyrgyz joint venture, the fourth largest gold mine in the world. The miners worked year round above the snow line extracting the gold. The mine accounted for about twenty per cent of Kyrgyz GDP and at least that proportion of the scandal. The minister in charge of the mine had recently changed. Kumtor had just paid for an all-expenses shopping trip for him and his wife to Amsterdam. One of the more famous scandals concerned a planeload of gold which never reached its destination. Despite the shipments having been secured with tamper-proof seals to ensure that no one helped themselves to a couple of bars in transit, the plane was empty when it arrived. The Kyrgyz government claimed that the plane was hijacked in mid-air. It is extraordinary that they thought that anyone would believe that several tonnes of gold could be shunted from one plane to another in mid-air; the word around Bishkek was that the gold never took off. Huge juggernauts rattled past us ferrying workers, equipment and possibly gold. At intervals, we came across signs saying, 'nature is the wealth of animals' and 'forests are the lungs of the world'. While such statements were laudable, it seemed slightly hypocritical coming from the company responsible for the massive cyanide spill into Issyk-kul.

At tea-time, we came across a family of Kyrgyz setting up their *yurt* among the boulders. All that was standing when we arrived was a circular trellis. A couple of women stood in the centre of the *yurt* with a long wooden prong supporting the wheel, while other members of the family slotted in the spokes and lashed them to the trellis with leather thongs. The *yurt* was then lined with *chiy*, long grasses, to keep out the insects and the dust. A layer of felt was wrapped around the frame and thrown over the roof.

A friendly wave from our host in the Barskoon Valley

Unlike the Mongolian tents, the door was not a normal wooden affair, but a flap of felt and *chiy*, tied to the entrance, which was rolled up above the doorway during the day and unravelled at night.

Once the tent was up, the women hung up decorative wall hangings around the side of the *yurt*; they were bold red with pink roses and an imperial purple brocade, threaded with simple woollen brocades through the spokes. A couple of colourful felt quilts, known as *shirdaks*, covered in a patchwork of simple geometrical designs, were scattered on the floor around a plastic tablemat. A steaming *samovar* was brought in from outside and they laid a selection of bowls on the mat containing thick fresh cream and rancid butter, and some hunks of bread. As the women prepared the *yurt* and made the tea, the men cleared the surrounding area of boulders and the young son led a miniature donkey up to the tree line in search of firewood. As I drank my tea, I looked up through the hole in the roof. Crossing through the centre of the wheel above our heads were two sets of treble tracks, the national symbol of Kyrgyzstan, silhouetted by the blue afternoon sky. A Kyrgyz *yurt* has forty spokes, representing the forty tribes of Kyrgyzstan. When there is a death in the family, one post is removed. The *tunduk* or opening in the top symbolizes family unity. The hearth of the *yurt* contains an eternal flame which burns for loved ones when they are at war.

After tea, we plodded up the road, hemmed in on either side by sheer rock faces, below frozen ice walls glistening thousands of metres above our heads. On the lower slopes, shale, rocks, boulders and the occasional streak of runaway snow warned of the perils overhead. The track coiled into a series of steep hairpin bends. By the end of the morning, we'd climbed another 1,000 metres. We entered a moonscape of rubble and snow, shed by the colossal walls of granite around us. Only the sky added colour to our monochrome surroundings. Jilda scampered over the rocks, chasing marmots. The inquisitive creatures sat outside their burrows, perched on their hind legs, staring at our caravan. Jilda slunk up to their holes like a wolf, freezing occasionally, one paw raised, sniffing the air. The head of the household always proved an invaluable sentinel, issuing a piercing whistle to warn the rest of the family. A flurry of fat bottoms and thick bushy tails scampered into burrows, out of sight.

By afternoon, we were trudging through a frozen wasteland. Jilda was gripped by a mad frenzy running round and round, tearing after an imaginary hare through the virgin snow, stopping occasionally to cool her tongue, relishing the crunchy snow like a child savouring an ice-cream. We crossed a small bridge over a stream; a small sign on our right indicated that we were crossing 'Arabel Su', the source of the Naryn River and the

Arabel Su. The source of the Naryn River also known as the Jaxartes

legendary Jaxartes. Known locally as the Syr Daria, it irrigates the cotton in the Fergana valley, rushes through Tashkent before doubling back into Kazakhstan, spilling over the lifeless Kyzylkum, watering the astronauts in Baykonour, the infamous Soviet Space Station, before dribbling into the Aral Sea.

The source of the Naryn River, a humble, pale blue, frozen alpine pool starved of water from the glaciers above, darkened to cobalt in the translucent evening air. Small, rebellious rivulets cut over the surface, clamouring for spring but were soon silenced by the icy twilight. The horses slipped on the slush, snow and ice as we followed a rock-strewn track, littered with the drop-pings of thousands of sheep, several days' journey ahead of us. We reached the top of the pass and gazed in awe at a concatenation of peaks, enormous frozen white horses, billowing, heaving and rolling snow as far as the eye could see. My head ached and I felt nauseous; the garlic, prescribed by our hosts by the lake, for altitude sickness, was burning a hole in my stomach lining.

As soon as we stopped, I set up the tent and lay shivering with a temper-ature, a headache and nausea. Ruslan was unsympathetic and kept asking when we were going to have supper. Feeling guilty, I struggled out of the tent and set about boiling some rice, meat, onions and beans.

Ruslan continued, oblivious of my ailments, 'I wouldn't put those beans in. They'll never cook, there isn't enough wood.' I poured them in anyway and we sat over a dwindling fire, fed by a pathetic supply of wood, which eventually flickered and died. 'I told you not to put in the beans. How am I supposed to eat this? The rice is mush and the beans are as hard as stones.'

'Fine, don't eat it, I'm going to bed.'

'You should have cooked the beans earlier when we were by the lake.'

'Why didn't you suggest it?'

'You're the woman.'

'If I sat at home all day, I wouldn't be paying you.'

'I can earn just as much fishing with my brothers,' he lied.

A concentration of peaks – the top of the Naryn Valley

As we descended down the valley, my headache began to evaporate. There was nothing to break the vast silence save the shrill, polyphonic calls of marmots. Flanked on one side by a large rock face and on the other by craggy tors, we headed towards a tiny lake, a pearl encrusted with ice. For a while we stood at the edge, skidding flat round stones across as Jilda gingerly paddled around, bathing her sore paws split by several days of futile, high-speed chases across sharp rocks in pursuit of marmots.

Ruslan showed Jilda up, catching a marmot with his bare hands; it was slow and it looked ill. I made him kill it and bury it. Many marmots carry bubonic plague; a foreigner had died of it in Almaty the previous year. I was armed with Amoxycillin in case I contracted it. It is said that it came to

Europe via the Mongols through the marmot population. It is highly conta-
gious, spreading aerogenically and is supposed to be able to last in human
spit for three months. During the siege of Kaffa in 1346, plague broke out
in the invading Mongolian ranks, who catapulted the infected bodies over
the city walls. From there it spread to Genoese merchants who carried it all
over Europe, wiping out a third of the European population. Marmots are
normally grassland animals but if they contract the plague, they move to the
desert, feeding off saxaul bushes, which are supposed to contain an antidote.

Picking our way across various ravines, which looked like massive earthquake faults, we sought out the only bridge over a river, swollen by the
melting glaciers. As we crested a fault-line, we startled a herd of half a dozen
Siberian ibex, which took off, springing out of sight with Jilda in hot pursuit.
That evening we wound our way down a small track. It began to snow, hail,
drizzle and finally bucketed down. Through the mist, we spotted a large
herd of yaks. Various inquisitive members trotted up, oblivious of the effect
that their massive woolly frames and menacing horns had on our horses. As
they danced out of control, Ruslan and I shouted and waved our hands. Jilda
sensed that there was trouble and took after the beasts, at least thirty times
her weight, barking furiously until I sensed she was dog-hoarse.

By the time we spotted a farm, we were soaked through, the rain barely a
fraction above freezing. Our hosts that night gave us bad news: the spring
thaw was setting in and dozens of swollen rivers stood in our way. Even if
we managed to cross them, the path was littered with landslides and in
places it had ceased to exist. The herders rarely took horses along the path
and many refused even to walk it. Our host pointed to a small river on the
map called Kashka Suu; a park warden lived there. Our host suggested we
should seek the warden's advice. Ruslan and I were initially horrified by the
idea of consulting the park warden. Again we had found ourselves in a
border area without permits; he could throw us out on a whim. However we
decided to try to offer to pay him and see if he was prepared to be our guide.

We started down the Naryn valley, a vast plateau, whose breathtaking
emptiness annihilated us: symmetrical triangular sheer faces, devoid of
snow, troughs filled with snow. A few lonely herds of yaks dotted the
biscuit-brown grass. The Naryn River doubled back on itself after Arabel
Su, and disappeared behind another mountain range, devouring a myriad
of streams in its path. Days before a small stream, it caught up with us
again, snaking lazily down the sweeping valley, several miles across, cutting
a deep rampart into one side; it was already impassable. The Central Tien
Shan range, which we had crossed the night before, was shrouded in cloud.
Bright shafts of sunlight were boring at the centre, causing a blinding white

glare. I could just make out one mountain in the distance, an inky smudge, fading in and out of vision. After skirting round a small settlement, we crossed a bridge and followed the left bank of the river. The river gouged its way through a narrow gorge; its languorous meander had become a furious dash. Our source of worry was wading through numerous mountain torrents cascading down from the surrounding glaciers.

We stopped for the night at a shabby brown *yurt*, made of a selection of skins and trussed up with string. The family goats clung to the side of the mountain as they grazed. Insisting on abiding by their traditions, our host, Hussein, slaughtered a sheep in our honour. It was an act of enormous generosity on the part of a family with only fifty sheep but the rite was performed with minimum fuss and maximum modesty. His wife, Nargiza, a portly motherly figure, prepared a delicious Kyrgyz speciality called *kurdak*: lamb fried with onions followed by *Beeshbarmak*.

Jilda was also in luck. For the past month, she had had to make do with scraps of bread, milk and fresh eggs. Whenever I found tinned meat, I'd surreptitiously feed it to her under the cover of night, always taking the empty tins with us. Meat was a luxury, saved for guests and special occasions and I dreaded the thought of being caught giving it to my dog. That night, Jilda dined on marmot, caught by the owner's swift-footed, stealthy dog. Unlike Mongolia and Northern Kazakhstan, it was regarded as inedible

Our Naryn hosts – Nargiza, Hussein and family

in Kyrgyzstan and Ruslan and I gazed longingly at the waste. Ruslan taught me how to skin the marmot: breaking off the bottom of its legs, one must make an accurate incision up the legs and the belly of the creature to save the pelt, several of which make a warm hat.

Nargiza insisted on preparing huge quantities of cream, butter and bread for our journey ahead. I tried to repay some of their kindness with matchbox cars, penknives and Polaroids. When her husband wasn't looking, I slipped her enough money to buy a sheep. Despite her overpowering need to accept, I had to force the money into her hand.

We arrived at the warden's bungalow at eight the following night, the horses stumbling over boulders waist-high in water in the dark. Luckily we hadn't missed dinner; the park warden, Beeshek, a slim, no-nonsense, practical man with closely-cropped greying hair, reserved the 'right' to feed off the gazelle and Marco Polo sheep, which he was employed to protect. Given his meagre salary of $20 per month, he was forced to dine on venison because he couldn't afford lamb. He fined us a paltry $10 for being in the park without permits and happily agreed to be our guide for $10 a day. We rose early and organized a family photo-shoot. His granddaughter, a shy 4-year-old with a lacy white bow in her hair, posed awkwardly alongside a home-made car. The chassis was made of coat hangers and aluminium

Beeshek's granddaughter and her car

sheeting, the latter also gracing the bonnet. The wheels were made of old pilchard cans and two red Coca-Cola bottle lids made the headlights.

Beeshek was impatient to get on, his fresh young Kyrgyz mountain-pony trotted several hundred metres ahead as our horses slogged behind. The path hung precariously over the angry river, climbing up several hundred metres into meadowland and plunging down to sandy coves. In the afternoon, we picked our way over rocks and scree, which clattered down into the river as the horses skidded on the cascading stones. Luckily, we were only twenty feet above the river.

We camped in a log cabin with a simple wood-burning stove and a large Central Asian equivalent of a wok. Beeshek cooked us a fine fry-up of potatoes, onions, garlic and copious quantities of venison, which I secreted in my pockets to give Jilda later. I slept well, perched in my sleeping-bag on a simple wooden shelf, with Jilda curled up underneath. We were up at dawn. As the others loaded the horses, I washed behind some bushes in a freezing stream.

As we continued downriver, the banks closed in on us creating a chasm, the thunderous torrent boring its way through the bedrock and forcing our narrow trail to headier heights. We picked our way over a massive landslide, the path barely thirty centimetres wide, the river foaming several hundred metres below. Ruslan and the warden stayed on their horses, I followed suit, dizzied by the noise of the roaring water below, my heart palpitating, the drop much worse for being in the saddle and not in control. My nerves were at breaking-point but I couldn't lose my cool. Then solid ground was underfoot again. We stopped to watch a herd of ibex leaping effortlessly up a vertical rock face on the opposite cliff. I was beginning to regain my nerve when Ruslan drew his horse up. The path had fallen away down a muddy ravine, leaving a sloping dusty pocket. Taking off the baggage, we led the horses over one by one, knowing that one slip and they would be history. As I led Wolf over the gap, one leg slipped. I was holding him near his bridle and somehow he kept his balance. Cakes of earth rolled down the side of the mountain, kicking up the dust.

Eventually we found ourselves in a small meadow. We stopped for some *koumiss*; I knocked it back, grateful for something to steel my nerves. Beeshek wouldn't let us stop for long and before my pulse was normal we were off again, re-living the same nightmares, taking the baggage off the horses and creeping around rockfaces. I insisted on taking off the baggage at all these junctures; trekking in Kashmir with my family, I once saw a horse carelessly brush a rock with its saddlebags. The force was enough to tip it over the edge into the river below; the icy current swept it to its death.

*

At mid-morning, we were ambling gratefully along a wide track a few metres above the river. Suddenly the track petered out.

'It was here a few weeks ago,' fretted Beeshek. 'It must have been washed away by the heavy rains. We'll have to turn back.'

I couldn't bear it. My nerves couldn't take a re-run of the morning's efforts. Ruslan and Beeshek set off on foot up the vertical slope and into the trees. Beeshek looked nervous; Ruslan was positive.

'I think we can do it, Achak. We'll leave the baggage horses down here and lead the other horses up to a safe place about a hundred metres up from here. There is no path but I think we can wind through the trees.'

The side of the mountain was so steep that, at times, we clambered up on our hands and knees, my horse struggled, tipping me back and at other times, nudging close behind before I had a chance to find my footing. After twenty minutes, we reached a clearing and I tied the horses up and stood guard while the others went back for the baggage horses. At least forty minutes passed and there was no sign of them so I left the horses tied to a tree and went back to look for them. I found them scrambling among the pines; Beeshek was steadying Wolf, whose saddle had slid under his belly, and Ruslan was struggling up through the pines having rescued Wolf's baggage. Tom, the other baggage horse, was tethered to a tree further back.

Ruslan relayed the story: 'Wolf was skittish and lost his footing, he fell a metre and I managed to hold on to him.'

It was lucky they were still in the trees. Barely a few metres further down the path, there was nothing to break the hundred-metre fall.

Ruslan shouldered the baggage and I led Wolf; Beeshek brought up the rear with Tom. A few minutes further on, Wolf stumbled and I held on for all I was worth as he regained his balance. My heart was drilling against my ribs and I could hardly breathe as I led him up through more pines. I lost my footing several times slipping on moss, hidden by crunchy pine needles. I knew I had to keep my nerve for both of us. Once in the clearing, I tethered him and went back to help the others. We waited for a while until we were sure Wolf had calmed down.

Finally, we came off the cliff edge and on to safer ground. It began to rain hard and I thanked our stars that the rain hadn't come earlier. The horses were tired but we urged them on; Beeshek had to be back home in the afternoon to receive a village elder and he needed to show us the route. Picking our way around large boulders in a brisk stream, the horses clambered up the bank. Three Socks got his front feet on to the bank and heaved himself up. Suddenly he lost momentum and we tipped back into the stream; I managed to avoid landing underneath him and fell heavily on my hip on to a boulder. I was momentarily knocked backwards by the current and fought to stand up. I saw my saddlebags floating past me and grabbed hold of them, stumbling out of the water. Three Socks was already shaking himself out like a wet dog, unhurt. We soldiered on in the rain, my teeth were chattering but there was no point in stopping. Finally the sun came out and we stopped for an hour so that I could change and dry out. Ruslan looked guilty as I laid my possessions out in the sun; it wasn't his fault.

'You should have secured your saddlebags properly,' he scolded.

'Thanks for telling me sooner,' I said through gritted teeth.

Beeshek left us on a grassy hill overlooking the distant red cliff-faces of Naryn. In the centre of a large meadow stood a truck, a white cupcake *yurt* and a pen containing several hundred sheep. Our host was a middle-aged, lively man named Karatar with fuzzy hair and a huge Latino handlebar moustache, barely discernible in the undergrowth of his face. Within a few minutes of our having dismounted our horses, Karatar had selected a goat from his pen. It was late by the time the goat was cooked and we passed the time drinking vodka and talking about potatoes. His brother, a potato farmer, was finding farming tough. When the Soviet Union collapsed, he could sell his potatoes in Almaty for export to Russia for ten som (fifteen pence) per kilo. Now the Kazakh border tariffs were so high, and the officials so corrupt, that he could only sell his potatoes in the local market, for a third of what he used to get. While borders were coming down in Europe, the opposite was the case in Central Asia; the leaders preferred building barriers around their fiefdoms. The presidents may have liked the sound of a unified Central Asia but each one believed that he should lead it. At the outset, the leaders spoke of high ideals and perhaps some genuinely believed in them. But in the end, they succumbed to greed and corruption; their principles were sacrificed in favour of bigger bank balances. Karatar's experiences as a herder were no better.

'Before *perestroika*, things were much better. I was a shepherd on a large farm. Now I scrape by looking after the village sheep. The young don't believe in working any more. They stay in the village and drink, while I look after their sheep. Half of them don't even bother to pay me.'

We stayed for a few days. After the exertion and frights of the previous week, the horses needed a rest. Wolf had lost quite a bit of weight and I bought seventy kilos of grain to try to fatten them up. I also found a local supply of corned beef, which I fed Jilda every night. While she enjoyed it, it made her fart and she was not the best sleeping companion. While we were there, Karatar's neighbour agreed to swap Jijig, whose saddle sore had put him out of action for several months. Jijig wasn't very popular with the other horses; he always seemed to keep himself to himself. The herder was

a palette of pastels, rose, lavender, peach and primrose, streaked with black clouds. It was almost dark by the time we reached the shore and we began a fruitless search for firewood. In the middle of the road, we came across a tethered horse and a donkey. There was no one in sight. As we debated whether or not to stop, a middle-aged man and his young teenage son crawled out of a hole under the road and invited us to stay with them. Clambering down the bank beside the road, we crawled inside the storm drain, three or four metres long covered at each end by a sheet of tarpaulin. Inside, a series of felts and thin sleeping-bags afforded slim protection against the freezing concrete tube and the bitter wind, which stole underneath the canvas. At the far end of the pipe a small metal bucket contained the day's catch.

'What are you doing here at the lake? Are you a fisherman?'

'No, I am the park warden. I guard eggs.'

'I'm sorry?'

'I guard eggs.'

'Whose eggs?'

'Goosey eggs.'

I fished out my book of birds and found that he was indeed still in possession of his marbles. The bar-headed Indian goose, a rare grey bird with a white head crossed with black bars at its nape, crosses the massive Pamir and Tien Shan ranges, flying at altitudes of up to 8,000 metres, to lay its eggs on the shores of Song-Kul. After the various protected species fed to me by the park wardens, I fully expected 'goosey' omelette. However, our warden had just retired and we feasted on *ooxah*, traditional fish soup made with noodles. He explained that now that he was retired, he supported his family through fishing. As he talked, he picked at his ear with a matchstick, absentmindedly examining the contents.

'We come here every summer to fish. Every few days, a friend drives up here, collects the fish and drives to the market in Bishkek. On a good day, we can catch ten kilos, which we sell for fifteen soms (twenty pence) per kilo. Sometimes we only catch a couple of kilos. It is difficult now. Many more people are coming here to fish. There used to be two trawlers, now there are ten. We only have our net and a small rubber boat.'

'Why don't you bring a *yurt* up? It is freezing in here.'

'I do in winter, but it is summer. The snow should have melted by now.'

Ruslan made space for the man and his son in his tent, which kept out the glacial wind. In the morning, we awoke to driving snow; thick, white snow clouds eclipsed the mountains. We decided to stay put until the storm cleared. At breakfast, a slim man with a moustache and a blue cloth cap appeared as we were stoking the fire for another round of fish stew.

'Are you a fisherman?'

'No, I guard the trees.'

'Where are the trees?'

'There are a few further down that way,' he pointed, tossing a few more logs on to our fire.

In the early evening, the clouds turned from steel grey to pink and lifted, exposing chains of snow-capped peaks. The next day we set off under a pale blue sky, the lake deep blue in the brilliant morning sunshine. The grass already seemed greener. The fisherman's son rode with us for a few hours, pointing out strange stone circles, the burial mounds of warriors of the sixth-century Turkish Kaganate. Each stone is said to indicate the number of people that the warrior slew before succumbing himself.

Sixth century burial mounds, Lake Song-Kul

We didn't get far around the lake. On the western shore, we met a group of Russian fishermen, who invited us to dinner. Ruslan was a little wary of the Russians at first, but soon he was in full swing, helped by a few friendly toasts of vodka. We began with an excellent fish salad: fish roe, fish liver, onions, chilli pepper and pungent vinegar, followed by *ooxha*. They cooked the fish heads in a sack and then removed them, creating a highly flavoursome broth to which they added potatoes, rice, chilli pepper and herbs. The fishermen stayed there all year round in a Russian army tent, sleeping on a wooden dais covered in warm quilts. The bedding, damp after many winter months, was drying in the sun, the first sign they'd had of spring.

> Here round the steppe, high hills everywhere.
> Here are high passes and mountain crests.
> Though on the heights no thick grass rests,
> Mountain sheep graze there, like grains of sand....
> Here are mounds, and gully and rock,
> Ledges and wedges of mountain crests.
> Here no sign of humanity rests.
>
> Manas

17

CONFRONTATION

Leaving the lake behind us, we rode up through the mountains, the ground squelching under the horses' feet, a plethora of tiny spring streams cascading in every direction. At the top of the pass, we met a Russian 'ornithologist' from St Petersburg, who had driven to Kyrgyzstan in a Lada to watch the birds. He didn't seem to know anything about the Indian bar-headed goose and I wondered whether he was casing the area. Ruslan was chuffed because he was given a packet of Russian cigarettes. We shared a loaf of bread and a can of pilchards with him and told him to seek out our 'goosey' egg man.

Not long after our snack, the path divided into a high road and a low road.

'I think we should go this way,' I suggested.

'No, this way,' Ruslan insisted.

'Fine. You go that way, and I'll go this way. I'll see you later.'

Poor Jilda scampered from one caravan to the other all afternoon, until we met up in the late evening. The track became increasingly dark and dusty. We passed a river cascading blood-red over a rockfall. Ruslan briefly forgot himself, taking photographs of the contrast between the muddy upper reaches and the rusty clay colour lower down.

Several hundred feet further down the valley, we could hear the loud thud and clang of excavators, ploughing into the open-face coal pits below. We were soon plodding through a small mining village. The workers were shuttled in by four-wheel drive, six-wheeled people-carriers and lived in shacks and caravans. It felt oppressive, suffocating and dangerous and we hurried through, walking for an hour in the dark. Finally we came to a couple of *yurts*. A young woman, in a blue silk dress and bright lipstick invited us to stay with her and her young son.

Later in the evening, we were joined by a couple of men, who seemed to be settling in for the night. It dawned on me that she might be 'servicing' the mining community and that we were sleeping in the tent normally

*The start of the confrontation. Ruslan takes the high road while
I take the low road*

reserved for clients. At first, I felt rather uncomfortable but soon we were merry-making, sharing several kilos of fish, washed down with liberal quantities of vodka. At midnight, the woman put her son to bed and began to yawn conspicuously. I made my excuses and went off to brush my teeth. I slept for a couple of hours and awoke to more revelry. The men were all quite drunk and our hostess looked decidedly jaded. Perhaps she wasn't what I'd thought she was.

'Ruslan, I think you should stop. We are her guests. If we stop, maybe the others will go and she can get some rest.'

'F…k off and stop being so bossy,' he slurred.

'Ruslan, we have a long journey ahead of us tomorrow. We have another pass to cross and two or three more after that. I think it would be wise to stop.'

'Fine. You go to bed and sleep. I can still do my job in the morning.'

'Have a little respect for this woman. You are keeping her son awake; let them sleep.'

'Just because you are paying me, you bitch, doesn't mean that you can tell me what to do. No one is my boss. I can earn just the same amount of money fishing. I quit. Tomorrow you can look for a new guide.' He slumped on to his sleeping-bag.

'You heard me, bitch. I want my money. Tomorrow you are on your own.'

I lay awake in my sleeping-bag, trying to work out what to do if I couldn't find a replacement. After my Mongolian experience, I knew that five horses would be impossible to handle, particularly through steep mountain-passes, where there could be snow.

In the morning, he seemed to have forgotten his threat. After getting the woman's number, he saddled the horses as usual. He wasn't in the mood to talk. We clambered up a steep goat track towards the pass, leading the horses. Ruslan paid for his revelling and his chain-smoking habit; every twenty minutes he stopped, crouched on his haunches and cradled his head in his hands. After a few minutes, he would look up to check that I wasn't too far ahead. I soldiered on, looking back occasionally to check that I still had a good lead, making him sweat.

At midday, we got to the top. A lip of snow and ice, several metres deep, blocked the path. I waded through the snow and found a place where the horses could pass. One by one we led them across. On the other side, we faced a steep descent of several hundred metres of boulders and scree, streaked with patches of ice, snow, slush and mud. A myriad of frosty trick-les, fed by the glaciers above, gained momentum as we descended and combined to form a substantial river. The path which I had hoped to follow was covered in snow. Rather than plunging down the valley, it teetered along the side of a steep wall of moraine. One slip would be fatal. We decided to descend on the other side of the valley.

The incline became gentler, green virgin pastures dotted with one or two abandoned shacks owned by the more adventurous shepherds, who hadn't yet moved their animals to their summer grazing. We didn't see a soul all day.

'Shouldn't we be going that way?' Ruslan pointed to a large track, which we had passed on the other side of the river.

'I'm sure we can go this way. Look at all of the animal tracks. This must be a tried and tested route.'

After an hour, we entered woods of Tien Shan spruce punctuated by the occasional clearing of lush tall grass. Passing a small empty wooden log cabin, we startled a fox, which stole into the woods with Jilda giving chase. As we plodded deeper into the woods, the path became steeper and narrower, and fallen trees blocked the way. The animals, whose tracks we had been following, evidently hadn't passed this way. We were stealing along the steep slopes of a canyon, several hundred metres deep. We finally reached a point of no return. Ruslan was angry.

'Now look where you've led us. I'll wipe my arse with your bloody map. What are we supposed to do now?'

'How was I supposed to know that the track had fallen away?'

We turned and trudged several kilometres back up the river, until we found a point where we could cross and follow the wider track that Ruslan had spotted earlier. From the other side, we could see how fruitless our efforts would have been. Huge chunks of the slope were missing. Even on our side, we were forced to climb up several hundred metres only to plunge down again into another stream-bed and up yet another exhaustingly steep slope. We stopped for something to eat, sharing our dry biscuits with Jilda. But we couldn't stop too long; my sweat-soaked shirt soon had me shivering. I began counting my footsteps, allowing myself 200 paces before I could stop to catch my breath. Finally, at around six o'clock, the path began to wind down towards a town in the bottom of the valley. We stumbled down the side of a steep meadow. My legs were shaking so much that I couldn't control my downward momentum, except by sitting down.

The path flattened out and followed the river. We found ourselves in a Garden of Eden, overgrown with wild rhubarb, lucerne and enormous plants, which looked like over-sized lilies. It is a sad reflection on the deterioration of nomadic traditions that some parts of Kyrgyzstan are bald from over-grazing, while others, inaccessible by motorized transport, are flourishing. We were desperate for somewhere to stay. Fed up with each other's company and exhausted, we couldn't face the idea of putting up the tents and eating our rice gruel with tuna yet again. Eventually, we happened upon a converted train-carriage with a small wood-burning chimney. The occupants were old, hospitable but not too inquisitive. Jilda made friends with a skeletal saluki with straggly hair and wispy ears. After a few bowls of yoghurt and litres of tea, I collapsed into a bunk for the night.

Our host guarded 'fresh water'. The small spring above their caravan was the only supposedly safe drinking-water in the valley. From a small waterfall above us, it made its way in insulated, lagged pipes down to Ming Kush, the uranium-mining centre of the former Soviet Union. Or at least that was the theory. In practice, the pipe was corroding, leaking and soaking up the escaping radiation from the plethora of uranium shafts in the valley, which had been hastily and carelessly closed up ten years earlier. In some areas of Kyrgyzstan, particularly near the Fergana valley, the mercury and stibium content in the soil is several hundred times above the norm.

Ming Kush, whose name means 'a thousand eagles', used to have a population of thirty-five thousand and relied on uranium and open-face coal mining. Until 1992, it was shut off to the world. After the Russians closed the uranium mines, the population plummeted to 6,500. Coal, however, is still being extracted in small quantities for local use. The town consists of colourful wooden buildings, which used to be painted red, white and blue on festivals, and a few concrete, three-storey apartment blocks situated in an ochre canyon in what seemed like the middle of nowhere.

The horses were in desperate need of re-shoeing. As I was making a few purchases in the local shop, a slight, neat woman tapped me on the shoulder.

'Do you speak English?' she asked in a flawless English accent. Maya was the local English teacher.

'This is the most exciting day of my life. After teaching English all my life, I have finally met a real English speaker.' Her eyes brimmed with tears.

Together, we tracked down the blacksmith's wife. She had horseshoes but none of them had any holes for nails; her husband would have to fit them for me.

'Please don't tell him that you bought them from me. If he finds out that you have paid me, he will take the money and drink it. Look at my children; I can't afford to buy them clothes; we don't even have enough to eat.'

We tracked her husband down in a round capsule, which served as the guards' quarters for Ming Kush's felt-tip factory, the only source of employment other than the uranium shafts. There was nothing to guard. It had almost entirely ceased operation. The guards sat inside drinking moonshine earned by whomever in the local community had managed to rub a few pennies together. The blacksmith promised to have the shoes ready in the morning.

Returning to Ming Kush, we searched for a safe place for the horses and opted for a small patch of grass in the fire station.

'They have a pistol. They can watch the horses,' explained Ruslan, who elected to watch the horses. Maya had family staying. After dinner, I was invited to stay with Oleg, the local heart surgeon, a Russian man with a ruddy face which radiated kindness, and a shock of frizzy strawberry hair. He had stayed in Ming Kush out of a sense of duty, earning a living as a bee-keeper and practising his medicine virtually for free.

'I am lucky that my brother married a woman of German descent. He now works in a car factory in Germany, earning twenty-five-thousand dollars a year. He sends money back to help us. Two years ago, he drove a car over from Germany for my father.'

'What work can a heart surgeon hope to find here?'

'Ming Kush used to have a population of twenty thousand. Now we have less than five thousand. No one can afford a doctor and state funding barely exists. I have no equipment and can only refer people to Bishkek. We have nine doctors here; we are all specialists: paediatricians, heart surgeons, obstetricians, but we spend most of our time treating cancer patients.'

A portly, shabby Russian lady spoke up from across the table. 'The mines were never closed properly. There is radiation in the water and even if we had clean water to drink, our animals are radioactive. Our hair is falling out, our teeth are falling out but the government doesn't care; the world has forgotten us.'

The next day I returned to the fire station. A sour old woman sat on a wall in the forecourt, dispensing moonshine on credit. After all, I owed the blacksmith and the guards money. The money would never make it back to the families. Like everyone, the old woman needed to earn a living but I couldn't help despising her for playing a pivotal role in ruining families like the one I had seen the day before. The men were huddled under a tall tree and as I approached, I realized that none of them could focus. Ruslan was playing king-pin and was even more drunk than the rest of them. His eyes were glazed over and he was having trouble registering anything. He had promised all those in the fire station a slice of the action. I was paying above the odds but I was happy to do so in order to get away.

'Come on, let's go.'

'I think we should wait until tomorrow morning.'

'Ruslan. These men are all drunk. They can't guard the horses. This place is scaring me.'

'Tomorrow morning, early,' he insisted.

'Let's go now.' Ruslan glanced anxiously over his shoulder to see if any of his drinking companions had heard. I started to load the horses, with the help of Oleg, the doctor.

When all the horses were ready, I handed Ruslan his reins, took hold of the baggage horses and rode out of the yard. I looked back in time to see someone giving Ruslan a leg-up on to his horse. He was slouched over the side of the saddle, trying to right himself. I walked ahead beside Oleg, joking that he'd do a roaring trade if he were a renal specialist.

'Are you sure you'll be OK with him?'

Ruslan trotted up behind me, and took hold of the reins of the baggage horses.

'I can look after these. You concentrate on staying in the saddle.' Ignoring Ruslan, I asked Oleg for directions to the next pass. He began to explain the way to Ruslan.

'There's no point telling him anything. He won't remember anything in ten minutes,' I said, half-jokingly but still seething at Ruslan's behaviour. Five minutes further along the road, we bade Oleg farewell. We rode on in silence until we were out of earshot.

'What did you say to him about me?'

'Nothing.'

He rode in front of me and turned his horse around, blocking the path. 'Don't lie. What did you tell him?'

'I wasn't talking about you.'

Grabbing my reins, he stopped my horse. 'I heard you. You said, "don't tell him the instructions, he's too drunk. He won't remember." You think I'm stupid?'

'No, you are drunk and someone needs to remember the way.'

'You bitch. I can remember the instructions.'

'Fine.' I dug my heels into my horse and trotted ahead but he followed behind, taunting me. After several minutes, we came to a crossroads in the track. A bus stopped in front of us and a dozen miners staggered out. Ruslan spent five or ten minutes discussing directions with one of them, while the others leered at me. I'm sure they'd only stopped out of curiosity, but I began to get very nervous.

'Come on Ruslan, let's go.'

'Can't you see I'm talking,' he slurred. Ten minutes went by; I could see that Ruslan had no intention of going. I tugged at his reins, but he kept his horse steady.

'Please Ruslan. It's late and we need to get away from Ming Kush. It is not safe here.'

'I told you, I'm talking.' I gave his horse a flick on its backside with my whip. It danced forward a couple of paces before he pulled it up.

'What did you do that for?'

'Please,' I implored the men standing around us. 'Let us continue on our way.' The men dispersed, clambering back into the bus and we were alone.

'Why did you speak to them like that? Why did you hit my horse?' I ignored him. I dared not reply, fearing that my voice would crack. Tears rolled down my face and I turned away from him before he had a chance to see them and wiped them away.

'Listen to me. How dare you hit my horse! Now it is my turn.' Blocking my path, he lashed out at me with his whip but I managed to steer my horse away. He tried again, this time with the force of his weight behind each stroke. He fell off his horse. I tried to use the opportunity to put some distance between us but it was difficult controlling three horses behind me. Ruslan caught up with us and grabbed my horse by the reins. His black eyes burned and I was convinced he was going to kill me. Whether or not he aimed at me, I closed my eyes and opened them in time to see that he had missed. Kyzylkum had blood trickling down between his eyes and Wolf had a gash on his neck.

'Help, please help,' I screamed, kicking the three horses into a trot, which was all I could manage, the horses weighed down with baggage and knocking against one another. My cries for help echoed off the valley walls. There was no one around to hear me. Ruslan was trying to remount Aykulak and kept falling off. Finally Aykulak took off without him; I caught him and continued walking. Ruslan hurried after us, swerving along the road as he ran. He finally succeeded in getting on to Aykulak. As he raised his whip again at me, I flinched and ducked. But the blow didn't come. He froze, arm raised, for a couple of seconds – the vodka had lost its grip over him. Disgusted, he threw the whip into the bushes and galloped away.

'He's got one horse and many of my belongings,' I thought. 'But I haven't paid him; we're even.' I was convinced that I had seen the last of him. Despite being alone again with five horses, this time I wasn't afraid. 'I'll find someone else,' I reassured myself. 'I can speak Russian. I am much better with horses than I was last time.' I didn't feel like crying; I just felt relieved and drained. Emotions were a luxury of the good life I had left behind. My life had been had been worn down to its bare sinews by the exertions of the past months; instincts had taken over; survival was all that counted and I was alive.

In the evening, I rounded a corner in the track. Ruslan's horse was tethered on the bank of a fast-flowing river. He was nowhere to be seen.

'Perhaps he's drowned or injured at the side of the road.' There was no sign of him by the road so I started towards the river and stopped. 'That's what he wants me to think. Perhaps he is waiting by the bank to push me in. If he whacks me over the back of the head and I fall in, it could look like an accident. He can take everything and return home with no consequences.' I stopped on the track, a good twenty metres from his horse and waited. After five minutes, he staggered up the bank, bare-chested, his face and hair dripping. So he'd gone there to sober up. Wordlessly, he rode up to me and took the baggage horses. We spent the next twenty minutes looking for a spot where the horses might cross the river to a *yurt* on the opposite bank. Finally we found a safe place and rode up to the *yurt*.

As we sat under the moonlight, drinking noodle soup and eating yoghurt with yet another warm and generous family, I felt an enormous sense of relief to be in company. I was shocked by the strength of Ruslan's reactions. I didn't want to continue on with him but I didn't have a moment alone with the shepherd to ask his help or to seek out an alternative. That night, I lay in my tent and thought about what to do. Ruslan had shown me a dark side, which I suppose I always knew was there. What could I expect from a young man living with alcoholic parents and alcoholic brothers? Vodka does horrible things to people. I'd seen the scars from his street fights; I'd known the risks. Deep down I knew that Ruslan was a sound guy who meant well. What was the point of looking for a new guide? Why swap a known entity for someone unknown? Ruslan was a bloody good guide; he was excellent with the horses. Was this what an abused wife feels when, yet again, she takes back her husband? Maybe it was exhaustion and resignation – perhaps I was too generous – but I decided to keep him on.

In the morning, I pointed at the scars on Kyzylkum and Wolf.
   'You did that.'
   'What.'
   'Look, here, here and here.'
   'Don't be so stupid. Of course I didn't.' That was that. No apologies, no recognition of his guilt. How does one start to apologize for such behaviour?
   We rode in silence for most of the day, snaking down a dusty track under wild cherry trees, alongside the river until our valley joined a much larger river, coiling sluggishly through a parched summer landscape. We escaped the midday sun, lunching with a man and his two playful daughters. His wife had died recently and his 10-year-old daughter now kept house. A passer-by sold us a couple of fish as the local store only had dried biscuits, cigarettes and rice.
   Later we climbed another steep mountain track, ducking to avoid Tien Shan spruce as we wound into a forest of conifers. We soon resorted to walking on foot, leading the horses and listening to the gentle thud of their hoofs as they tripped over old roots buried under a carpet of pine needles on the forest floor. The path was steep and became progressively narrower. Despite the fact that it was already late, neither of us relished the idea of camping in the trees, under the watchful eye of bears and wolves, preferring instead to soldier on up several hundred metres in the twilight. Finally, we found a beautiful meadow above the tree-line a thousand feet up from our lunch spot. We camped beside a mountain stream bang in the middle of the territory of two possessive stallions, one of which had a very deep sore in its back. They kept challenging our horses to a duel and every time we heard the aggressive neighing of our horses, we resorted to our armoury: stones, starter pistol and Jilda.

While Ruslan prepared a delicious fish stew, Jilda kept running up to the baggage and disappearing behind a tree. We soon found out why; she had found our only loaf of bread. I can imagine her thoughts:

'They won't notice if I take a tiny bite. Gosh that was good, surely they won't miss a bit more? Oh dear! The damage is rather noticeable, I'd better take the rest.' I wasn't angry. She was hungry and we didn't deprive her of her share of the fish stew.

The hard uphill slog continued the next morning as we crested a series of false summits towards our 3,700 metre pass. Before long, we were skirting large patches of snow, winding steeply up the stark mountainside, threaded with boulder-strewn streams. We had to pick our way carefully, trying to keep in the sunshine, where the path was relatively dry. Some areas in permanent shadow were buried under deep snow and spring avalanches. A small path wound over the top of a narrow gully. It seemed relatively dry and we decided that it would be the safest option. Fifty metres up, we came to a muddy slope, terraced with small trails and chequered with patches of snow. I led Three Socks and Kyzylkum along one of the trails. When I was almost across, Three Socks' back legs gave way underneath him and he slipped on to the trail below, before recovering his balance. I led my horses across to a safe, gentle slope and went back to help Ruslan.

'Ruslan, I think we should lead the horses across here, one by one. Three Socks slipped up there.'

'Don't worry. I can handle it.'

I walked ahead and he led Aykulak, Tom and Wolf, tied head to toe, along the track. Suddenly, Wolf lost his nerve, jerked his head back and stumbled down on to the trail below, pulling Tom down with him. Both horses collapsed on their sides, with their feet facing uphill. It was impossible for either to get up from that position. Aykulak was straining to keep his balance on the path.

'Achak. Hold Aykulak.' Ruslan cascaded down the mountain on his bottom towards Wolf. I dug in my heels and leaned back, trying to use my weight to balance Aykulak. Wolf tried to get up and began slipping towards the edge of the deep gully. My feet began to slide along towards the edge of the path.

'Achak, you have to let go or they will pull you down with them.' I clung on until my toes were dangling over the edge and let go. It was a nightmare in slow motion; my three best horses rolled down the side of the mountain together. I closed my eyes and waited for them to plunge over the edge.

'Achak, quick, the knife.' They were lying a couple of metres from the edge, their fall stopped by Aykulak, who was facing uphill, his front legs clawing the mountainside as he strained to break the slow slide of the others. We clambered down the side of the mountain. I held Aykulak, while Ruslan cut the other horses loose. As Ruslan cut Wolf's baggage loose, I wrestled with the cold muddy knots on Tom's baggage. Dragging the baggage aside, Ruslan held the reins of the other two horses. Wolf struggled to his feet and I led him slowly up the slope along the path, past the muddy gashes, clawed by their earlier struggles, petrified that he would baulk again. I led the others over while Ruslan lugged the baggage up. We stopped in a small meadow, where we sat eating dry biscuits until the horses had calmed down.

After a couple of hours, we resumed our climb. On the map it looked as though, once at the top, the path would skirt left along a shoulder for a kilometre or so before a final ascent. When we got to the top, I could see a gap between the boulders in the distance, where the path should be.

'It doesn't look right. Maybe we are already at the top,' I thought; my compass was buried at the bottom of one of my saddlebags.

'Let's go down here.' The path looked well trodden. After a couple of hours, we were back in the trees. Dogs barked in the distance. Suddenly two mongrels charged at Jilda, one jumping on her back and sinking its teeth into her fur. My starter pistol wasn't at hand so I slithered off my horse and beat the dogs off with a whip. One of them had a clump of Jilda's fur in its mouth. I waited until its owner, our host that night, was not looking before hurling stones at it in revenge.

Our host had shot a deer and we ate venison until we were at bursting point. His Russian canvas tent supported by beams, felled from the surrounding trees, was the only one in the vast valley and he could hunt with impunity. He only had forty goats. If he didn't hunt, his family would never eat meat. He informed us that we had taken a wrong turning and the next morning we'd have to climb 1,000 feet back up the mountain to the pass.

So we retraced our steps back up the valley. Our host's brother, Talai, accompanied us. On the way up, he spotted something in the woods and shot at it. The wounded animal limped into the bushes and Talai chased after it with a large chunk of wood and beat it over the head. He came out of the trees holding up a large badger, which he hung from a branch to collect on his way back.

I was limping; my feet were covered in blisters and I had stabbing pains in my knees.

'Why don't you ride your horse?' Talai kept asking.

'Because he's tired,' I gasped, stopping again. Ruslan stayed a metre behind me, wheezing and coughing but refusing to fall behind in company.

'Why do you keep on stopping, Achak? Are you finding it too difficult?'

It was worth the struggle. All around us stood steep, snow-fed, green mountains with white coronets. Talai handed around a couple of bowls of yoghurt, which we drank crouching on the snow behind a rock, an icy wind licking at our sodden shirts. We descended into verdant pastureland, carpeted with over-sized dock leaves and dotted with numerous *yurts*. We were invited into one for tea. A well-dressed young man in his mid-twenties was visiting his mother for the weekend. He worked in the gold factory in Kazarman and was there for the weekend.

'Watch out in Kazarman. It is not safe. At night it is crawling with drug addicts and gangsters. You don't want to camp anywhere near it.'

We were quickly on our way down a rocky road, covered in landslides and large boulder-filled streams, which jarred the horses' legs and had me wincing with every step. By nightfall, two of the horses had lost all four shoes and Aykulak was limping. We couldn't find anywhere to camp. Finally we hit a dust track, silver under a bright moon, and followed it until midnight when we happened upon a field in which we tethered the horses. It was warm enough to dispense with my tent and I lay on a mat, my sleeping-bag draped over me, a gentle breeze blowing on my face, gazing at the silhouettes of the horses, munching by the riverbank.

I woke at dawn; dew had drenched my sleeping-bag. We realized that the horses were grazing in some poor farmer's winter pasture. Hurriedly saddling the horses, we were on our way by six, stopping for breakfast in a small village, where an old man gave us some extra nails to reshoe the horses. After breakfast, a large group of schoolchildren fell in with us. Ruslan, to his great amusement, soon had them all marching in a perfect four by four in front of us until we reached their school – a group of large Russian canvas tents. The school building had been washed away in spring floods and the new school had not been completed.

Down in the valley, it was incredibly hot and dusty. Rows of poplars stood in neat rectangles around the fields and our path was dotted with simple, gingerbread cottages with white roofs. That night we slept on the floor in an abandoned farmhouse. We dined on potatoes, wild garlic, corned beef and noodles, cooked using old planks from the fence as firewood. The horses ate their fill of every imaginable kind of grass which grew in metre-high abundance.

The next day we began to climb towards the final pass that lay between Kyrgyzstan and Uzbekistan's Fergana Valley. Ruslan resumed his standard complaint; that the road was 'like a big snake' and 'why can't we travel in a straight line'. Halfway up the road, a young boy, who might have been eleven at a push, failed to cadge a cigarette off Ruslan. This unleashed a torrent of abuse in Kyrgyz; a few of the expletives were familiar to me as Ruslan's favourites. As we rounded the corner, the boy began to hurl stones at us. Ruslan took out my starter pistol and fired a few shots in the air. The imp darted behind a rock, jumping up occasionally to make faces at us and hurl more abuse, and bobbing back down at the sound of the shots, which sent Ruslan and me into fits of laughter.

Near the top, we followed some steep animal trails until the path became impassable. Packed ice glistened ahead on the trail, a drop of several hundred metres to the road below. We couldn't risk taking the horses over it and turned back. We found a steep meadow, which we led the horses down. The final ten metres down to a safer track was a landslip of shale, and cakes of dry, loose earth. I led my horse down, a petrifying experience as it gathered momentum behind me, skating on cascades of dust and small stones until I thought it would crush me. I didn't have the courage to lead any of the others down, preferring to lumber down with the baggage.

The last pass before Kazarman

Our detour lost us a good deal of time and we reached the start of the descent in the moonlight. The dark contours of the mountains behind us were crystal clear in the alpine air. The sky was peppered with billions of bright stars. In that perfect immensity the outside world seemed insignificant. My brain once cluttered and tense was now empty. I felt remote from everything, at the limits of the earth and completely at home. Ruslan didn't want to tarry so we kept going, looking down towards Jalalabad and Osh, the start of the densely-populated Fergana valley. All I could see was the lingering heat and haze of the desert. The thought of riding across Uzbekistan filled me with dread.

The road descended into the haze. Sheer rock-falls on either side ruled out the possibility of camping for the night. We limped on; Ruslan also had terrible blisters. The moon illuminated the road ahead into a series of glistening coils, which looked like a giant snail's trail. At two in the morning, we found a small terrace of grass where the horses could graze and we could lay out our sleeping-bags and collapse.

Late the next morning, we came across an old couple, living in a *yurt* secluded in the trees, who invited us for lunch. The old man topped up his miserable pension by cultivating bees. I'd noticed that beehives in Kyrgyzstan were often portable; the bees lived on the back of a lorry and moved from place to place, to maximize potential to pollinate. He served us litres of *koumiss* with what looked like bird droppings floating on the top. As I scraped off the black scum and braved a third bowl, my hosts ticked me off for getting rid of the best part. The congealed cow's fat, blackened with juniper smoke, was a delicacy which enhanced the flavour!

We continued our descent through pristine woods of walnut, large fields of sunflowers in full bloom and parched fields, full of neat haystacks of winter grass. At every opportunity, we stuffed our saddlebags with wild cherries, apples and rhubarb. It was strange to have skipped into summer, missing out on spring. Only a week before, we had been shivering in a blizzard in Song-Kul. Jilda kept stopping and hiding in the shade of trees until we were almost out of sight.

We were now only a few days' ride east of Jalalabad and the Uzbek border. Ruslan was impatient to get home; he didn't want to miss his brother's wedding. We were both exhausted and had had enough of each other but I was sorry that I'd have to say goodbye. Our shared experiences, good, bad, and even terrifying, had formed a strong bond. I felt that we had been through more together than many people do in a lifetime. I dreaded the thought of looking for a new guide.

Dropping down several hundred metres, our surroundings became increasingly autumnal. The horses were tired and the heat was beginning to take its toll. We were spending most of the day on foot rather than exhausting them unnecessarily. Walking in the heat was thirsty work and by early evening, we were parched and we desperately needed to find grazing for the horses. But the grass was owned by a 'synacuse', a cooperative, farming grass. Whereas in the mountains, we had found grass in abundance, there it was harvested for people in the large towns, who kept half a dozen sheep in their backyards for meat. Despite Ruslan's entreaties, no one was prepared to let us graze our horses. Whatever sum we offered, it would have to be ratified in a village pow-wow and couldn't be agreed at such short notice.

'There is one place we can stay but there are lots of children and it is very small. We will have to make our own tea.' Assuming the bit about the tea meant reluctant hosts, we continued our search until dark.

'We'll have to stay with the people with the children. We have no other choice.' A young, untidy teenager with a cheeky smile and lively face greeted us outside a hut the size of a small greenhouse. Puffing out his adolescent chest authoritatively, he explained the ground rules to us.

'You can graze your horses here, but you must tether them. Our land stretches from the cart to the electricity pole. The grass will cost you.' He paused for a moment. The corners of his mouth curled into a pawky smile, like a salesman clinching his first big deal. 'Five som (sixpence) per horse.' He held his breath as Ruslan translated from Kyrgyz into Russian.

'Fine. Thank you.' I watched his chest relax and the corners of his mouth turn up; he ran the back of his hand over his mouth to hide his evident pride.

As we unloaded the horses, Ruslan surmised the situation.

'I don't know where their parents are. The boy and his twin sister are looking after their three young siblings. She has gone next-door to borrow some bread.' We sat on the floor around a low wooden table. A young toddler was curled up on some cushions in the corner. The other two children, one with a badly sprained wrist, looked on as we ate our bread and yoghurt, which we washed down with tea. When we'd finished, they clustered around the table and devoured the rest. Ruslan and I slept outside so that we could keep an eye on the horses and ensure that they didn't stray outside the fifty-metre perimeter, delineated by a wireless pylon and a shabby wooden donkey-cart.

At breakfast we drank tea, thickened with a few spoonfuls of flour.

'This is terrible Achak, children living alone. We don't have hunger like this in Kazakhstan.' He pushed aside his half-finished bowl.

'Ruslan,' I muttered, 'finish your food and stop being so ungrateful.'

'Perhaps you should observe a little before criticizing me. They have given us their tea.' I looked around the table. The youngest two were eating, the other three were watching.

'Ask them how many animals they have.'

'One donkey and a cow.'

'How about land?' He pointed to the grass and a patch of sunflowers the size of a postage-stamp. I was torn between outrage and tears. I tried my best to find out something about the parents. I was petrified that they were alcoholics or worse. The eldest son hinted that it was time to settle up. I called him and his twin sister behind the hut. After paying the bill for the horses, I gave him a wad of dollars.

'On Sunday, you must go to the bazaar and change this money. It is enough to buy two cows, which you can breed. There should be enough left over for several sacks of flour and some tea. Don't tell anyone about this. I will come back in a couple of weeks and I expect to see results.' He nodded seriously, a toothy grin stretching from ear to ear as he explained the deal to his sister. As we left, we gave the girl all the food we had. She was playing with the infant in a chicken-coop, which she was using as a crèche. I hoped the parents wouldn't arrive home and drink the money.

When we got to Jalalabad's bus station, Ruslan was in a hurry to leave. He had five days to get back for his brother's wedding. I found a tea-service and a silver-plated cutlery set in a battered leather box for him to give his brother as a wedding present. I paid him his salary and a good tip. As we sat eating congealed dumplings in the bus stop, I extracted a promise from him that he'd spend the money on livestock. We joked about how he would be the catch of his village in Kurchum.

'Achak. I am sorry for Ming Kush.' He faltered nervously. 'But we are friends now, yes?'

'Yes.'

'Achak.' He stared at the ground. 'If I had been six years older, would you have considered marrying me?'

'Maybe.'

'When I get married, you will come to the wedding, won't you?'

'Of course.'

'You will call, won't you?'

'Yes.' He gave me a shy peck on the cheek and hurried into the minibus where he sat in the window waving and making hand signals for me to call.

I felt uncomfortable being alone again. I found a farm on the outskirts of Jalalabad where I could leave the horses while I planned the next stage of the journey. I needed to find a Kyrgyz guide with Uzbek paperwork, who would be able to cross the border with me. I couldn't be sure that the sedentary Uzbeks would know how to handle horses; I was entering the land of cotton fields and rice paddies. I was worried that I didn't have the right veterinary certificates to get the horses into Uzbekistan and even if I got the right paperwork, I wasn't sure that I would be allowed to cross the border with my horses. I couldn't risk dodging the official border-post as I knew that the Uzbeks had mined the area.

It was a stroke of luck that I met Faisul in the bazaar. He was well turned-out in a crisp blue cotton shirt, his growing middle-aged paunch spilling over pressed trousers. With his silvery-grey hair and clean-shaven face, he had a no-nonsense air around him – a man who looked used to getting things done. I persuaded him to help me to find a guide and to sort out the necessary paperwork. I promised him $100 if he could find me a guide and see me safely across the border. As a traditional Muslim, I suspect that Faisul found himself rather thrown off-balance by his encounter with a modern Western woman. As he drove me around in his battered Jeep, he would lament the fact that he was married: Kyrgyz women were too subservient – he would love to have married a strong woman. He was probably trying his luck and I didn't find his overtures threatening.

Faisul organized for a vet from the local department of sanitation to inspect my horses. The vet injected each horse with a faded brown mixture which he extracted from a dusty old bottle, reassuringly using the same syringe for each inoculation. After scribbling down a few notes detailing the colour and age of the horses, he issued them with a 'passport', which he assured me would get them across the border: a single flimsy piece of paper, which was good for all of the horses. Like so much of the paperwork, it still bore all of the hallmarks of the Soviet Union including 'SSSR', which he scribbled out and replaced in a scrawly hand with 'Kyrgyzstan'. The official process governing the movement of animals seemed to have been carried over as if nothing had changed.

'What is your final destination?'
'Ashkabad.'
'So you are transiting through Uzbekistan?'
'Yes.'
'What is your *marshoot*?'
'My what?'
'Through which cities in Uzbekistan will you pass?'

I reeled off a list, not quite understanding what business it was of the Kyrgyz department of sanitation. After all Uzbekistan was another sovereign state. I thanked him profusely for the paperwork, which cost $6, inclusive of the jabs. Little did I know at that stage what a barrier-opener the passport would be.

A few days later Faisul managed to find someone whom he thought would be a suitable guide. We rode out to the middle of a rice-paddy to a slight, hunched, weather-worn Kyrgyz who was weeding the verges of a small plot. Ravshan had lived most of his life in Uzbekistan, returning to claim his family house several years previously. When he smiled, he bore a kind, grandfatherly expression but such occasions were rare and his natural demeanour was pinched, fatigued and slightly mean. He avoided looking me in the eye and I was undecided whether he was being self-effacing or shifty. A rice-farmer by trade, he used to herd the family animals when he was young. Although only fifty-four, he was already frail, and I was doubtful that he would be able to cope with the physical exertions of the journey. I was reluctant to take him on until he invited me to his house for tea. He was a father of twelve and they were obviously struggling to make ends meet. I felt guilty that he needed to undertake such an arduous journey to feed his family and I resolved to look after him as best I could.

The author with Ravshan on her left and Faisal on her right

Sweet to ride forth at evening from the wells
When shadows pass gigantic on the sand,
And softly through the silence beat the bells
Along the Golden Road to Samarkand.

We travel not for trafficking alone:
By hotter winds our fiery hearts are fanned:
For lust of knowing what should not be known
We make the Golden Journey to Samarkand.

We are the pilgrim's master; we shall go
Always a little further: it may be
Beyond that last blue mountain barred with snow,
Across that angry or that glimmering sea:
White on a throne or guarded in a cave
There lives a prophet who can understand
Why men were born: but surely we are brave
Who make the Golden Journey to Samarkand.

J.E. Flecker, *The Golden Journey to Samarkand*, 1913

18

FERGANA

On 1 July, we headed towards the border in the fierce heat. It was so hot that I found it impossible to think; I just wanted to curl up and sleep under a tree. I knew that it was going to get worse. By mid-July, the temperature would climb into the mid-forties. Ravshan wasn't interested in chatting. Whereas Ruslan had regarded his job as an adventure, Ravshan could not disguise the fact that he regarded it as burden that he had to endure to provide for his family. He rode several hundred metres ahead of me in a new straw hat, which I'd bought him, a white, damp hanky wrapped around his head.

We arrived at the first border-post at dusk. It was closed. Continuing terrorist activities in Batken in Southern Kyrgyzstan had led to the closure of all of the smaller border crossings. I attempted to negotiate with the guards, all armed with automatic weapons. They wouldn't let me past and kept talking about quarantine. As I tried in vain to negotiate, a small boy of about ten used me as a diversion to scuttle a jerrycan full of petrol across the border. It was heavy, he wasn't quick enough and the can was wrestled from his grasp.

Downcast, we had to make a diversion to the other crossing, forty-five kilometres away. The border procedure was time-consuming. First I had to leave Kyrgyzstan, which meant going through passport control and then customs. It took me half an hour to fill out the paperwork declaring what I was taking out of Kyrgyzstan and another hour for a scribe to translate it into Russian. The officials were all very friendly and laid-back. Zigzagging through a series of concrete barriers, we passed through no-man's land and into Uzbekistan. All the soldiers at the border were wearing brown camouflage and carrying automatic weapons. I was escorted into an office and spent two hours sitting behind a desk while an official in brown combat fatigues processed my passport and customs declaration. I didn't declare my knife but all the rest was on the form: two cameras, GPS, a starter pistol, cash, one gold ring, five horses and a dog. They had to get me for something.

One of the final valleys before the Uzbek border

Unable to fault me on my paperwork, they hauled me up for littering the streets. My horses left a series of unwanted deposits on the road and I was instructed to clear them up!

We hurried along large tree-lined avenues in the outskirts of Khanabad. It was hard to lead Jilda on an enormous two-metre lead with one hand and the spare horses with the other from the saddle, in busy traffic, and I was grateful when we finally turned off and wound along a track through a series of small villages and patchwork fields. In the early evening, we watched workers cycling home, dressed in stripy shirts and signature embroidered skullcaps, like the Uighurs. The shirts seemed to be uniform in the Fergana valley. Wide black and white vertical stripes graced the backs of most labourers in the fields. While they picked cotton, they sweated in polyester. Occasionally we heard the tinkle of a bicycle bell, the back wheel weighed down by bales of freshly cut grass. Children squatted by the side of the road, cutting grass with scythes. None of the fields contained animals. They were all devoted to wheat or cotton. Cows, donkeys and sheep grazed on verges beside the road and returned to court-yards at night. I didn't see any horses.

As we looked for somewhere to camp, a handsome Uzbek, with Persian features, fell in step with our horses. He was dressed in a *khalat* – a long lightweight cloak with green and mauve stripes, tied at the waist with a sash – rather like an English smoking-jacket. He invited us to stay on a nearby *kolkhoz* or collective farm devoted to cotton, where he was on night-duty with a couple of men. We shared a couple of tins of sardines with them: they made tea and brought grass for the horses. I was surprised, given the Fergana Valley's reputation for Islamic fundamentalism, when a bottle of vodka appeared in our midst. We slept on a large wooden dais, looking out over the cotton fields.

The following day we made a detour to visit Ravshan's sister in a small white-washed mud-brick house which stood back from a shady courtyard, covered with trellises heavy with grapes. She was several years older than him, petite and stooped, a heavily lined face rejuvenated by a turquoise floral headscarf. She hadn't seen Ravshan for two years and was bowled over by the surprise. Immediately, she started preparing *plov*. Her husband bought a couple of bottles of beer and vodka. They were not well-off; a couple of pieces of lamb and a few pieces of processed meat graced a mound of rice and carrots. Our hosts barely touched the meat and kept moving the precious pieces into my part of our shared plate. Within an hour of our arrival, about fifty people from the village were huddled in the room.

Woman baking bread in a traditional clay oven – our lunch in one of the Kyrgyz villages

'I left Uzbekistan two years ago. I lived here for fifty years. These people are my old friends. This village is seventy per cent Kyrgyz.'

'What do they do here?'

'They work in the rice paddies or the cotton fields.'

'What about their herds?'

'We used to keep animals in this valley until a few years ago. Every spring, we would herd them up into the mountains in Kyrgyzstan and return in the autumn. Now the laws have changed. We cannot even drive over the border, let alone take our animals. Only the super-rich can afford to pay to take a car across the border. Some Kyrgyz work on the *kolkhoz*, and some of us have returned to Kyrgyzstan.'

The villagers were very curious. They had never met a foreigner before. They leafed excitedly through the guidebooks and postcards of London and bombarded me with questions about my journey. Many brought family photos for me to sign, which I found rather embarrassing. After dinner, they sat around in a circle singing traditional Kyrgyz ballads, while some of the more adventurous women danced in the middle.

It was still dark when we got up and we were on our way by seven – Ruslan would have been impressed. Unfortunately Ravshan wasn't very good at saddling the horses. The girth was always too loose; he didn't have the strength to secure the baggage and I had to redo his knots. There was no question that the physical burden of the next stage of the trip would fall on me.

Despite the early hour, women in printed dresses and colourful silk head-scarves were already hard at work in the fields, tidying irrigation trenches in rows of dark green cotton while others were bent over knee-deep in rice paddies. The cotton was already beginning to ripen; white puffs and white flowers with pink edges were visible on some of the plants. We rode to the sound of water trickling through hundreds of irrigation canals and trenches and the smell of newly cut straw. Cows were grazing in the shade of trees. Occasionally we heard the lonely bleating of a couple of sheep, or the distant whirr of a tractor or gigantic mechanical rakes with huge claws furrowing the trenches. Frequently, we saw large threshing-machines, which looked as if they dated from the 1950s, beside the road. Piles of wheat were placed in the road for passers-by to ride, cycle or drive over, separating the wheat from the chaff.

By midday, the virulent heat was insupportable, at well over forty degrees. I wanted to stop but there was nowhere for the horses to graze. Several hours further down the road, we sought refuge under avenues of poplars. The horses had to graze in the sun and were soon sweating heavily. A worker in a neighbouring paddy field bought us some tea. Despite the shade, Jilda lay on the ground panting hard; I covered her in a wet towel and she slept.

The Fergana Valley is the most densely populated area in Central Asia, with 18 million inhabitants. It was not horse country. There were no tracks through the cotton fields and deep irrigation channels criss-crossed the countryside, confining us to the main road. I felt incredibly self-conscious riding through the large villages. Despite my conservative *shawal kamize* and head-dress, I couldn't escape attention, riding at the head of a caravan of five horses. Some people were curious and stopped to talk to us; many had never met a westerner before. Others, possibly strict Muslims, gave me reproachful looks and made me feel like a fallen woman on parade. Ravshan relaxed into his role of spokesman, explaining that I had ridden from Mongolia and boasting to everyone we came across that I was paying him $10 per day.

At dusk, we rode through narrow, dusty back-streets in the outskirts of Andijan. Walls on either side of us, broken at intervals by intricately carved wooden doorways, veiled the inhabitants from the outside world. Occasionally we stole a glimpse through half-opened gates into shady courtyards, canopied with grapes, peach, apple and pomegranate trees. From his majestic palaces in Delhi, Babur wrote wistfully about the 140 varieties of grapes and watermelons produced in the Fergana Valley.

Despite our entreaties and heavy cash incentives, no one wanted five horses in their courtyard and we moved on. As we rode on in the dark, a group of young children ran after us, hurling stones. No one made any effort to stop them. One teenager encouraged his dog to go after Jilda. I shot at it with my starter pistol and it scurried away.

Just when things were getting really desperate, an old man ushered us through a doorway into a dusty courtyard at the centre of which stood a half-finished house with cement bags piled up on the porch. He moved a few of the bags so we could roll out our sleeping-bags. The bare, parched ground was covered in rubble and cement dust. There wasn't a blade of grass to be seen. After a while, the man came back with three or four bales of hay, which we split between the horses. Within twenty minutes it had disappeared and the horses were pawing hungrily at the ground. He brought us a couple of beers and we shared some of tins of sardines and a loaf of bread. I laid my sleeping-bag out on the doorstep of the construction site and slept. At midnight Ravshan shook me. A couple of policemen wanted to see our passports. I handed mine over.

'Where is your registration? Every foreigner must register here within seventy-two hours.'

Jilda having a hard-earned rest and feed

'I don't need to register yet. I have only been in Uzbekistan for two nights. I will register tomorrow.'

'We will take your passport to central office. You can collect it in the morning.'

I took my passport back, explaining that if he wanted to take my passport to the police station he would have to take me and the horses. A common trick in Central Asia is to confiscate passports, forcing the owner to buy them back. The policeman began to look edgy.

'Where is his passport?' He scowled at Ravshan, who produced an old Soviet passport.

'This passport is no good, it is old. Where is your new one?' Ravshan looked towards me for help. He looked nervous.

'You know that this is a perfectly legal travel document in Uzbekistan.'

'I will take this passport to head office.'

'I am sure we can sort this out quickly,' I said. 'I will come down to the police station and make a call to Tashkent. My friend is head of the KGB there. I play tennis with his wife. He can tell you if the passport is valid or not. I hope he won't be angry that I am calling him so late.'

'Thank you madam. But that won't be necessary. I am sorry to trouble you.'

As they left we breathed a huge sigh of relief and I wondered whether the head of the KGB had a wife. Over the course of the journey, I would get to know her rather well!

The next day I left Ravshan with the horses and tracked down the local branch of the Ministry of the Interior, known as OVIR, responsible for tagging foreigners. The official wasn't pleased that I had been staying in local homes; foreigners were meant to stay in hotels. Luckily I had an article about my trip in Russian and joked that inns on the Silk Route no longer catered to horses. A wry smile broke through his mask of officialdom. He registered me as resident in a hotel in Andijan for the duration of my trip. I had to pay for my registration stamp at the local bank. It was barely past the age of the abacus. Huge volumes of paper retarded every transaction. The process of form-filling in triplicate, in words and numbers, was further complicated by the fact that the bank clerk was unable to spell the word 'twenty'. In order to make a clean break from the Soviet Union, it had been decided that all government business should be conducted using the Roman alphabet. Most people of working age had been educated in the Cyrillic script. Even those who were familiar with the Roman script, did not know how to apply it to strange-sounding Uzbek words.

Back at the construction site, the whole neighbourhood had turned out to see us off. Before we were allowed to go anywhere, we had to have lunch

'The whole neighbourhood had come out to see us off'

with a neighbour. We sat in the shade of an apricot tree, on a raised dais known as an *ayvan*, which stood in the corner of a large courtyard. Despite the shade, it was unbearably hot.

'I love having guests,' she sighed languidly, mopping her sweaty brow and spreading her corpulent form over several cushions, while her daughter rushed back and forth with stew, melon and yoghurt. 'It is nice having you here. You must come back. I have a spare house. You can come and live here. My son's wife left him, maybe you would like him.'

As we saddled the horses, I noticed that Ravshan was trying to cover up a sore on Kyzylkum's back underneath the waterproof cape attached to the back of his saddle. Despite my entreaties to let me know if any of the horses developed problems, he had been covering it up for several days. Maybe he was worried what my reaction would be. I injected Kyzylkum with antibiotics and removed the plastic cape which was responsible for the sore promising Ravshan a thirty per cent bonus if all the horses reached the end of the trip in good health.

Over the next few days, I realized that grazing was going to be a serious problem. None of the farms on which we stayed had any grass and it was impossible to buy it so the horses frequently had to make do with straw. By midday, it was always too hot to go on and we would look for pathetic patches of grass in the shade where they could graze. At lunchtime, Ravshan would lie on his back, snoring lightly, and I would try to negotiate with villagers for corn. Ravshan made a couple of nosebags out of old

Cotton fields in the Fergana Valley

saddlebags and we tried to give each horse at least five kilos of corn a day. I took lunchtime feed and he was on evening duty. Sometimes someone from neighbouring houses would bring us bread, apples, tomatoes and tea.

The heat was incredibly draining and I fought to stay awake guarding the horses. All day, I could see Ravshan's head lolling and twitching. Several times a day I would holler as his horse began to swerve into the road. He was permanently drowsy, like an old dormouse, and he happily surrendered more and more of the daily tasks to me. We were surviving on five hours' sleep per night. My glands were up, my throat hurt and my body felt like lead. Although there were mountains on either side of the Fergana Valley, they were rarely visible in the dusty haze. Occasionally, if it was windy, I would catch a glimpse of the mountains and I longed to be back in their cool green pastures.

A week into Uzbekistan, we were heading for the lights of Boz. We decided to turn off the road on to a small track, which criss-crossed a series of canals. After a half-hour search, we found a couple of fields of stubble. A beautiful man with delicate features and skin like alabaster lay sprawled on a mattress under a small straw canopy. As we approached, he beckoned us over, stretching dreamily.

'How wonderful to meet a real English lady,' he pouted, ushering me to a seat and pouring me some green tea. 'I love England. One day I will visit London and then Rome.'

He sent his brother off to fetch us some *plov* and as I ate, I tried not to look him in the eye, for fear of giving too much away. We chatted for a couple of hours until the conversation started to take a dangerous turn.

'Your back must be stiff from a day in the saddle. You need a good massage to relax.'

Luckily the temperature dropped several degrees with the arrival of four policemen with flashlights. I had to give them credit for tracking us down so quickly. Three of them picked over my documents asking to see everything, including the papers for the horses, before handing them to the chief. The chief was determined to find fault with my paperwork. As usual, my new fairy godmother, the wife of the head of the KGB in Tashkent, worked her magic and they left bobbing politely. I laid out my sleeping-mat in the field of straw with the horses. Jilda curled up next to me. I declined the beautiful man's offer to sleep under the canopy with the weak excuse that I had to watch the horses.

The following day the heat was even more intense. Tom had bad diarrhoea all morning. At midday, he began to retch, his belly heaving as he dribbled slimy green mucus on to the ground. I had no idea that horses could be sick, let alone how to treat them. I decided rest and shade were probably the best course. We stopped underneath some trees beside a canal and tethered the horses. I found a few patches of lucerne. While Ravshan rested, I cut grass for the horses and gave them their corn rations, keeping them in the shade. The heat was also taking its toll on Jilda. She kept sitting down and hiding in the shade, licking her paws. She had begun limping and had taken to bathing her paws in water channels beside the road. Every day, I inspected her paws but I couldn't see anything. I made her some boots using a few pieces of felt for the soles and some ribbons to secure them to her paws. They were a disaster and she quickly pulled them all off.

A few days later, her paws split open; the blistering had been too deep to see. I stopped in a small kiosk and found her a few pairs of striped baby-socks. I lined the bottom of the sock with felt and patched up the blisters with gauze, securing the socks around her ankles with several rolls of plaster. She seemed much happier, trotting beside me on her lead for an hour without limping much until she found a small canal and stopped to drink and cool her feet. The socks were soon sodden and stretched and, after slip-slapping along the road for a couple of paces, they fell off and the dressings came off too. I got off my horse and applied new dressings and four new socks. She found another muddy stream five minutes later, lost all the socks and hid under a tree. I felt as if everyone was staring at me as I stood in the muddy stream, sweat pouring down my back, tears running down my cheeks, trying to retrieve the socks. Ravshan was half a kilometre further ahead and continued to ride on.

As Jilda limped on beside me, I tried not to look. I was so hot and so tired that I could no longer control my emotions, alternating between fits of temper and tears. I could no longer remember the reason for the journey; it seemed insane to be putting myself through this. We stopped at midday in a small roadside *chaikhana* where there was a little shade and grass. I bought several kilos of kebab meat, which we shared with Jilda. I slept for several hours and recovered my sanity. I resolved to fight back. I found another pair of socks for her and made a new pair of shoes and, in the early evening, as the sun lost its intensity, we saddled up and rode on.

The next afternoon we crossed the Syr Daria, known to Alexander the Great as the Jaxartes. It was here that he inflicted his final defeat on the Persian army. Darius, their 'Great King' was dead, slain by his own generals led by Bessus, who had seized control of the army. Alexander made an example of Bessus. First he was paraded in front of the whole army, naked save for a wooden halter. His ears and nose were then cut off, and he was sent away for a grim execution. Once a small icy stream we'd crossed in

Kyrgyzstan, the Syr Daria now irrigated the whole of the Fergana Valley, gushing through thousands of canals and dykes known as *ariks* into cotton fields, rice paddies and fields of wheat. When Ella Maillart crossed Uzbekistan in the 1930s, she reckoned that the canal network stretched to 25,000 miles. *Aksakals* or 'white beards' were responsible for the maintenance but it was the rich Begs who owned them. The Emir levied a tax supposedly calculated on water usage, but the heavy burden often simply corresponded with the individual Beg's greed.

As the canals entered the little villages, more water was siphoned off through a series of home-made water wheels, using recycled paint pots to scoop the water up into primitive pipes or small trenches, which watered houses and allotments alike. It filled me with horror to think that this was the same water in which I had seen countless Kyrgyz performing ablutions ranging from laundry to nose-clearing and I felt guilty remembering Jilda's preference for peeing in streams.

One evening, ten days into the journey, as the light began to fade, we began seeing fewer irrigation channels. The tree-lined road flanked by green fields of cotton gave way to a large baked plain, rising towards a pass. A couple of shabby cafés and *shashlik* outlets were plying a busy trade for lorry drivers and cars *en route* from Tashkent to Fergana. I talked one of the owners into letting me graze the horses in the orchard behind his café. The only clean water stood in a large vat behind the café, which we carried by the bucketful to the horses; the large horses drank five buckets each. I sat talking to the owner of the *chaikhana*, who spoke Russian, drinking beer and eating *shashlik*. Ravshan ate his meal watching the horses. He seemed happy enough: I bought him a couple of vodka shots and a bottle of beer to wash down his meal.

At dawn the next morning, we were already on our way; I wanted to be across the baking plain and into the hills before the sun was too strong. By ten o'clock, we had left the plain and climbed four or five hundred metres through a series of predominantly Tajik villages. For the next few days, we would be riding through a narrow corridor of Uzbekistan, sandwiched between Kyrgyzstan in the north and Tajikistan in the south. The Uzbek government was very jittery about the activities of the Islamic militants who had invaded Kyrgyzstan from Tajikistan the previous summer. They were taking every precaution to ensure that they did not enter Uzbekistan.

We stopped in a Tajik village. As we ate our brunch, a funeral procession rushed past. A dozen men were running along shouldering a body on a stretcher, which was covered in a blue shroud. Ravshan explained that, according to Uzbek tradition, if a person dies in the morning, the body has to be interred by nightfall. In Kyrgyzstan, they allow three days. His mother had died when he was young; he had been up in the mountains with the flocks. They didn't find him in time and he missed the funeral.

It was cooler in the mountains but the fresh air did little to improve my mood. The horses were tired and the grazing was no better in the pass, the grass parched and sparse. It was still a battle to find them something to eat. Jilda continued limping, Ravshan was tired and I was shouldering more and more of the physical burden, petrified that he might suddenly keel over. Early that evening, I spotted a large green patch in a gorge beside the road. On closer inspection, we discovered an orchard overgrown with fine grass and watered by a clean stream. After protracted negotiations with the owner of a small roadside guesthouse, a plump, surly woman with greedy eyes, we agreed on five dollars for her grass. I had my first wash for at least a week in the stream behind a bush.

Families planting rice in the Fergana Valley

At five the following morning, she turfed us out.

'Get out, get out,' ranted the owner. 'Your horses have eaten too much grass. You must go now!'

Wearily, we saddled and loaded the horses and set off up the road. Lorry drivers kept slowing down and sounding their horns, yelling at us.

'These people are disgusting,' Ravshan muttered.

'What are they saying?'

'Dirty things.'

'What things?'

'They think you are my woman. They are saying filthy things about an older man with a younger woman.' Ravshan looked old enough to be my grandfather; I felt sick at the thought. For the rest of the afternoon I returned the filthy comments with equally filthy hand signals.

By early evening, Jilda was limping very badly. With Ravshan's help, I hoisted her on to my saddle and sat on a cushion behind her. We found a short-cut down the side of the valley, which cut out several kilometres of the looping road. At the bottom of the track, we were ordered to stop. Two young men were pointing machine guns at us over the top of a ruined turret.

'Stop! Who are you?'

'Please put down your gun, I am a British tourist not a terrorist.'

'Where are your papers?'

'Here.' I waved my passport at them. They refused to come forward to check them and kept their guns trained on us.

'The Uzbek government shouldn't give automatic weapons to children.'

'I'm not a child; I am married and my wife has just had a son.'

'Congratulations! Please will you kindly behave like an adult and come and look at my papers.'

The father approached us, leafed through my passport and handed it back. He held his gun up to my head.

'Tell me the time.'

'I will when you put the gun down.'

'What is the time?'

'Tell them the time, Clara,' implored Ravshan.

That night we settled for another roadside café, whose garden, the size of a small London lawn, would have to make do for the horses. Within half an hour of our arrival, each horse had polished off a neat circle around its tethering rope. I tried my best to locate some corn but there was none around. In the morning, we found a path running through the mountains, parallel to the road. The horses had a few hours' grazing on the mountainside. I slept in the shade of a bush while they ate. Jilda was much happier with grass underfoot and scampered around like the old times.

However, after a few hours, we turned on to a rough, stony track, which wound through a series of villages. Now that we had lost height, it was hot again; Jilda was limping and kept hiding to escape the heat. For a while she hid until we were out of sight, which necessitated a painful trot to catch up with us. Finally she gave up. I called out to her and she didn't come. I went back to look for her and found her hidden under a trailer. She growled and snapped at me as I tried to pull her out. Finally she relented and walked behind us for another five minutes before disappearing again. I found her hidden under a bush. I prodded her on the bottom with a stick but she refused to get up. I knew she had given her best and couldn't go on.

I picked her up and put her on Aykulak but he couldn't walk up hill with Jilda and me. I tried to balance her on the saddle and lead Aykulak but she kept slipping off. Repeatedly I lifted her up again, struggling under her weight. Ravshan was nowhere in sight. Finally I gave up and burst into tears. A heavy-set, middle-aged lady, stopped to help. She looked like a good witch with thick black eyebrows and a large mole, sprouting several long hairs. She soon realized that my situation was hopeless and invited me to come to her house for tea. There was nothing else I could do and I accepted willingly. After a few cups of tea and a bowl of yoghurt, I collapsed on to a mattress in a cool, dark room at the back of the house. When I awoke, it was dark.

Ravshan was up at 4.30. I pretended to be asleep. I couldn't face getting up. Now that I had given in to sleep, I felt utterly exhausted.

'Clara, Clara. Time to go.'

'No. I'm not going.'

'What do you want to do?'

'I'm too tired. I can't go on. I can't watch Jilda suffering like this and I will never leave her behind. Let's stop here for a few days. We can both rest and we can look for a cart to carry Jilda and corn for the horses.'

We stayed for five days. Ravshan went to the dentist to have one of his remaining teeth pulled and I bought corn for the horses. I passed the time learning how to dye my eyebrows with crushed leaves. Our host, a tubby wrinkled woman, her hair swept back under a scarlet scarf, sat us down with her 11-year-old daughter for our makeup lesson. The daughter, whose Persian face with thick dark eyebrows that didn't look as if they needed accentuating, crushed the leaves with a pestle and mortar. Her mother showed me how it was done, drawing a thick, bright-green monobrow. Our host oohed and aahed her approval as she deliberately drew attention to her massive mole with a blob of dark green dye.

'Now you will find good Uzbek man,' she assured me. As it dried, the dye became quite black. Next our host set about applying her home-made mascara. I blinked by mistake, my eyes filled with what felt like chilli paste and I spent ten minutes rolling around on the floor in agony. When I could finally open them again my eyeballs were angry red, tinged with green, and I was crying Martian's tears. The dye was semi-permanent.

While we were staying with the good witch, I had my first run-in with Ravshan. I found out that he had been reselling the corn which I bought to fatten up the horses. When I questioned him about it, his face contorted in a miserly expression and he shrugged his pathetic shoulders in denial. A collection of bottles in his room gave the game away; he had drunk the difference. The horses looked thin and worn. I was angry; I had looked after him well, shouldering all of the heavy labour. I knew he had a big family and I had wanted to be able to reward him and pay him well. Now I just didn't care any more. There were plenty of honest men with big families who would appreciate the work. I made enquiries about other guides but everyone was busy bringing in their potato harvests and I was forced to stick with Ravshan.

A few days later, I found a support vehicle for $50. It looked like a large wooden bathtub, with a mysterious hole in the middle, big enough to suck a person through. Its only fixture, a large wooden plank, possibly good for soap and a flannel, didn't look as if it would be particularly comfortable for Ravshan's backside. The back wheels had been stolen from a Russian motorbike, the front wheels, about six inches in diameter, were made of wood coated with a small strip of rubber. Now there would be no more loading and unloading, no more sores on hungry horses and no more blisters for Jilda. On the first day, I had to tie her down in the cart to stop her

Jilda in her new cart

from jumping out. From then onwards, she realized which side her bread was buttered. She lay in the cool under a tarpaulin which I rigged up. When the worst of the heat was over, she would emerge from her burrow and sit upright in the cart looking back at me and smiling, her big ears standing to attention.

As we approached Angren, military and police check-posts became increasingly frequent. We stopped at a *chaikhana*. I got talking with a taxi-driver over a cup of tea and some greasy *shashlik*. He was the first person that I'd met in Uzbekistan who had dared to criticize its leader.

'Once we were part of a great nation. Now we are as poor as Africa. In the Soviet Union, I was an engineer. Now I am nothing. I don't even know how to work a computer. Karimov has turned Uzbekistan into a police state. Everywhere you go there is police harassment.'

'Surely the police are just doing their job? Uzbekistan has everything to fear from the Islamic Militants' Union. These men are terrorists, trained in Osama Bin Laden's camps. The government is trying to keep them out of Uzbekistan.'

'Karimov exaggerates the terrorist threat to repress all Muslims, good and bad. As for the police, they don't care. They are only interested in making money. That car could have guns in it, that one might contain a bomb,' he said, pointing to passing cars, 'but the police won't look inside if you pay them. They always stop me and hassle me for money. While they are hassling me, the real criminals are driving past. Even if they found a bomb in a boot, they wouldn't know what to do with it. Sometimes I feel like putting a timer in the boot, just to see their reaction. I can just see them … tick, tick, tick … frowning, throwing up their arms and running in the opposite direction.'

Angren was an industrial graveyard. We rode around a massive black crater in the centre of the valley. The open-face coal pit, which fed the Russian war-machine in the 1940s, is one of Angren's few industries to escape extinction. Dinky excavators worked like mechanical ants in the depths of the pit. Large chimneystacks of a redundant power station soared heavenwards like minarets, towering over broken windows and industrial debris. Their days of belching smoke died with the collapse of the Soviet Union.

As we rode out of town, we were confronted by a series of menacing police checks. At the first checkpoint, I argued for twenty minutes about Ravshan's out-dated passport. Fifteen minutes later, a military Jeep screeched to a halt in front of us. A corpulent chief demanded our papers, while his sidekick kept his machine-gun trained on us.

'What are you doing in Uzbekistan?'

'I am a tourist.'

'What do you think of Uzbekistan?'

'I'd like it a lot more if he put the gun down.'

'Don't you ever get bored riding?'

'Not when I have machine-guns pointed at me every other day.' He got the hint and waved the other man's gun down. 'Sorry for the trouble. Enjoy your journey.'

Twenty minutes later we went through another police post.

'Where are your papers? Why does this man have an old Soviet passport? It is no good. I will have to call the chief.'

'I have just been through this whole business twenty minutes ago. What has changed in the last one and a half kilometres?' As our passports were carted off again, I asked a young policeman what was happening.

'Big problem. Nineteen Wahhabists have crossed into Uzbekistan from the mountains. They are hiding in these villages. One person has been shot. This morning we saw soldiers, guns, tanki-pankis. It is very bad.'

Throughout the next day, convoys of military Jeeps swept past us. Later on came huge white vehicles, with six sets of wheels, which looked like lunar-cruisers. I learned later they were probably Uzbek Spetznatz vehicles. At the last checkpoint of the day, the policeman was more interested in our well-being than our paperwork.

The author chatting up an Uzbek policeman at a checkpoint

'There are Wahhabists everywhere,' he warned. 'You must not stay out after dark. They may try to kidnap you. They kidnapped four Japanese geologists in Kyrgyzstan last year.'

Wahhabism is a strict eighteenth-century creed which originated in Saudi Arabia, to counter widespread Sufism amongst the Bedouin. The secular and oppressive Uzbek government found it convenient to use the term quite widely from those who were simply trying to practise their religion to members of the outlawed IMU. That year, the IMU were invading over the low green hills which separated their bases in Tajikistan from Uzbekistan. The IMU's leader, Juma Namangani, first came to prominence as a paratrooper sergeant in the Afghan War, fighting alongside his Muslim brethren to rid Afghanistan of Soviet troops. Just before the collapse of the Soviet Union, Muslims seized the Communist Party building in Namangan after they had been denied land to build a mosque. The collapse of the Soviet Union led to an Islamic revival and mosques, funded by the Saudis, sprouted throughout Central Asia.[25]

However, Karimov was wary of the growing power of the mullahs and throughout the 1990s he instituted a series of crackdowns against Muslim parties with links to the Wahhabis in Uzbekistan. Many Islamic parties including Birlik and Erk were banned and there was no democratic outlet for Islam. Karimov went on to ban all political opposition and had opponents kidnapped or committed to lunatic asylums. In January 2000, even the opposition candidate, Abdulhafiz Jalalov, voted for Karimov! Continued crackdowns on Islam, including imprisonment for growing a beard or wearing a veil caused many Muslims to turn militant.

The IMU were driven out of Uzbekistan into Tajikistan, where some remain today in their strongholds in the Tavildara valley. Karimov was very angry when the Tajik president, Rahmonov, formed a coalition with the Islamic Revolutionary Party in 1997, and he successfully forced Rahmanov to evict the IMU. Osama Bin Laden took advantage of the situation, offering them sanctuary in Afghanistan. They formed the vanguard of the fighting force in Mazar-e-Sharif against the Americans. Karimov continued to strong-arm the weaker Central Asian states, in particular Kyrgyzstan and Tajikistan, to deal with their Islamic militants. The events of September 11, unfortunately gave Karimov a shot in the arm. America sorely needed his air bases during the bombing of Afghanistan and had to turn a blind eye to his gross human rights violations. Karimov had refined the art of playing the Americans off against the Russians, who did not want to lose Uzbekistan from their sphere of influence.

The jury is still out on the other main Islamic party of Central Asia,

Hizb-ut-Tahrir, which wants to unite Muslims by non-violent means under a caliphate modelled on the seventh-century caliphate in Saudi Arabia. Hizb-ut-Tahrir is popular amongst intellectuals as opposed to the IMU which has support in rural areas. While the Hizb-ut-Tahrir support non-violent means for achieving their objectives, they had close talks with Bin Laden and the IMU in September 2000 and made it clear that they would support an IMU invasion of the Fergana Valley. Whether or not Hizb-ut-Tahrir turns out to be as bad as the IMU, the cause of the radicalization of Islam in Central Asia needs to be addressed to avoid the spread of fundamentalism. Many Muslims in Central Asia are being driven into the arms of radicals by poverty, corruption and political and religious repression. Until something is done to address these issues, the security situation could get much worse.

That night we were still on the road at dusk, holding out for a field of grass for the horses. Finally we found a large apple orchard. The owner agreed to let us stay there. As the sun set in an orange haze behind the low hills marking the Tajik border, I wondered whether they were full of IMU guerrillas. We didn't put up the tent, for fear of drawing even more attention than we had already attracted. I lay under the cart and slept with my knife down my sleeping-bag. Despite my fear, I couldn't keep awake. During the night, a turbaned man rode into our campsite. I battled with sleep, trying to will myself to wake up. I was convinced we were done for. I heard Ravshan talking.

'Who is it?' I murmured.

'The orchard guard.'

Seconds later, I was asleep again.

Now that I had a cart, I could carry from fifty up to a hundred kilos of corn with me but there wasn't much about; the last year's stocks were running low and this year's wasn't ripe yet. One day we stopped at a small village bazaar. I offered a hefty premium over the normal price and, suddenly, corn was available. As we waited for our sacks to arrive, we dined in the local café. Jilda sat underneath the cart and no one dared to approach it. Dima, a mousy Russian, his top lip partially obscured by bum-fluff joined us for *plov*. He cycled alongside us for most of the afternoon. He came from Solkhoz Gulistan, a small collective by Russian standards, which used to employ 50,000 people, ninety per cent of whom were Russian. Only five Russian families remained; the Solkhoz was bankrupt.

The author and her cart, in bandit country near the Tajik border, Uzbekistan

'There is eighty per cent unemployment in the Fergana Valley. I cannot find work on a farm so I took an apprenticeship and now I repair televisions. We don't get much business but at least the competition is less than in the city. With the money I am studying. I like computers. I know Windows 95 and 97. I am also learning Arabic.'

However, all good impressions of Dima evaporated when I invited him to have lunch with us. Spotting a lush garden behind one of the roadside cafés, we stopped for lunch and persuaded the owner to let us graze the horses in his garden. As we dined on *shashlik*, bread and tomato salad, Dima showed me his 'dark side'.

'I used to have a dog like that,' he said, staring at Jilda who was panting heavily under the table. 'I ate it.' There was no trace of humour on his face. Dima proved difficult to shake off, continuing to shadow us all afternoon.

'It's late now, you'd better head home or you won't make it there until dark.' Finally he got the hint.

That night we stayed in a cotton factory; there was not a blade of grass to be seen but at least the horses were safe behind the solid factory gates. The workers organized a factory tour. The cotton plant, which flowers in the summer, is ready for picking in the autumn. When it is ripe, a tufty ball of cotton wool bursts out of the large brown pod. Were it not for the seeds, it would be good enough to use, indeed many of the Uzbeks do use raw cotton. Frequently I have found a bucket of it next to the thunderbox; in the West such a luxury is reserved for babies' bottoms. The brown kernels are separated from the cotton and are used to make cotton oil, for cooking, soap and even as a mix in horse fodder. The cotton itself is pressed into long thick strips and folded into bales. From Fergana much of it is shipped to Manchester and Liverpool via Singapore.

The Chinese used to believe that cotton came from water sheep! Cotton was one of the reasons that attracted the Russian imperialists into Uzbekistan. Russia was highly dependent on Uzbek cotton, particularly during the American Civil War. Cotton imports were draining foreign currency reserves; by 1863, Russia was spending 4 million roubles a year on Uzbek cotton. The Uzbeks were also muscling in on a traditional Russian preserve; in the sixteenth century, slavery was the second biggest Russian export after silver and gold. While the Russians were happy to trade in slaves, they drew the line at foreign Christians. In 1717, a Bukharan ambassador's request for nine Swedish girls was not well received. As the Russians began to lean on their Bukharan competitors to release Christian slaves, the reply came to release Muslims. For the next century, the Khivans, Bukharans, Turkmen and Kazakhs increasingly relied on kidnapping to subsidize declining incomes from the Silk Route. As more and more Russians were captured, calls to avenge Russia's humiliation grew more vociferous.[26]

In Soviet Uzbekistan, every square inch of land was devoted to cotton, to the exclusion of food staples such as rice and wheat. The land was over-worked and laced with toxic fertilizers and pesticides, which polluted the water-table. The raw cotton was bought for a fortieth of the international price and only five per cent of the processing was done in Uzbekistan. An Uzbek mafia grew up around the Uzbek party chief, Sharif Rashidov, falsi-fying cotton production figures. It is estimated that he and his cronies pocketed $2 billion in fifteen years under Brezhnev. When Soviet satellite pictures displayed the extent of the scandal, an investigation was launched, which went right to the top. Rashidov is supposed to have built thirty mansions for entertaining Brezhnev, which he sold for a million dollars apiece. Brezhnev's son-in-law, Yuri Cherbanov, was found guilty of accept-ing a suitcase containing $200,000 from Rashidov.[27]

Early the next evening, we entered into territory oft-described as 'the hungry steppe': mile upon mile of monotonous wasteland, bare of almost any plant life. At dusk we rode into a small town and turned into some side-streets. Standing in our stirrups, we peered over walls looking for grazing. Finally we happened upon a smart bungalow surrounded by a huge field of lush, tall grass.

'This is where we are going to stay.'

As we parked the cart outside the gates a few women peered out of the windows at the filthy western woman, clad in a smelly *shawal kameze* and Russian army surplus boots strolling up their driveway.

'You can stay here but you cannot come inside; this is a sanatorium.'

Initially, I was rather perturbed.

'Perhaps they are looking after old people; we shouldn't disturb them,' suggested Ravshan.

'We might catch something funny,' I said. 'Perhaps they are looking after people with incurable diseases.'

Our fears were soothed with a pot of tea and reassurances from our hosts.

'This isn't a hospital. It is the recreation ground for the Syr Daria football team.'

I woke at 5.30 to angry shouts. I wriggled free of my sleeping-bag and crawled out of my tent to see what the fuss was about. A stout man with a white beard was hobbling towards Ravshan, shouting and wielding a big stick.

'Get out of here. You are stealing my best grass.' While I was slightly bemused about how I would tackle this raving geriatric, Ravshan didn't seem keen to take him on and rapidly began packing. The old man seemed unconcerned that we had an invitation and ignored pleas from the manager of the home to leave us alone.

'I will report you to the police,' he shouted, waving his stick above his head and marching off towards the town centre.

As we were leaving, three policemen appeared. They examined the scene of the crime. A large pitch, knee high in grass the night before, was neatly mown in circles around the tethering ropes. The caretaker of the football club was questioned, followed by the team captain. Although he didn't own the land, the old man claimed an exclusive right to graze his sheep on it, because 'he always had'. The police chief apologized and advised us to leave. The old man looked crestfallen, perhaps convinced that we would be paraded through the streets in cuffs. I turned down the chance to see a football match and hurried out of town.

As we rode alongside the deep canals, I envied the naked children with glistening brown backs jumping in and splashing around in the cool water. We found a secluded spot and I went for a swim in my *shawal kameze*. Further downriver, a couple of boys were washing a petrified sheep. Later in the morning, we passed three Ladas, red, white and blue, which were being washed in the river.

At lunch, we spotted a small patch of grass beside the road and decided to give the horses a couple of hours' grazing. A young man invited us to his

Boys washing sheep

house for tea. He led us along a path, which wound through tall marshy elephant-grass to a small hut. Outside, his elderly father, clad in an olive green *khalat*, was reclining on a rusty iron bed, brushing marsh flies out of a generous white beard. As we drank tea, he proudly showed us his rice paddies, which were hidden behind the long grasses.

'The land is not mine, it is the government's. Our annual quota is ten tonnes. Any surplus we can keep or sell.'

'How much rice can you produce?'

'Twenty tonnes.'

That wasn't bad; he could earn sixty dollars per month, a pretty good income for Uzbekistan.

'But we have to work very hard. In a bad year, it is difficult to achieve the government target. We have many mouths to feed. He has to feed his family.' He pointed to a silent, good-looking young man, who was crouching under the tree.

'He is a Tajik.'

'Where are your family?'

'My wife and children are here. My parents are in Khodjent with two brothers. There are no jobs in Tajikistan.'

That night we camped in the middle of a tractor track, running through four huge sunflower fields. The horses eyed the sunflowers wistfully but had to content themselves with the grass verge. At two o'clock, Jilda woke us up, barking furiously. Thinking we were being robbed, I struggled out of the tent, my sleeping-bag around my ankles. Jilda was chasing Aykulak, who had broken his tethering rope and was making a beeline towards the road. Rounding on him, she barked incessantly, stopping him in his tracks until I managed to catch the reins.

Several days later, we reached Tamerlane pass. Ravshan steered the cart along the road while I shadowed him several hundred metres above in the rolling hills, parched golden brown and punctuated by clumps of copper thistles. We camped in a chocolate-brown field full of straw stubble, a few hundred metres from a police post, which marked the boundaries of Samarkand. As I lay in my tent, I could hear the distant hum of a threshing-machine, whose headlights danced on the horizon. Trucks rumbled through the border-post and occasional raised voices kept me awake. At one point, Jilda began barking aggressively. I let off a couple of shots from the pistol, hoping it would deter any opportunists. I had taken to wearing the pistol down the back of my trousers. When I saw someone menacing and I was sure they were watching, I stretched and shoved it down the front of my trousers.

Any illusions that I might have had of my machismo were dashed at lunch the following day. We stopped at a roadside *chaikhana* and I went off in search of the loo. As I pulled down my trousers, I heard a clatter and looked down just in time to see the gun fall through the hole. Despite feeling the urge, I couldn't pee on my gun. Ravshan was eating *shashlik*.

'Where have you been?'

'My gun has fallen down the loo. I need a torch.' I rushed back to the loo, hoping that no one had got to it in my absence. The aperture to the cesspit below was only three or four inches wide and it was difficult to angle the torch. Two or three metres below, I could see the gun floating on brown sludge. Frantically, I began looking for something I might be able to use to fish it out. The acrid smell of crusty urine made me want to retch. Finally I capitulated and solicited the help of the restaurant manager.

'Excuse me. I dropped my gun in the loo.'

'Sorry?'

'I dropped my gun in the loo. Can you help me?' Expecting a sharp rebuff, I was pleasantly surprised by Sultan's efficient response. He surveyed the scene and set about looking for a piece of wire from one of the surrounding fences. I was charged with angling the torch while Sultan fished with a large coat-hanger hook cobbled together with two strands of wire that he'd pulled from the fence. After half an hour bending over several thousand watery stools, he looped the wire over the handle and raised it to the surface: slimy, brown and exceedingly smelly. We hosed it off, doused it with disinfectant and slung it into the bottom of the cart. I tried to eat my lunch but all I could smell was shit and it didn't do wonders for my appetite.

For the next two days, we rode along the main road to Samarkand. The belching fumes from passing juggernauts stuck in my throat. It was difficult to keep the horses under control. On one occasion, the sight of a young boy rolling a tractor tyre along the road sent the horses into a panicking canter along the tarmac. Later all the horses refused to pass two white donkeys, grazing by the side of the road, and we were forced to take another route. We stopped at the October Kolkhoz, a farm run by the sixth brigade, just outside Samarkand. We were now four days' ride from the Turkmen border. The horses needed a rest. Our hosts had a large apple orchard overgrown with lucerne; I paid them three dollars a day for grazing and went off in search of corn.

I consulted one of the villagers, a retired major, a wiry Uzbek in mufti, neatly trimmed moustache, brown slacks, pressed blue shirt and gleaming shoes. The major invited me to lunch at his home, a simple one-storey building made of local mud bricks. He was thrilled to practise his English.

'My English used to be good, but I have forgotten so much. I was an interpreter in the army.' We sat at the table, picking at *ouriouks* (apricot kernels) and drinking tea. He was keen to help me with the next stage of my journey. While we were about 150 kilometres from the Turkmen border, the last stretch was semi-desert and it would be even hotter.

'You think it is difficult to find fodder in Uzbekistan; wait until you get to Turkmenistan. I served there as a young officer. At this time of year, the temperature in the desert can reach fifty degrees and the sand can reach seventy degrees. In such conditions, you would be doing well to cover five kilometres per day. You need to wait at least a month before you go.' I asked him what chances I would have selling my horses or finding a good home for them in the neighbourhood but the major wasn't positive. A drought that year meant that there wasn't much grass; the fodder was too expensive. Only butchers could afford to buy my horses; they could recoup their money the next day selling sausages in the market. His young local wife, a scuttling shadow, appeared with a bottle of vodka and scuttled away.

'My first wife died seven years ago. It broke my heart. Her husband also died. She's a simple country girl. She doesn't speak Russian.'

By the time the *plov* arrived, the major was thoroughly morose. Casting his hand over dozens of first editions from Dostoyevsky, Pushkin, Tolstoy to Chekhov, he tried to persuade me to take them.

'These are useless to me. No one here is interested in Russian literature. My son will never read them; he doesn't speak Russian. They are only good for toilet paper.' By this stage, he had returned to the table in his full major's uniform. Concerned for my femininity, he had given me a thimble for my vodka; he had a mug. I made my excuses and left before he lost his dignity completely.

The next day, he offered to take me into Samarkand to buy corn and to take Ravshan to the bus station. As we sped along, he pointed at rusty holes in the footwell through which I had the dizzying sensation of watching the road rush beneath my feet.

'I am sorry about this old car. When I bought it, it was a great privilege to own a car. I was one of the only people in my neighbourhood with one. I do not use it much any more. I can't afford the petrol.'

'Surely the Uzbek army pays you a good pension.'

'I was a major in the Soviet army,' he boasted, 'not the Uzbek army. After independence, the Russians forgot about us. My pension is fifteen dollars per month. That is barely enough to buy rice. I would be a taxi driver, but no tourists would want to come in my car.'

'Why doesn't the Uzbek government help you?'

'Karimov sees intellectuals as a threat.'

As we approached the outskirts of Samarkand, the portal of the Bibi Khanum Mosque loomed into view, clad in scaffolding and arching high above the sprawling bustle of modern Samarkand. Tamerlane wanted it to surpass all existing constructions in the Muslim world. He ignored both architectural guidelines and seismic activity in the area. It was hurriedly completed in five years using the combined muscle of ninety-five elephants from India.

It was doomed from the start. The architect was besotted with Tamerlane's Chinese wife. She held out for months, trying to redirect his ardour elsewhere, which he said was akin to comparing water with wine. Finally she consented to a single kiss, which left an indelible mark on her cheek. Tamerlane quickly spotted his wife's love-bite and had her hurled from the top of the minaret. The architect was lucky. As he fled up the tower, he turned into a winged bird and flew back to Meshed. He left behind a crumbling thirty-five-metre gateway. Like his taste in women, it was distinctly over-ambitious. It collapsed in an earthquake in 1897. Reconstruction work is now underway.[28]

I tried to distract the major but he was on a roll.

'When we get to the market, you must keep near me and I will do the talking. The people here are all dishonest. They are too ignorant to understand the benefits which come from treating tourists well. These people are nothing without Russia.' I felt rather sorry for the major. He was a Russian soul trapped inside an Uzbek skin, stranded in a village of simple cotton pickers. Clinging hopelessly to his position in an élite which deserted him, his condescending attitude to fellow Uzbeks left him isolated, impoverished and embittered.

> Look 'round thee now on Samarcand!
> Is not she queen of Earth? her pride
> Above all cities? in her hand
> Their destinies? in all beside
> Of glory which the world hath known
> Stands she not nobly and alone?
> Falling – her veriest stepping-stone
> Shall form the pedestal of a throne –
> And who her sovereign? Timour – he
> Whom the astonished people saw
> Striding o'er empires haughtily
> A diadem'd outlaw!

Edgar Allan Poe, *Tamerlane*, 1827

19

CHANGE OF PLAN

Samarkand was one of the most important trading towns on the Silk Route, which split in two near the Zerafshan valley, one branch going to India and the other to Persia. Known as Maracanda by Alexander the Great, it was here that he slew his friend Clitus and married Roxana. Below the enormity, symmetry and colour of the Timurid capital, archaeologists have found the remains of Graeco-Bactrian pottery, Soghdian frescoes and the temple of the goddess Nana, destroyed by the Arabs in AD 712.

It is said that some Muslim missionaries in Central Asia were boiling a sheep on the hill where Ulug Beg's monastery stands. One pulled out the head and remained in Samarkand, one got the heart and went to Mecca, the third extracted the hind legs and went to Baghdad. Henceforth Samarkand became a thriving city known as the 'head of Islam'. After the departure of the Arabs, it was the preserve of Persian Samanids and later the Seljuks, until it was flattened in 1220 by Genghis Khan.[29]

At the same time as Genghis Khan was successfully expanding his empire westwards, Khwarazm Shah Ala al-Din moved eastwards and captured Samarkand in 1210. Genghis Khan sent three envoys to the Khwarazm Shah with a condescending message to his new neighbour:

'My country is an anthill of soldiers and a mine of silver and I have no need of other lands. Therefore I think that we have an equal interest in encouraging trade between our subjects.'

He signed it 'God in Heaven, the Kah Khan, the Power of God on Earth. The Seal of the Emperor of Mankind.'

The Shah responded by murdering one envoy and shaving the beards of the other two. In 1218, the Shah's governor in Utrar captured a caravan of four hundred and fifty Mongolian camels, laden with goods, and killed all of the tradesmen. The Shah's army was almost double the size of the Mongol force but he deployed them badly in a thin line of defence across the Syr Daria. The Mongols punched through it with little difficulty. Using the cover of the Kyzylkum desert, they stole four hundred miles into the Shah's territory, capturing Bukhara and massacring its Turkish garrison. Genghis Khan rode into the largest mosque and converted the cases that held the Koran into mangers for his horses. Climbing into the pulpit, he preached to the terrified congregation:

'I am the scourge of God. If you had not committed great sins, he would not have sent a punishment like me.'

Captured Bukharans became 'hashar service' or cannon fodder, as the Mongols marched on Samarkand. They took it within five days, massacring 30,000 people, raping the women and carrying off thousands of slaves. After a five-month siege, the Mongols took the city of Utrar. Genghis Khan ordered that the governor be taken alive. They took down the armoury, where he was hiding, brick by brick. He was carted off to Samarkand for a painful death: molten silver was poured into his eyes and ears.[30]

All that remains of pre-Mongol Samarkand are the brick walls around Shah-I Zindah and the shrine of Kussam Abbas, a first cousin of Muhammad. Kussam was decapitated while fighting the Christian infidel in Samarkand. Picking up his head, he jumped down a well. At some time, he will emerge and continue his fight. Shah-I Zindah was rebuilt and now houses the tombs of many of Tamerlane's relatives and generals. Away from the bustle of the city centre, we stopped below a hillside, dotted with graves. A cluster of peeling blue domes, growing tufts of grass, dwarfed the modern headstones. I walked up a stairway and down a cool, narrow alley, clustered with cubic mausoleums. Stopping at Kussam's shrine we listened to the soothing prayers of a young student from a local madrasah.

After the serenity and understatement of Shah-I Zindah, I was struck dumb by the enormity, symmetry and colour of the Registan. No number of superlatives would suffice to describe it. An inscription reads:

The architect has built the arch of this portal with such perfection that the entire heaven gnaws its fingers in astonishment, thinking it sees the rising of some new moon.

I entered an imposing square, the enormous portals of three madrasah covered in intricate geometric tiling rose around it. In perfect symmetry, minarets flanked the madrasah to the left and right. Symmetrical portals flanked the madrasah ahead. A blue mamelon dome rising on its left side broke the symmetry, as required in the Koran. The symmetry was all the more surprising given the fact that it was built in three different stages. Originally Tamerlane commissioned it as a bazaar, ordering that the main street in Samarkand be cleared and replacing it with a broad new street lined with shops covered in a dome. His grandson, Ulug Beg, renowned for his giant sextant which accurately depicted degrees and minutes, remodelled the Registan. Changing its purpose to official functions, he built a large *madrasah* and a mosque. An almost perfect replica, the Shir Dor *madrasah*, whose taboo scene depicted a tiger attacking a deer, was added in the seventeenth century.[31]

The Tilla Kari (gilded) Madrasah, Samarkand

In the afternoon, I sat in the shade under the bazaar near the Bibi Khanum, scooping the delicate, sweet-tasting flesh from an enormous melon with my penknife and watching workman restoring the building to its former glory. I listened to the loud hum of activity broken by raised voices as women haggled over brightly-coloured spices and metre-long melons. I thought about my options. The horses were already tired and skinny. Was it worth exhausting them further for the sake of linking two points on my map to ensure that I made an unbroken journey from Ulaanbaatar to Ashkabad? What would I do with the horses when I reached Turkmenistan? Surely the horses deserved more than slaughter after the 3,000-kilometre journey.

And what of Jilda? She couldn't survive the desert heat. Her paws would blister again on the hot sand. I had already decided that I would take her back to England with me. Perhaps this would be a good time to send her back? I turned these thoughts over and over in my mind as I continued to explore Samarkand.

In the evening the fluted cupola of Tamerlane's mausoleum cast a long shadow over the neighbouring *madrasah*. The sun shimmered on the golden-buffed bricks on the drum beneath the dome. Beneath it, in bold, white Kufic characters, ten feet high, the inscription read: 'God is immortal!'

A large slab of dark green jade, broken down the middle, lies over Tamerlane's tomb. The mausoleum was built for his grandson, Muhammad Sultan, who was mortally wounded in the battle of Angora against the Turks. Tamerlane oversaw the reconstruction of the complex of Gur Emir, 'the Great Prince', insisting that the dome and drum be completely rebuilt in two weeks. At the time of construction, he did not know that he was designing his own mausoleum. In 1941, the Soviet Archaeological Commission opened the tomb and found: 'the skeleton of a man who, though lame, must have been of powerful physique, tall for a Tartar and of a haughty bearing. They examined the skeleton and the remains, which included fragments of muscle and skin, and some hair of the head, eyebrows, red moustache and beard. The skull indicated Mongol features.'[32]

Tamerlane was born into the Barlas clan within the Chaghadayid Khanate, a legacy of the Chinggisid dynasty. He claimed that his mother had been inseminated by a ray of light. His name comes from the Persian *Timur-i lang* on account of the lameness in one leg which he wounded in the battle of Sistan. Apart from the lameness in his leg, he also lost two small fingers on his right hand, cut off by a blow he received as a child for stealing sheep. After the collapse of the Mongol dynasty, the nomadic way of life continued in much of Central Asia and the nomads dominated the sedentary peoples. With no overall leadership, the former khanates became a shifting question mark of alternating alliances and political intrigue. Although a man of insignificant lineage, Tamerlane was able to take advantage of changing allegiances, and through outside help from Moghulistan, he manoeuvred himself into the position of Khan of Chaghatay.

Once in power, he invoked his Chinggisid lineage, inherited through his wife, and called himself the 'Royal Son-in-Law'. His rule was, in many ways, a blueprint of that of Genghis Khan: ceaseless military activity in which he expanded his empire towards the former Chinggisid boundaries.

His army plundered Persia, flattened Khorezm, ravaged north-western India, sacked Moscow and went on to take Georgia, Anatolia, and later Syria and Damascus. He maintained control by breaking up enemy tribes and distributing them into different units. He established and promoted a new élite from his personal following whose prestige and wealth derived from conquest and plunder.

His cruelty often surpassed that of the Mongols such as cementing people in towers, a punishment meted out by the Taliban today. During the siege of Sivas, Tamerlane promised that he would not shed the blood of a number of the chiefs if they delivered him a ransom in silver and gold. Once the money was in his possession, he spared the bloodshed, as promised. They and 4,000 others were buried in a pit. The children of the city were trampled under the hoofs of his cavalry and 9,000 women were carted off to join the imperial harem.

Like previous khans, he maintained a lavish court, which was documented in great detail by Clavijo, the envoy of Henry III, King of Spain. His palace was surrounded by a deer park and an orchard of assorted fruit trees, planted in avenues which led to a small artificial hill, surrounded by wooden palisades and streams, where the palaces stood. Tamerlane's tent was a magnificent affair, lined with ermine, crimson tapestries, silk hangings embroidered with gold, and topped with a huge silver eagle in the cupola and three smaller falcons below. Tamerlane sat on piles of silk cushions on a raised dais in front of a fountain, which threw water backwards and was full of bobbing red apples.

Entertained by troupes of performing elephants, the guests engaged in huge binges of feasting and drinking. The court dined on roast horse washed down with litres of *koumiss* and wine, which according to Clavijo they quaffed, 'at such frequent intervals that the men soon get very drunk.... The whole of the service is to keep on giving cup after cup of wine to the guests ... when one server is weary, another takes his place.' Sixty-gallon wine-jars dotted a field near the royal enclosure, guarded by marksmen who shot arrows at anyone caught near the booze:

> We noticed that many had thus been wounded for their inadvertence and some had been thrown out for dead and were lying at the gates of the enclosure.

By 1402, Tamerlane controlled all western Asia from the Aegean to Turkestan. In November 1404, he set out to conquer the 'Pig Emperor' of China. Wintering in Utrar, he fell ill and died in February 1405. Jealously guarding his power throughout his highly personalized reign, Tamerlane left no one capable of succeeding him. His nominated successor, Pir Muhammad, governor of Kabul, was too far from the action to establish control. After a fifteen-year power struggle, another son, Shah Rukh, inherited a considerably smaller, fractious empire, which had already fallen into decline.

The major offered to look for a buyer for the horses and suggested that, while he did so, I took some time off to go to Bukhara. We agreed that if he hadn't found a buyer by the time I returned, I would take them back to Kyrgyzstan. I was loath to leave Jilda behind so I took her with me.

We arrived in Bukhara in time for a *shashlik* lunch and sat beside the Labi Haus, formerly the principal reservoir for Bukhara, drinking tea and watching young boys jumping, diving and flopping into the murky green pool. As one of the last places to receive the waters of the Zerafshan River, the Labi Haus was the perfect breeding-ground for the guinea worm. Anthony Jenkinson, an Elizabethan merchant and sailor, who was probably one of the first Englishmen to enter Bukhara, wrote in 1558:

> The water thereof is most vnwholesome, for it breedeth sometime in men that drink thereof, and especially in them that be not borne there, a worme of an ell long, which lieth commonly in the legge betwixt the flesh and the skinn, and is pluck out about the ancle with great art and cunning, the Surgeons being much practised therein, and if she breake in plucking out, the partie dieth, and every day she commeth out about an inche, which is rolled vp, and so worketh till she be all out. And yet it is there forbidden to drinke any other thing then water and mares milke....

After the bustle of Samarkand, my footsteps echoed through the sun-baked side-streets of Bukhara. Rows of little doors led into warrens of student cells in numerous *madrasahs*. Many of the courtyards had been given over to carpet-sellers, whose brightly coloured rugs restored colour to arches denuded of their lapis and turquoise tile-work. Outside the domed bazaar, an old man watered tangerine flowers in the shrubbery, holding up his trouser legs to stop them trailing in the water.

I climbed the Kalon Minaret, which cast huge shadows over the sandstone ground. From the top, I could see the turquoise onion-shaped domes of the *madrasah*, the thick buttressed walls of the ark, framed in the small arches in the top of the minaret. Distant trees broke the dryness and yellowness. The pale blue-white hot sky cast a haze over the low, washed out mud-brick houses of Bukhara.

The Kalon Mosque – an aerial view of Bukhara from the Kalon Minaret

Bukhara, whose name comes from Bikhara meaning 'convent', reached its intellectual zenith in the ninth century under the Persian Samanids. One of its finest thinkers, Avicenna, translated Aristotle into Arabic while also finding time to write the Qanun, a medical compendium spanning ten centuries, containing sources from China, Greece, Persia, India and Egypt. The Pope was so impressed that he issued a bull insisting that all medical faculties in Europe should study it.

When the Russians took Bukhara, it had 197 mosques, 167 *madrasahs* and 20,000 students. The Bolsheviks shut down all the *madrasahs* bar one and turned the Kalian mosque into a warehouse for shoes. The Mir-I Arab, built from the proceeds of the sale of several thousand Shiite Persians into slavery, was the only *madrasah* in Central Asia which remained open. After the break-up of the Soviet Union, the number slowly increased.[33]

While the *madrasahs* represent an enlightened period in Bukharan history, the Kalon Minaret conjures up the iniquity of Bukhara under the Emir, Nasrullah Khan. Genghis Khan spared the 170-foot 'Great Minaret', whose bands of geometrical patterns entirely in brick never repeat themselves. In the nineteenth century, it became a tower of death; the Emir's victims were stuffed in sacks and hurled from the top.[34]

In October 1843 Wolff, a local clergyman, set out from London in search of two of Nasrullah's victims: Stoddart and Connolly. He was too late. Stoddart, a British envoy sent to reassure the Emir about British activities in Afghanistan, had gravely insulted him. Riding in the ark on horseback, an offence in itself, he carried a missive from the Governor of India. The Emir expected a letter from Queen Victoria herself. Stoddart was slung into the bug pit. Three years later, Connolly arrived to rescue him. He joined Stoddart in the deep well, full of specially bred vermin and reptiles. After two months confinement, much of their flesh had been gnawed off their bones. When the Emir heard news of the British retreat from Kabul, he decided Britain was not a power to be feared. When both men refused to embrace Islam, they were made to dig their own graves and were executed in the public square.

The chief executioner was sent to Wolff to ask if he would embrace Islam. He refused. When Wolff came before the Emir, he was dressed in full canonicals with a bible under his arm, causing the Emir much amusement.

Carpets for sale in a madrasah in Bukhara

At the last minute, Wolff decided to do thirty prostrations crying *Allahu Akbar*, as a sop to the Emir. He was let off and a band from Lahore played 'God Save the Queen'. The Bolsheviks finally put an end to the Emir's rule, burning his palace. He escaped to Kabul with 175 million dollars' worth of jewellery and a harem of young dancing boys. Locals claim he returned several times, disguised as a pilgrim, to mourn his loss.[35]

Outside Bukhara, I passed through fields of cotton, orchards and flat-roofed mud houses and stopped outside the mausoleum of the fourteenth-century Bakhauddin Nakhshbandi. One of the founders of Sufic Islam, he was the holiest Sufic saint. Sufism, whose name comes from the Arabic for wool, is still the predominant religion of Central Asia; its appeal to the previously animist nomads was its simplicity, its tolerance for other superstitions and its direct communion with god, without the necessity for priests.

Several buses were parked outside and the shrine was milling with pilgrims. A student, fresh out of a *madrasah*, was reciting prayers in Arabic on a raised dais, under a mulberry tree, surrounded by half a dozen countryfolk. Lids were lightly closed over big almond eyes, his delicate boyish face was relaxed, serene in contemplation as he cupped his hands and muttered his prayers. Shadows of the leaves from a mulberry tree overhead played on his thinly-striped *khalat*. At the end of each prayer, he passed his hands over his face; the pilgrims followed suit. Each pilgrim had brought an offering: fried pastries, cream or a shoulder of lamb. A group of about twenty old men in black and white *khalats* were sitting cross-legged on a long red prayer-mat in cloisters, supported by carved wooden colonnades. Each man, his shoes discarded nearby, was cupping his hands at the start of prayers. A party of women circled the trunk of an ancient mulberry tree, caressing the bark and touching their foreheads in the hope that it would bring them luck and fertility.

I sat in the cool grey shadows of the colonnades out of the burning sun, staring at Nakhshbandi's tomb, a simple square with four arches. The colours were rich under the deep blue sky, the greens of the mulberries, the sandy minaret, the brick reds, the baked yellow cobbles and geometric patterns in tiles of sapphire blue and turquoise amid a sea of black and white skullcaps. I sat there for several hours; it was an extremely peaceful setting and I could feel my mind unwinding. I wondered whether the major had had any luck selling the horses; I was not hopeful. The only place where I could guarantee the survival of my horses was back in Kyrgyzstan. Perhaps I should return there while I waited for the Karakum desert to cool. I could explore the Pamirs and visit Tajikistan. Perhaps I could send

Prayers under a mulberry tree at
the Bakhauddin Nakhshbandi
Mausoleum

Jilda home early; by plane. Some friends in Brussels had offered to look
after her to avoid quarantine. The sooner she got to Europe, the sooner she
could get to England. While none of this was in my original plans, it seemed
the most sensible option and the most humane thing to do.

> Villain, I tell thee, were that Tamberlaine,
> As monstrous as Gorgon, prince of hell…
> Three hundred thousand men in armour clad,
> Upon their prancing steeds, disdainfully
> With wanton paces trampling on the ground;
> Five hundred thousand footmen threatening shot,
> Shaking their swords, their spears, and iron bills,
> Environing their standard round, that stood
> As bristle-pointed as a thorny wood;
> Their warlike engines and munition
> Exceed the forces of their martial men…
> Nay, could their numbers countervail the stars,

Or ever-drizzling raindrops of April showers,
Or withered leaves that autumn shaketh down,
Yet would the Soldan by his conquering power
So scatter and consume them in his rage,
That not a man should live to rue their fall…

Smile, stars that reigned at my nativity,
And dim the brightness of their neighbour lamps;
Disdain to borrow light of Cynthia,
For I, the chiefest lamp of all the earth,
First rising in the east with mild aspect,
But fixed now in the meridian line,
Will send up fire to your turning spheres,
And cause the sun to borrow light of you…
And on the south, sinus Arabicus,
Shall all be loaden with the martial spoils
We will convey with us to Persia.
Then shall my native city Samarcanda,
And crystal waves of fresh Jaertis stream,
The pride and beauty of her princely seat,
Be famous through the furthest continents;
For there my palace shall be plac'd,
Whose shining turrets shall dismay the heavens,
And cast the fame of Ilion's tower to hell.

Christopher Marlowe, *Tamburlaine*, *c*.1587

20

SAVING THE HORSES

The major hadn't managed to find a buyer for the horses but he found me a lorry big enough to transport them. Our journey took us via Tashkent where I bought Jilda a passage on a Lufthansa flight to Europe. While I was making the arrangements, I installed the horses in the local hippodrome. Finally, the lorry came to take us to the Kyrgyz border. On the night we were due to load the horses, Three Socks, the young horse which I had ridden across Kyrgyzstan, fell ill. I found him rolling around on the ground in agony. He hadn't eaten or drunk anything since the morning. I was sure it was colic. When I suggested puncturing his stomach, as we had done in Mongolia, I was told that it was barbaric and no one would help me. We hurried to the nearest telephone at the fire station and called the hippodrome vet. He couldn't be bothered to come out on a Friday night but suggested some medicine over the phone.

'Have you got it?'

'Yes.'

We rushed back to the hippodrome and administered the dose.

'What is it?'

'A painkiller.'

'What use is that? A painkiller won't expel the gas.'

We massaged his stomach with a long pole, which two of the hands rubbed along his stomach, while a third steadied him as he lashed out with his hind legs.

'We must puncture his stomach.'

'If you do that, you are on your own.'

I couldn't control the horse and puncture his stomach. I was nervous. I had only seen it done. I couldn't remember if I had to drive the screwdriver in between the third and fourth rib or the fifth and sixth. I tried the vet again but he wouldn't come to the stables. I was told that he mustn't lie down or he'd twist his gut. For several hours, I fought to keep Three Socks on his feet, beating him when he lay down and chasing him round the paddock. He soon became oblivious to the blows and lay down regardless. I moved a bed outside and lay down beside the paddock. Three Socks lay down on the other side of the fence and stretched his head under the fence so that I could stroke his head. Every now and then he rolled, groaned, got up, walked around and slumped down again.

In the morning he seemed a little better. The vet finally arrived and gave him an injection for colic. He managed to pee and I walked him around the hippodrome to expel the air. Any optimism I had was soon quashed. His belly started swelling again and the vet decided to puncture his stomach. The methane gas hissed out but the damage was already done; he had blood poisoning. His temperature began to fall rapidly, his nose was numb, he started shivering violently and stumbling. I phoned another vet and asked him to come and put Three Socks out of his misery. He said he would be with us within the hour. It was too late. With one last effort, Three Socks pulled himself up, walked to the far corner of the paddock, stumbled and collapsed. I ran over to him but he was already dead. His legs stretched out, his mouth wide, teeth bared in a last gasp, eyes horrified. We buried him in the grounds of the hippodrome. One of the stablehands saved me one of Three Socks's shoes. I burst into tears: it was such a waste, he had come so far and he would have been back in Kyrgyzstan the following day.

I arrived in Osh in time for the Sunday market. As I rode alongside a canal towards the market, I heard the antiphonal calls to prayer, echoing across the hillside. It was the first time I'd heard it since I'd arrived in Central Asia. Unlike their countrymen over the border in Uzbekistan, the Muslims in Osh were free to practise their faith. The market, which the locals called the *malbazaar*, was still quiet when I arrived. Several sheep bleated in a corner and a plump mare was pawing the ground at the far end. I left my horses with the owner of the mare and went off for breakfast in a converted animal stall, with a mud floor and large wood-burning oven in the corner. Groups of old men were hunched over greasy plastic table-cloths, sipping green tea out of small, chipped bowls. The tables were distinctly divided. The nomadic Kyrgyz were selling the animals. They were dressed up in conical *kalpak* hats and shabby suits, ill-disguising bow-legs, tapering down to boots covered in patches. The Uzbek butchers, in cheap imitation leather jackets, white shirts and white embroidered skull-caps, sat in another corner. In the centre of the eating area, a young boy was fishing fried meat-pastries out of a huge black cauldron while an old lady boiled tea in an industrial-sized *samovar*. The whole place reeked of congealed lamb fat.

Agreeing on the price of a sheep in the Sunday market in Osh

By the time I had finished breakfast, the market had turned into a sea of hats: white conical caps with black turnups belonging to the Kyrgyz, the skull caps of Uzbeks, Russian hats, woolly hats, trilbies and baseball caps. The pens were writhing with lowing animals and their bartering herders. On one side, fat-tailed sheep of various hues, which were sometimes hard to distinguish for the mud and dung, were tied head to toe along a low railing. Near the entrance to the bazaar a woman in a white headscarf, black paisley shirt, leggings and cut-off wellington boots was squatting beside some bags of flour, a cigarette in one hand, a bundle of banknotes in the other.

A couple of men were discussing the merits of a fine sheep. The owner, a Kyrgyz in his Sunday best, an old suit-jacket with one ripped pocket and no buttons, proudly grasped its fat hindquarters. The prospective buyer, an Uzbek dressed in a long *khalat* topped with a black and white skull-cap, was shaking his head, but his longing gaze gave him away; he looked as though he might eat it there and then. An old man, with a drooping white moustache and tufty white beard leant on a cow with a bony hide and looked on as they bargained.

A young calf lay close to its mother, which was licking it protectively. Nearby, two men were in advanced negotiations over the price of a bull. The owner was showing him off, holding its sharp horns which curved heavenwards like bicycle handlebars. The butcher had his hand half way up the owner's sleeve; a series of secret hand-gestures, hidden up an ill-fitting Western corduroy jacket, were not giving anything away. Another butcher, in a brown trilby, which cast a shadow down to his neat moustache, stood someway back from the negotiations, where he thought he was blending with the crowd. His eyes never left the sleeve, lest something were given away or the sale fell through. It wasn't to be. The hands emerged from the sleeve and an old man in a Kyrgyz hat came forward. Pairing the two hands together, as though officiating a wedding ceremony, he shook them up and down three times and pronounced the sale complete. The purchaser extracted a wad of notes and started counting.

A crowd was beginning to gather around my horses. A few old Kyrgyz men were admiring Tom, but it was the men in leather jackets who were making the offers. After several minutes of pointless negotiations, I walked off and sat down. A young man approached and asked if he could try Tom. He jumped on to him bareback and put him through his paces, galloping across the field, bringing him up sharply, turning him around on a sixpence and encouraging him to rear. Signalling to a friend, who jumped on Wolf, they began jostling the two horses against each other, rearing and cantering side-by-side. The older men looked on appreciatively. While their equestrian skills were in no doubt, the horses were frightened, their nostrils flaring, their mouths contorted on a short rein.

'He is a good horse. Well trained. They are looking for horses to play *ulak*,' said the owner of the mare. This month, Osh is celebrating its 3,000th birthday. A huge celebration has been organized, which will take in horseracing, eagle hunting and the local version of polo, played with a headless goat's carcass.

'We'll give you one hundred and fifty for the big one.'

'I'll give you one hundred and eighty,' countered the fat butcher.

'I'm not going to sell my horses for meat, I'm sorry.'

'That horse will be sausage anyway. After the games, they will sell him for meat. I'll give you four hundred for all the horses. Take it or leave it.'

'Thank you, but no.'

While various people felt up the bellies of the horses, I chatted to Yesen, the owner of a chestnut mare. Dressed in a grey suit which had seen better days, Yessen's pale blue eyes looked out of place under a Kyrgyz conical hat. He told me that he had been a local journalist but after the collapse of the Union, the paper had closed down and he had been forced to return to herding. Despite his relative isolation, he was still extremely knowledgeable about current affairs, eking out international news from local papers, radio and news programmes from Moscow. I asked him about the recent incursions by the Al Qa'eda-trained Islamic Militants' Union into Kyrgyzstan and the kidnapping of the Japanese geologists from a neighbouring valley. As I suspected, each summer, Islamic fundamentalists from Pakistan had been penetrating the Allai Valley and trying to persuade local herdsmen to join the jihad. Fortunately, local herdsmen in the area were not interested 'in the politics of religion', as Yesen called it; they had their animals to look after and were not interested in fighting a jihad with people whose outlook was alien from their own.

Yesen was the only voice in the marketplace whom I felt I could trust. He had nothing to gain from me but he freely offered his advice: he was holding out for $200 and advised me to do the same.

'This isn't a free market any more. The butchers have created a cartel. They fix the prices way below the rate in other parts of the country. The herders are forced to sell their livestock at rock-bottom prices, knowing that their animals will be transported to another part of the country and sold at a huge profit. Only the butchers can afford to buy horses. They pay today and profit tomorrow.'

As the day wore on, the butchers became frustrated at their failure to break my resolve. I found myself face to face with the bazaar chief.

'This is a bazaar, not a shop. If you want to sell your horses, you must bargain.'

'These are my horses. If you want to buy them, you must pay.'

Before long, a policeman was sent over. He demanded to see my passport but couldn't find any faults and slunk off.

I began to think that I wouldn't manage to find a good home for my horses. I wondered whether Yesen would look after them. I started to ask him questions about his farm, how much land he had, how many animals and whether he had good winter pastureland. When I was sure that he would be able to look after them, I made him an offer that he couldn't refuse: he could treat the horses as if they were his; he could work them in his fields, he could use my stallions for breeding but he was not entitled to sell any of my horses or kill them for meat. I would come back each summer to ride them. Yesen readily agreed to the terms I had set; he was very excited about the possibility of mating Aykulak with his mares: they would be the finest foals in the valley. We took them to his house in the mountains; he lived in a two-roomed house off the main road, leading to the Pamir highway. Other than the mare, he owned a dozen turkeys and several sheep. The horses were put out to graze in a grassy gorge next to Yesen's potatoes and sunflowers. When she wasn't making tea, his wife spent most of the evening lying down, cradling her stomach. She had been menstruating for over a month and her eyelids were almost white. She described her symptoms; it sounded like the onset of menopause. I offered to take her to the doctor the next day.

The family was jinxed: their eldest son was dropped on his head as an infant and was mentally disabled. Their 9-year-old son, had a pronounced limp. Three years before, he had been severely scalded by a pot of boiling milk. Rolling up his trouser leg, he showed me his war wound, a huge scab behind his knee, which still hadn't healed.

'They operated on it when it happened. There isn't enough skin behind his knee, so it tears open every time he bends his leg. He is always running around, he loves football. It will probably never heal.' In the morning, I took the mother to a gynaecologist, who treated her for menopause and contacted a local aid agency and arranged payment for plastic surgery for her son's leg.

Yesen and I went riding. He took me to his favourite spot and from our vantage point by the river, we looked up a valley which, he assured me with pride, was intensely green in spring. At the bottom of the valley, clusters of trees were wearing their autumn best: brilliant reds, yellows and orange. The gentle slopes gave way to steep, narrow, grassy walls, dotted spruces rising up between two rocky arêtes. It struck me how the hardships he and his family had endured hadn't dented Yesen's dignity. Age hadn't dimmed the evident love between him and his wife. Yesen was testament to how little in life we need to survive. Their uncluttered lives boiled down to the essentials: the companionship of two people, pride in and devotion to their children. Theirs was a proper accommodation between man and nature, untouched by the excesses of consumerism. Their simple, modest, yet dignified existence was in harmony with their stupendous surroundings. The pace of life was as it should be; they lived off the land, the surrounding springs ran clear, and the air was so clean and crisp that you wanted to savour every breath.

Yesen invited me to stay for a few days to watch a pageant to mark the 3000th birthday of the city of Osh. Osh's central stadium looked like the scene of a medieval pageant. The pitch was decorated with a dozen of Kyrgyzstan's finest *yurts*. The regional *ulak* teams were congregating, ready for a parade. Each team was cloaked in squad colours: long imperial-purple capes clashed with orange and turquoise. Golden eagles and falcons perched on many arms. A wizened man, in chain mail and a visor, headed the team from Talas. On a ridge behind the stadium, local residents peered into the stadium from the vantage point of their horses.

As the children warmed up for the horse race, an old man with a shaky voice belted out Kyrgyz ballads on a crackling microphone. Spectators crowded around the commentator's tower, and some weighed up the bloodied carcass of a headless goat which lay in a pool of blood at the foot of the tower. Two bare-chested, flabby men of sumo proportions were demonstrating *urdarysh*, wrestling on horseback, which detracted from the arrival of President Akaev. A few people in the audience began to slow clap him. One wrestler hung over one side of his saddle, all his weight on one stirrup as he yanked at his opponent.

With the president's arrival, one of the main events – the horse race – began. At least thirty horses flew around twelve laps of the track, kicking up sludge until their riders were muddy ghosts with peep-holes for eyes and the spectators were in fits. Suddenly something large flew past me, knocking over a spectator. A young rider had lost control of its horse, which took off into the middle of the hippodrome. As the children circled the track, an aged man with a large golden eagle resting on his arm was hoisted up on a ladder fixed to the back of a truck. Below him an unsuspecting dove was released into the air. It never had a chance. Within a couple of seconds, the eagle was contentedly pecking at it, its huge wings spread out protectively around its prey. Occasionally, it stopped, looked up and puffed out its chest before returning to its meal. The highlight, for some, was a half-drugged fox cub. It stood stationary, dazed by the enormous shadow swooping towards it. The eagle, thinking it was dead already, continued its flightpath over the fox and landed in the audience.

A Kyrgyz man with his eagle at the Osh 3000 celebrations

The horse race came to a crescendo, the young riders flogging their exhausted mounts. It was difficult to tell who had won. The muddy horses and mud-splattered riders were indistinguishable from one another. The winner, a muddy apparition, was paraded, shivering and dazed, in front of the presidential box, by a proud father. They won a Volga: an old-fashioned Russian poor man's saloon, rather like India's Ambassador car.

Finally it was time for the game of Ulak (known more commonly as *bushkashi* in Afghanistan). The umpire hauled up the goat's carcass, securing it under his leg. He charged into the middle of the pitch and dumped it in a muddy puddle in front of the two teams. A rider leaned out of his saddle and scooped it up. It was already slimy and he struggled to pinion it under his leg, his stirruped foot far forward. He managed a few metres before he dropped it. A team-mate charged to the rescue turning his horse in tight circles in an attempt to block his opponent. He stretched down and down and down until only one knee was securing him in his saddle as he struggled to get a grip on the slippery decapitated goat. Resting it on the pommel of his saddle, he began to canter towards his goal. The other players swarmed around him, blocking the path. Suddenly he had a break; with

A headless goat – the 'ball' used in Ulak, Kyrgyz polo

the goat now nestling in his armpit, he charged at his goal, which looked like a large bagel, cushioned on the outside by an assortment of rubber tyres. He threw it over the edge; it sailed over the wide rim and disappeared down the hole. The crowd was ecstatic.

They returned to the scrum, barging horses trampling over the carcass, which had merged with the mud. The umpire ruled a play-off between two horsemen. As his opponent turned blocking circles, the wily horseman from Osh positioned his horse's neck across his opponent's. Turning his horse around, he used his mount's backside to barge his opponent out of the way. Osh had possession to cries of 'eeh' by the commentator followed by 'ay yie yie ya' as it slipped from the rider's grip several paces later.

The opposition took control; as a rider raced towards his goal, he was surrounded, and manoeuvred offside. Activity was soon centred back on Osh's goal; a team member was trying to pick up the straggly goat. He reached over further and further and dived headfirst out of his saddle. Shaking off the worst of the mud, he raced off after his horse, which was making a bee-line for the spectators' tent. A couple of umpires took off after the horse to cheers and whistling from the audience.

As the game continued in the middle, the crowd were distracted by a game of kiss-chase, known as *kyz-kuumai*, on the race-track. A young damsel, her blue silk saddle-blanket fluttering, a purple cape flying behind her, was chasing down the track, whipping her horse. A young man, several lengths behind her, never got close. Had he caught her, he would have been entitled to kiss her. Denied his kiss, he had to suffer the humiliation of a role-reversal. He charged back, desperately clinging on to his peaked hat, the girl in hot pursuit with a whip. As she drew up alongside him, she began flaying him as tradition allowed her to do. His hat flew off and he wrestled to catch it as she flew past.

Kyz-kuumai reflects Kyrgyz wedding traditions; after a formal betrothal has taken place, the groom will ride up to the bride's *yurt* on his horse and literally sweep his bride off her feet and carry her back to his *yurt*. Yesen explained that unfortunately in some of the villages near the Tajik border, the tradition was open to abuse.

'Many of my friends in the smaller villages send their daughters to stay with relatives in Bishkek when they reach puberty. Local gangs have been known to take advantage of our tradition and kidnap our teenage daughters when they are working in the fields and take them home. By the time they are tracked down, they have been robbed of their innocence and no one wants them as a bride. One of my friends managed to stop gangs from taking his daughter several times, but they can turn violent if you try to stop them and they have been known to beat up fathers who try to stop them.'

A game of 'urdarysh' – horseback wrestling at the Osh 3000 celebrations

I was sad to say goodbye to Yesen and very sad to be parting from my faithful four-legged friends which had served me so well. Knowing that the horses were in good hands, I returned to Osh and found a lorry park from which Yesen had assured me that consignments of aid left for the Afghan border via Tajikistan. A group of drivers were sitting on their haunches, chain-smoking while they waited for their grain consignments to leave the warehouse. A few tones above the Turkic strains of the Kyrgyz drivers, I heard a sing-song lilt coming from a couple of mousy Tajik drivers, one of whom had green eyes. I agreed on $5 to ride 728 kilometres across the Pamirs to Khorog.

Ascending mountain after mountain, you at length arrive at a point where you might suppose the surrounding summits to be the highest lands in the world.... So great is the height of the mountains, that no birds are to be seen near their summits. Here there live a tribe of savage, ill-disposed and idolatrous people, who subsist upon the animals they can destroy and clothe themselves with the skins.

Marco Polo on the Pamirs

21

THE ROOF OF THE WORLD

I boarded a lorry bound for Tajikistan driven by Esaubeck, a chunky Kyrgyz who looked like a Tibetan herdsman. Every time he smiled, rows of gold molars winked at me. He had a familiar, jovial manner and seemed trustworthy. The main thing was that he was young and fit enough to cope with the stress, plying the route three times a month.

We set off up the pass. On the steep slopes, the lorry coughed and wheezed and the speedometer quivered at ten kilometres an hour. The orderly collage of Uzbek fields of sunflowers and wheat gave way to *yurts* and small farms. The grass was scorched golden brown and the earth was baked hard. Large carts, pulled by horses and miniature donkeys and piled high with freshly cut grass,

Collecting grass for the winter

creaked along the middle of the road. Preparations for winter were well under way. Grass was piled up on the roofs of the small stone houses with blue window-frames and farmers were preparing haystacks in the fields. Groups of women crouched beside small streams, washing grain and drying it in the sun, ready to make their winter flour. Other women were stooped over rakes, preparing potato patches. Carpets and quilts hung over the edge of white picket fences for their last airing before the winter.

The engine spluttered and died after twenty-five kilometres. Esau grinned nervously and enlisted the help of a couple of drivers along the road. We stopped for the night at the house of a friendly mechanic. He wasn't much use, swaying before us in a vodka-induced haze. Several times in the night, I was shaken awake and offered a shot. Esau was forced to sit up with our host. I finally persuaded him to grab a couple of hours' sleep. It didn't do him much good; within ten minutes of our departure, he was falling asleep at the wheel. An hour later the engine gave up again.

Luckily we had broken down outside the house of a fellow lorry driver. I nodded off to the sounds of tinkering under the bonnet as Esau changed the accumulator. The 'new one' came out of his friend's lorry. As the engine surged to life, I tried to see humour in the situation:

'It reminds me of the joke: "I change my underwear every day. I change with him, he changes with her...."'

Esau looked blank for several seconds and chuckled politely.

Twenty-five kilometres further up the road, it became apparent that the accumulator worked no better in our lorry than it had in its former home, our battery alternately overcharging and then not charging at all. We stopped in yet another village. Esau sat on the bonnet, pretending to do some good, while a couple of Kyrgyz herdsmen did the work. We stopped for a snack at a small roadside café next to the Kyrgyz customs post. A crowd of officers was hanging around on the road. A man was racing up and down in a new Toyota convertible, giving the officers a spin. While most of the heroin leaving Afghanistan crosses the desert into Turkmenistan, the Pamir Highway is also an important conduit. Many of the drivers delivering aid to Afghanistan via Tajikistan were returning to Osh with more lucrative cargo than the wheat and oil that they'd brought in.

As we crawled over a 3,500-metre pass, the rolling grass hills gave way to boulders and scree. As the engine began to overheat, Esau let off steam, driving with the bonnet up, which meant that he could only see the road by hanging out of the door. At the top of the pass, we drove into a wide valley of boggy, high-altitude pasture and grazing yaks. To our south lay the Pamirs, a regiment of 5,000-metre peaks. Peak Lenin glinted imperiously from its 2,000-metre vantage point. Small villages huddled against the sides

Washing grain – Pamiri women preparing for the winter

of the valley. Long black yaks' tails hung from poles in a graveyard, buffeting in the wind over the graves of those who had died with a pure heart.

At mid-morning, Esau announced that we wouldn't be going any further. A slow puncture and our faulty accumulator had put paid to progress. We stayed with a fellow lorry driver, a small roly-poly man with a small moustache and creases for eyes, who lived in a leather jacket. He insisted that vodka stopped him falling asleep at the wheel. Coca Cola and coffee were a poor substitute for Esau, forced into being a party pooper by his pushy English passenger. Our host spent most of the day arguing with his mother, who objected to him drinking the housekeeping. As the vodka began to fuddle his mind, he called on his daughter to show off her command of English. Angry at her stage fright, he succeeded in reducing her to tears. When enough damage was done, he went outside, threw up and ambled off to bed. His understanding wife left a bucket by his bedside, ready for the inevitable.

With the help of a drunken entourage of drivers, Esau managed to get the lorry repaired. Another accumulator appeared out of nowhere. He patched up the hole in the inner tube with sticky black paste and lined the inside of the tyre with pieces of blown-out inner tube. Fifteen minutes into the journey, Esau nodded off, jerking awake as we hit a pothole. I force-fed him Coca-Cola and kept him talking. As we approached the Tajik border, we passed through the first of dozens of check posts, none of which was particularly menacing. At the first post, the guards siphoned off some petrol in exchange for letting us through. At the next post, Kyrgyz soldiers showed me round their bunker and offered me a bullet as a souvenir. They proudly showed off Kyrgyzstan's centrepiece in her border defence, a solitary tank, fit for a museum. Further down the road, I met a few Russians on military service, cursing their luck at being billeted in a converted oil drum in the middle of the Pamirs. Excited by a piece of skirt, a particularly handsome soldier proposed to me. I told him I'd give him my answer on my way back!

Kyrgyz family drying grain

We rattled along the rutted road to Karakul, a large sapphire lake in a denuded moonscape, four thousand metres above the sea-line. Yaks were the only creatures which could survive up there, feeding off clumps of tough grasses and lichen, their shaggy woollen coats protecting them from the icy wind which fell seventy degrees below zero in winter. After hand-ing round our peanuts, the soldiers agreed to let me photograph the lake from their watch-tower. From Karakul, we crawled up the final pass with the bonnet open. I had developed an abscess on one tooth. I could feel my lower gum swelling with every metre we climbed towards the 4,600-metre crest. The altitude, combined with the incessant rattling of the truck, left me in agony. Despite popping three Panadol, I felt no better. We had barely descended a hundred metres when we had a blow out. Two small, skinny boys with dirty, wind-burned faces clambered out of what looked like an abandoned farmhouse and helped Esau change the wheel. Satisfied with his handiwork, Esau put the tyres to the test as he thundered down towards Murgab, barely touching the brakes. Needless to say our puncture returned.

The next night we stayed with a couple of Kyrgyz tradeswomen, who had just got back from a birthday party. They were legless. I couldn't sleep on account of my toothache and watched them take turns to vomit outside, when they were lucky enough to make it. Esau accepted that his tyre was a write-off and went off in search of a new one. We spent the morning looking around dusty small streets, punctuated with hundreds of telegraph poles, which looked like ships' masts. I couldn't understand how the townsfolk could eke a living from the desolate, windswept surroundings.

We were soon hurtling along the road again past a large salt lake. As clouds swept over, the colours deepened: violet, turquoise to deep blue. Some of the surrounding rocks had been split down the centre by seismic

Esaubeck breaking down yet
again on the Pamir Highway

activity, revealing bands of colours: granite, clay and sand, like rings in an old tree. All around us was a high-altitude desert of naked, crumbling rock-faces. Suddenly we witnessed a high-altitude mirage. We cut through a green marshland broken by streams and small lakes, dotted with yaks and Kyrgyz *yurts*. Many Kyrgyz were stranded in Tajikistan when the new borders were drawn. Several thousand Kyrgyz families are scattered throughout the Pamir Valley. In the winter, they retreat to small stone houses with pin-prick windows which keep out the wind. They make a living bartering their yak meat and lake fish for petrol, flour, tea and cigarettes. Unfortunately they can't sell their sheepskins. Demand for Kyrgyz wool, which doesn't meet international standards, has plummeted since the collapse of the Soviet Union. They use what they need for making braids for their *yurts*, jacket linings and throw the rest away.

We stopped for the night in a Pamiri house, which was wooden and open-plan. In the centre was a large pit with a mud floor surrounded by four raised platforms. Five pillars, representing the prophets, supported the roof, which was made of four squares (the elements) stacked diagonally above each other in a star shape, the smallest on top. Each platform had a

A Kyrgyz woman in the Pamirs

purpose; one was the kitchen, while another was reserved for the bride to dress on her wedding day. A small hole in one of the platforms was for storing wood, another for baking bread. Our host, a rather camp engineer, was already tipsy and had eagerly invited three passing lorries and their passengers to stay. Miraculously, vermicelli and potatoes for twenty appeared on the table, along with an assortment of bottles of vodka and home-made wine. After slinging back a few more glasses, he insisted on dancing with me until his father ticked him off and told him to go home to his wife.

The final stretch towards Khorog took us alongside a steep stretch of contiguous landslides. The road was protected in the most vulnerable areas by a series of tunnels; the roof of each was weighed down with boulders. Khorog, a one-street town of 24,000 inhabitants, sits alongside the Gunt River in a narrow valley, flanked by crumbling mountains. The Gunt roars down into the Pyanj, a couple of kilometres away, then winds along the Afghan border until it becomes the Amu Daria or the Oxus. Perched on the hillside, a patchwork of postage-stamp, irrigated fields, some in the path of landslides, others under perilous overhangs, contains wheat and vegetables. Lower down the valley, orchards of mulberries and apples break the line of traditional wooden houses.

The wheat we were carrying was destined for Afghanistan. The worst drought in thirty years was threatening the country with widespread famine. Several days before, the Taliban had taken Taloqan, the political headquarters of the Northern Alliance. Ahmed Shah Masoud, an ethnic Tajik, had withdrawn to the border close to Badakhshan, leaving him with only five per cent of Afghanistan's territory. Aid agencies were concerned that 150,000 Afghans might seek refuge in Tajikistan. Of greater concern was the possibility that the Taliban might try to spread their control into Central Asia. Tajikistan would have been a very good starting point.

It is impossible to look at the history of Uzbekistan, Tajikistan, Afghanistan and Persia in isolation. Under early Saka kingdoms and the rule of Cyrus the Great, all four countries formed part of contiguous empires. They were conquered by the Alexander the Great and the Mongols. Afghan culture flourished under Tamerlane and Babur, who both originated in modern Uzbekistan. Until the Russian Revolution, successive Emirs of Bukhara ruled northern Afghanistan and Tajikistan. The fusion of Turkic nomadic and urban Persian civilization has left its mark. Waves of civilizations have washed up an extraordinary spectrum of tribes, such as the Shiite Hazaras of eastern Afghanistan, supposedly descendants from the Mongols. Uzbeks constitute a quarter of the Tajik population and 1 million Tajiks live in Uzbekistan; 2 million Uzbeks and 4 million Tajiks live in Afghanistan. The

Harvest in the postage-stamp sized fields in the Pamirs

national spectrum of Afghanistan is further coloured with a million
Turkmen and several hundred thousand Kazakhs and Kyrgyz.

The precedent for American and British help to the Mujheddin during
the Afghan War was set fifty years earlier, when the British encouraged
the Basmachi movement in Fergana to take advantage of the fall of the
Tsar and expel the Russian imperialists. The Basmachi set up the
Provisional Kokand Autonomous Government, which was run in accor-
dance with Sharia law, not dissimilar to the demands of the Islamic
Militants' Union today. The Bolsheviks under Marshall Frunze embarked
on a campaign to eradicate the Basmachi. Lenin nominated an Ottoman
Turk, Enver Pasha, to wipe out the Basmachi and use Central Asia as a
bridgehead into India. Enver Pasha defected to the Basmachi and captured
Dushanbe. Sponsored by the King of Afghanistan, he rallied 20,000
Basmachi to his jihad: the creation of a pan-Turkic empire in Central Asia.
However, the movement could not stand up to the might of the Bolshevik
military machine. Enver Pasha was driven back to the Aqsu River, bordering Afghanistan, where he made his last stand. Charging the enemy with
ten bodyguards, his sword drawn, he was easily cut down by the Reds'
machine-gun fire. The Islamic movement in Central Asia was driven
underground. Many of the Basmachi fled to Mazar-e-Sharif in
Afghanistan. During the Afghan War, the Russians colluded with the

Uzbeks to create a cordon sanitaire to prevent Islamic fundamentalism spreading to Central Asia. With aid from Moscow and Tashkent, General Dostum, an Afghan Uzbek, controlled six buffer provinces, preventing the Mujheddin from spreading the conflict northwards.

After the collapse of the Soviet Union, the Islamic Revolutionary Party emerged as a strong force in Tajikistan, winning thirty-four per cent of the vote. Nabiev's Communist Party, which drew its support from the Tajik Uzbeks in Khodjent, refused to accommodate the Islamists in any coalition. The Communist Party took advantage of age-old tribal tensions in Tajikistan, allying itself with the citizens of Kuliab against the pro-Islamic areas of Kurgan Tube and Garm. Karimov, the President of Uzbekistan, threw his weight behind the communists. The Afghans, soon joined by the Iranians and Pakistani Jamiat-e-Islami, supported their Muslim brothers. Both Masoud and his rival Gulbuddin Hikmetyar helped to arm and train the Islamic Revolutionary Party.

The war escalated. Yeltsin ordered 10,000 extra Russian troops to be deployed on the Afghan border in the hope of keeping Afghan subversion out. The communists freed 300 hardened Kuliabi prisoners and turned them on the people of Kurgan Tube. The conflict spread to Dushanbe. Led by Sanjak Safarov, who had spent twenty-three years in prison for murder, the Kuliabis seized four tanks and began a pogrom of murder, rape, extortion and torture resulting in 5,000 deaths, including many Pamiris who had no connection with the conflict. Aided by Uzbek helicopter gunships and CIS troops, the new President, Rakhmanov, a communist from Kuliab, succeeded in flushing out the Islamic Revolutionary Party. But the civil war continued to rage until 1997.

Fear of the Taliban, who had conquered much of northern Afghanistan, brought the Islamic Revolutionary Party to the negotiating table. The Deobandi strand of Islam, promulgated by the Taliban, is at odds with Central Asia's traditions of Sufism, which combines Islam with older nomadic traditions of animism and mysticism. An agreement, brokered by Russia and the UN, was reached in July 1997. Sporadic fighting still continues around Garm. The civil war resulted in 50,000 deaths and created 500,000 internal refugees, ten per cent of the population.[36]

Ironically, the tables had turned again. Masoud was now receiving aid from the Russians via the Kuliab airbase. Dostum, who had switched sides several times, had now joined forces with his arch-enemy, Masoud. Uzbekistan's President Karimov had continued to repress Islam at home. His stringent laws, which punish the growth of beards and women wearing the veil, had driven the Uzbek Islamic movement into the arms of the extremists. The Islamic Militants' Union, under Juman Namangani, continued the Basmachi cause, seeking the creation of an Islamic state in Fergana based on Sharia law. Trained in camps in Afghanistan and funded by Osama bin Laden, they had launched a series of invasions of Kyrgyzstan and Uzbekistan, which had almost reached Tashkent.

Esau dropped me in the main street and I went off in search of accommodation. A petite, blue-eyed woman named Nina, who worked for one of the NGOs, invited me to stay in her apartment. She was half-Greek and half-Russian; her mother lived in Kurgan Tube. We sat in her dining area, on a raised platform, watching women collecting water from the Gunt River and sipping tea sweetened with generous spoons of condensed milk.

'It is terrible. We live ten metres from a huge river and yet we don't even have cold water. Every day I have to collect water from the river in buckets.'

Occasionally, the water would come on and all the residents of the apartment would fill up every receptacle within reach.

'Do you like working here?'

'Yes but I miss my mother, she is ill; I wish I could be near her but it is no longer safe for me in Kurgan Tube. The Kuliabis took our home and they killed many of my friends. One day a group of Kuliabis stopped in my neighbourhood. They said they were looking for Pamiris. My neighbour said he was a Pamiri so they took him away and shot him. He was such a nice man; whenever the water was cut off, he would always invite people to take water from his well.'

That evening, Nina laid out some quilts on the floor next to her bed.

'Do you mind if I read for a while,' she asked.

'Not at all. What are you reading?'

'The Bible. Have you read it?'

'Yes. But I don't like some bits of it. The Old Testament is shocking in places.'

'Don't you believe in God?'

'Sometimes I wish I believed in God but I can never quite bring myself to. I don't like institutionalized religion. Too many wars have been fought because religious leaders have manipulated the masses.'

'You should believe in him. He loves you very much. He gave his life for us. I will pray for you. Believe me, God will save you. He saved me.'

'What did he do?'

'He saved me from a terrible man.'

'How?'

'I was walking down a side-street with my mother. A Kuliabi commander followed us. He held a gun to my head and began to rip at my clothes. My mother was screaming; I was frightened she would be next. I saw a

*Pamiri village on the way
to Lake Saryez*

bright light and I heard an explosion. His gun was in my hand and he was dead. I don't remember what happened.'

'God must be a great comfort to you.'

'He killed the man; he saved me. Now it is my job to help others.'

Nina refused to take any money for rent. I went to the local bazaar in search of goodies to stock her cupboards. The Tajiks were trading their surplus vegetables for flour, rice, vodka, beer, cigarettes, cheap Chinese clothes and electronics from Osh. Many of the women were very beautiful, their thin faces, wide eyes (often blue or green) and Roman noses were testament to their Indo-European descent. Their dress, bright *kurtas*, shot with gold thread and matching headscarves, could easily deceive one into believing they are quite well-off. The average salary was $4 per month.

I spent a fruitless morning trying to persuade the head of the KGB to let me visit the source of the Pyanj, which rises in the Wakhan corridor. The

Russians had stepped up security on the Afghan border in response to Taliban successes in northern Afghanistan. It was off-limits. A small fault in my paperwork was a good pretext to send me packing. I decided to climb up to Lake Saryez instead. In the middle of the night in 1911 a powerful earthquake swept a village down the mountainside, plugging the Bartang River with twelve square kilometres of loose earth and rocks. Formerly grazing ground, the natural dam now contained twenty-three cubic kilometres of water, half the volume of Lake Geneva. Geologists were petrified that the landslide might not be able to contain Lake Saryez. Huge scars along the bare, rocky cliffs beside the lake, warned of further landslides. Recently, one such landslide had caused a fifteen-metre tidal wave at one end of the lake. Luckily, by the time the wave reached the dam, it was only two metres high. While I was there, geologists were monitoring a large, unstable overhang which, if it fell, could generate a tidal wave 150 metres high. If that happened, the natural dam would burst and the floodwaters would rush down the Bartang valley, thunder into the Pyanj and the Amu Daria and on to the Aral Sea, potentially drowning 5 million people in its path.

The road up to Lake Saryez, in places barely wider than our Jeep, sliced through bedrock and boulders, switching over fragile wooden bridges and hanging over the white horses of the Bartang River. We wound through many villages struggling to eke a living. A mosaic of plots the size of tennis courts, strewn with boulders or hanging on to the sides of mountains, were shared between several families. Every bridge that we crossed seemed to be financed by the Mountain Villages Support Programme, an arm of the Aga Khan Foundation.

The Aga Khan, an English-speaking, Swiss-born, horse-breeder is a strange hero for the Ismaeli people, tucked in a far corner of the Pamirs. He is a direct descendant of the twelfth Caliph of Egypt, whose offspring founded the ancient terrorist organization, the Assassins. In 1094, a schism had developed in the Egyptian Fatimid dynasty over who should succeed the deceased Caliph of Cairo. The defeated candidate Nizar, left Egypt, escaping to the castle of Alamut in the Alburz Mountains in northern Persia, near the Caspian Sea. From the safety of his 'eagle's nests', high in the mountains, the cult of the Assassins or Hashashins began. Hasan i Sabah, also known as Aladdin, persuaded atheists and Sunnis to join the sect. Aladdin drugged young men with hashish. When they awoke, they were in a beautiful garden, which they assumed was Eden. Drugged again, they woke up in the real world. The only way back to Paradise was through successful assassination trips. Recently, parallels have been drawn between the Assassins and Al Qa'eda: even at that time, rulers were at a loss as to how to fight a movement whose chief weapon was the suicide mission. It is

said that a group tried to murder Edward I of England. The Mongols are
supposed to have foiled an attempt on the Great Khan's life by four
hundred 'assassins' and decided to eliminate them. Edward Gibbon wrote
that the Mongols rendered mankind a great service by eliminating the sect.
To destroy their strongholds high in the mountains, the Mongols hired
thousands of teams of Chinese engineers to manufacture siege machines
capable of firing huge boulders, which had to be lugged up the mountains.
Those who survived the Mongol onslaught gave up their terrorist beliefs.
Some settled in the Pamirs, others continued down to India and on to West
Africa. Ismaelis now straddle the Wakhan corridor, living in the frontier
areas of China, Pakistan, Tajikistan and Uzbekistan and clinging to a small
branch of Shia Islam in an otherwise overwhelmingly Sunni region.[37]

At intervals, we picked up villagers along the road. Men and women, who
normally walk the seventy kilometres in one stretch, got in and out of our
Jeep with various bundles: half a cow, a Pamiri songbird, which is worth a
fortune in the local market, sacks of flour and many wives' tales, including
one about the lake.

'A traveller, possibly Allah in disguise, was looking for shelter in the
Saryez Valley. Due to his ragged appearance, he was turned away from
many homes. A humble woman, with four eggs and a chicken to her name,

The author resting on the long haul up to Lake Saryez

took him in and offered to cook her chicken. Refusing any food, he told her to take a carpet and her chicken, climb to the top of the nearest mountain and wait until morning. When she woke, the valley was flooded and her village was under water.'

On the final stretch to the lake, we left our jeep as the path had narrowed to the width of our miniature donkey, which trod steadily along vertiginous overhangs and landslides and leapt from boulder to boulder like a chamois. At one stage, it got too much even for the donkey. The precipitous, rubble-strewn path became steep enough to justify a ladder. Shouldering the baggage, I clambered on all fours between boulders which shielded us from vertiginous falls, kicking up dust as gravel gave beneath my feet. The owner of the donkey staggered up behind me, his shoulder pressed into its backside as it skated on the shale.

I was exhausted by the time we reached the top but the exercise wasn't over yet. We had to row into the wind for half an hour across a small section of the lake to a solitary hut, which housed the park wardens. One of the wardens used to live in Afghanistan. He had walked through the Pamirs into Tajikistan. Two of his party never made it; wolves had picked them off on a night march.

At daybreak I wandered down to the lake. Waves danced on seventy miles of deep, inviting aquamarine and the wind stirred up the dust on desolate, disintegrating rusty rockfaces. From a distance, avalanches of rocks, which had been pummelled to dust, looked like patches of snow. I tried to pick my way over the landslide around the lake, hugging huge buttresses, which leaned out at forty-five degree angles over the water. Rocks which looked like promising anchors, crumbled in my hands. The only way around the lake was along the tops of the denuded mountains. Huge scars criss-crossed the cliffs waiting for the next earthquake to dislodge thousands of tonnes of rock into the lake, threatening to create the greatest tsunami ever seen inland. In each direction the icy summits of large, jagged saw-toothed peaks glinted in the distance.

A group of Russian geologists invited me for a spin around the lake in their dinghy. They were there to monitor the perilous overhangs and any seismic activity in the area. They had moved all their equipment, including the dinghy, up by donkey and lived off the land. They had recently shot a Marco Polo sheep; we lunched on meatballs and stew.

We set off down the mountain much later than we had planned. The donkeyman went the long way round and I rowed across the lake with the park warden. On the other side, the night was closing in rapidly as we ran at break-neck speed. I stopped to adjust my shoes. Two enormous water blisters had formed on my left foot and I was soon limping badly. The warden kept up a good pace while I limped behind. I could feel the skin breaking around the blisters. Soon it was dark and my eyes strained to adjust as we tried to make out the tiny track hanging above the river, which rumbled far beneath us. At times, I could make out the silvery trail in the moonlight. Occasionally the moon disappeared behind a mountain and I had to resort to my head torch. Vertigo and paralysing paranoia reduced me to scrambling on all fours where I thought there were steep drops. The warden tried to calm me down, but my heart continued to pound for two hours as we felt our way along the cliffs. Finally we spotted lights in the distance but it took another hour to find the right path down to the village.

Later that week, Nina invited me to a Tajik wedding in Khorog's only restaurant. Although superficial elements of the wedding were western cliché, the spirit was definitely Tajik. The bride, dressed in a white wedding-dress, sat with her husband at the far end of the restaurant. Two tables of guests lined each side, while the middle was left open for dancing. Ismaelis don't hide their women under a *burka*. The single women, wearing bright pantaloons and floral scarves danced in small groups, their friends clapping along as they twirled around snaking their arms and shaking their hips in time with the music. Occasionally a group danced in unison up to the top table to pay their respects. The bride and groom stood up to receive each approach but were otherwise rather cut off from the merrymaking. The bride looked downcast.

'She isn't marrying for love,' Nina explained. 'He is a kind man and she is frightened of being left on her own.' There was very little alcohol circulating and what was around seemed to be circulating in our corner. I managed to swig a couple of shots for Dutch courage before being dragged off into the centre of the room to dance with a group of women. A confident woman in a fawn suit showed me how to dance, twisting and swooping like a swallow. After a few dances, we went out on to the balcony to cool off. It took a couple of sentences to scratch beneath the veneer of self-confidence and find a typical Tajik tragedy.

'Are you Pamiri?'

'No, I am from Kulyan Tube. I am a refugee. The Kuliabis took our house and I escaped to Khorog with my husband and three children.'

'Is your husband here?'

'No. I don't know where he is today and I don't care. He is an addict and he has robbed us of all our savings.' She began to cry.

'When I married him, he was a sweet, gentle man. A few years ago, the dealers started to give away heroin. When they had enough addicts, they began to charge; it is a good way of recruiting smugglers. It is hard to earn enough money in the bazaar to feed my children. My husband is always asking for money.'

'He still lives with you?'

'I cannot turn him away. He would die on the street. He is my husband. I loved him once.'

In 1998, 200 kilos of heroin, worth $300 million, were seized on the Afghan border. Despite heavy policing from Russian troops, every day one tonne of heroin was crossing the border.

A young man called Dima whom I met at the post office gave me a guided tour of Khorog's museum. He whizzed me past blown-up bladders used to ford rivers, wooden household utensils, saddles, and communist memorabilia and dawdled in front of the semi-precious stones.

'That is lapis. Over the Chinese border near Murgab, the ground is strewn with lapis. It is difficult to get to it. Two hundred kilometres before the official border, the Chinese have built a huge electric fence. Many soldiers patrol the area but nomads can still cross the border. I have friends who can smuggle me in. I have to support my family.' He wrote to me some months later; arrested at the border, he had spent three months in prison.

As we left the museum, he bumped into a friend. They locked fingers in the air, each kissing the outside of the other's hand in the briefest embrace.

A Pamiri greeting. Dima greets a friend in Khorog, Tajikistan

In repayment for my tour, I bought him lunch. Over a stringy steak and a plate of cold chips in Khorog's premier restaurant, he told me that 7,000 people in Tajikistan died because of honey.

'Honey?' I asked incredulously, convinced that my Russian was failing me.

'Yes, honey. A man went into the bazaar with his cat to buy some honey. He asked the stall owner if he could have a taste. While he was trying it, he spilled a drop. His hungry cat licked it up. The stall owner's jealous dog attacked the cat and killed it. 'You killed my cat,' the customer shouted. 'I will kill your dog in return.' The vendor, enraged by the sight of his dead dog, killed his customer. A brawl ensued....' Dima was sure that the story was true. He couldn't remember in what paper he had read it.

> And the first grey of morning fill'd the east,
> And the fog rose out of the Oxus stream ...
> ... Through the black Tartar tents he pass'd, which stood
> Clustering like bee-hives on the low flat strand
> Of Oxus, where the summer-floods o'erflow
> When the sun melts the snows in high Pamere;
> Through the black tents he pass'd, o'er that low strand,
>
> ... The sun by this had risen, and clear'd the fog ...
> From the broad Oxus and the glittering sands.
> And from their tents the Tartar horsemen filed
> Into the open plain ...
>
> ...First, with black sheep-skin caps and with long spears;
> Large men, large steeds, who from Bokhara come
> And Khiva, and ferment the milk of mares.
> Next, the more temperate Toorkmuns of the south,
> The Tukas, and the lances of Salore,
> And those from Attruck and the Caspian sands;
> Light men and on light steeds, who only drink
> The acrid milk of camels, and their wells.
> And then a swarm of wandering horse, who came
> From far, and a more doubtful service own'd;
> The Tartars of Ferghana, from the banks
> Of the Jaxartes, men with scanty beards
> And close-set skull-caps; and those wilder hordes
> Who roam o'er Kipchak and the northern waste,
> Kalmucks and unkempt Kuzzaks, tribes who stray

Nearest the Pole, and wandering Kirghizzes,
Who come on shaggy ponies from Pamere;
These all filed out from camp into the plain.
And on the other side the Persians form'd –
First a light cloud of horse, Tartars they seem'd,
The Ilyats of Khorassan, and behind,
The royal troops of Persia, horse and foot,
Marshall'd battalions bright in burnish'd steel....

Matthew Arnold, 'Sohrab and Rustum', *Poems*, 1853

22

TURKMENISTAN

There was a growing chill in the air and I could feel that winter was approaching. With some reluctance, I left Nina and made my way back across Uzbekistan to the Turkmen border. Before I crossed the border, I stopped in Khiva. The city was deserted save for a small wedding party. The bride, dressed in a white wedding dress posed for photos under the stumpy Kaltan Minaret. Designed to be the largest in Central Asia, its progress was foreshortened when under the tsar's orders, its patron, Madamin Khan, was executed by a band of Turkmen. I wandered around the mausolea, admiring the rich variety of motifs, including many taboo vegetal and floral patterns. Outside the thick, clay walls, a group of old men in long white shirts, baggy trousers and black boots were gossiping outside a mosque after lunchtime prayers. A strong wind was blowing dark clouds over the sun, which occasionally broke through for long enough to illuminate the yellow and green tiles of the Kok Minaret. From the top of the Islom-Huja Minaret, the sun cast black shadows over the black sands of the Karakum.

The Turkmen settled in the Karakum desert from the Altaic region in the tenth and eleventh centuries. The Turkmens' ancestors are the Oguz tribes that moved west in the tenth century and eventually settled in Iran and Anatolia. The Turkmen are highly tribal and these divisions, Teke, Yamud and Ersari, still play an important part in politics today. The Teke tribe is the most powerful; its members dominated the communist party élite and still eclipse other tribes in the government ranks today. Limited grazing and water continuously brought them into conflict with other tribes and made them more tempted to plunder the wealth of neighbouring sedentary people. As trade along the Silk Route declined, Khivan khans began to trade in slaves, snatched by Turkmen raiding parties. In the nineteenth century alone, they captured over a million Persian slaves and sold them in the markets of Bukhara and Khiva. The khans of Khiva not only encouraged the trade in slaves but also in enemy heads. Raiders were rewarded with golden robes, graded twelve, twenty and forty-head robes, depending on how many heads rolled out of the sacks in front of the Khan. Like their Mongolian forbears, the Turkmen's strength was based on their blitzkrieg tactics as desert horsemen. The desert was their weapon and when outnumbered, they drew their prey into the sands. Their horses, named after the biggest tribe, the Akhal Tekke, were believed to sweat blood. It is only appropriate that Alexander the Great's famous horse Bucephalus was an Akhal Tekke.

The Turkmen made a fatal mistake when they began to trade in Russian slaves. Not only did this cause uproar among civilians in Russia but it also gave the Russian army the excuse they were looking for to expand southwards towards India. However, the Turkmen cavalry was not a pushover; the first punitive expedition, launched in 1877 under Lomakin, ended in Russian humiliation. Determined to avoid disgrace, General Skobelev built a light railway to transport a terrifying array of artillery to the area. The Turkmen, armed with a solitary smooth-bore, captured rifles, and razor-sharp sabres, never stood a chance. The Russian artillery blasted through the earth walls of Geok Teppe. As the military bands struck up, they stormed the city, massacring 6,500 people within the walls and at least eight thousand without. According to a witness, 'They lay in rows like freshly mown hay, as they had been swept down by the *mitrailleuses* and cannon.' For years to come, the Turkmen prostrated themselves on hearing a military band begin to play.[38]

The Turkmen were not the only ones making people 'disappear'. Even the *caravanserais*, lodgings for travelling merchants, were not safe. Khoja Khan, an innkeeper, dispensed with over four hundred of his guests with his tarantula brandy. Tarantulas were sealed in jars with pieces of apple and apricot. The irate arachnoids injected their venom into the fruit, which was then distilled into a poisonous potion, which paralysed its victims. A pet bear, trained to savour human flesh, cleared up the evidence. When Khoja was finally caught, he suffered a fitting death. He was tied to a couple of incandescent camels, whose bottoms had been stuffed with chillies. His body was scattered across the sands![39]

At dusk, I crossed the Turkmen border. The border guard, who shared a birthday with me, didn't seem to care that I didn't have a special permit for Dashoguz. The border-post was littered with dozens of posters of the president, Niyazov. Underneath a picture of a fat man trying to smile, a slogan says: '*Halk, Watan, Turkmenbashi.* The people, the nation, Turkmenbashi.'

Niyazov was the communists' idea of a perfect leader. Like Karimov, he was orphaned; both his parents died in a devastating earthquake in 1948, which killed 110,000 people in Ashkabad and only left the statues of Lenin,

Pushkin and the high school for girls standing. He was therefore brought up in a communist orphanage. Brainwashed from childhood, he remained steadfastly loyal to Moscow. When Turkmenistan found itself independent, Niyazov could be accused of taking Stalin as a role model. Banning all opposition, he finally conceded to elections in 1992 and promised to transform Turkmenistan into a Central Asian Kuwait. So far, the dream has failed; Turkmenistan has no outlet to the West for its gas. In a recent election, he allocated himself 99.5% of the vote, perhaps deciding that the half of a per cent of the votes he failed to get were calculated to represent those too infirm to make it to the polling station. Confident of his popularity, he has awarded himself divine status; in Ashkabad, a rotating twelve-metre golden statue of Turkmenbashi, built atop a seventy-five-metre tripod, welcomes the sun in the east and bids it farewell in the west. Since I left, he has arbitrarily changed the days of the week, the months of the year, naming January 'Turkmenbashi', and has banned right-hand-drive cars from all motorways!

In Dashoguz, I tracked down the office of an American water project. The boss, Syrdar, was a handsome Turkmen whose face combined strong, aquiline Turkish features with high cheekbones and slightly oriental eyes. He kindly offered to help me to find a guide and some camels. He suggested I travel west to Turkmenbashi to track down the Charvak people, nomads who tend their camels and goats at the fringe of the Karakum Desert.

On the way to Turkmenbashi, I made a detour to Konye Urgench. Known as Gurganj, it was the undisputed centre of the Islamic world in the eleventh century. Subjugated by the Seljuks, it continued to flourish as a trading centre on the principal caravan routes. It became the seat of the Khorezm Empire, which by the reign of Muhammad II, extended to Iraq, Azerbaijan, Ghazna and Transoxiana. Its heyday was short-lived. After the fall of Bukhara, Genghis Khan sent a detachment to Khorezm commanded by his two sons Chagatay and Jochi, who captured the heavily fortified town street by street. Its inhabitants were driven out and those who were not artisans or fit for slaves were massacred. They destroyed a dam on the outskirts and flooded the area.[40]

Two hundred years later, the city was once more threatened, this time by Tamerlane. The Gurganj's khan, Yusuf Sufi, challenged Tamerlane to a duel but never showed up to fight. Tamerlane let bygones be bygones and sent the khan a fine melon on a gold platter. The khan gave the platter to the gatekeeper and threw the melon in the moat. Like his forbears, Tamerlane razed the city to the ground and ordered that barley be grown on the site. It is a miracle that anything survived.

The half-covered turquoise conical cupolas of Sultan Tekesh and Fakhr ad-Din dignify an open, arid plain. The earth is strewn with the remnants of the Mongol and subsequent Timurid destructions. Walking past the stump of an eleventh-century minaret amid the fragments of bone, pottery and pale-blue glaze, I could almost hear the rumble of the hordes. Inside the various mausolea, rows of tagged fragments were waiting to be pieced together. The minaret, the highest in Central Asia, was tilting to one side and in danger of losing its top. The Russians did a quick fix, coating the outside in concrete, covering the bands of stylized Kufic. A British team is painstakingly removing the cement. In a cross-section of the citadel, one of the thousands of skeletons mown down by Timur was on display where the unfortunate victim fell. On top of the citadel, a small square of earth was dotted with thousands of miniature cradles, lovingly sewn by a succession of infertile women praying for children.

A fertility prayer – miniature cribs sewn by infertile women at the citadel at Gurganj

A burly man, called Kootlebai, with a head of thick unruly black curls and a large moustache, greeted me at the office in Turkmenbashi and offered his services as my fixer. After dining on *plov*, he proudly showed me pictures of his former life; he was Turkmenistan's answer to Houdini. The photos depicted a youthful Kootlebai lying on a bed of nails with six men standing on a board balanced on his chest, bouncing thirty-kilo weights off his belly and bending steel bars with his teeth.

Before heading off to the Charvak settlement, I filled up my canisters at the American-sponsored de-salinization plant as there was no drinkable water in Turkmenbashi. Every day, a large tanker did the rounds, distributing five-litre rations per person. Like many villages in the Amu Daria delta, it had suffered the effects of years of over-irrigation and abuse of pesticides, herbicides and defoliants including Agent Orange and DDT. That year there had been no rainfall. Most of the crops had failed. Irrigating the grey Turkmen soil is an art form; too much water will cause the salt to rise to the surface by capillary action. In the worst-case scenario, the land can be reduced to a salt marsh where only saltwort will grow. Water experts generally hold that cotton growers are using two to three times more water than they need. Once the fourth biggest inland sea, the water level in the Aral Sea has shrunk by sixty per cent since 1960. That year marked a step-up in the production of cotton. Much of the new production was targeted in arid areas unsuitable for cotton production, requiring massive irrigation. For twelve years, the Syr Daria didn't make it to the Aral Sea. The problem now lies with the Amu Daria: Turkmenistan's 1,400-kilometre Karakum canal robs the Amu Daria of its water, much of which evaporates in the desert.

The Charvak settlement lay at the foot of the sharp cliffs of the Ustyurt plateau, which marks the end of the steppe and the beginning of the desert. To protect this route from Turkmen raiders, the Khorezmians built a band of fortifications, signal towers and small forts along the whole of the plateau. Kootlebai gave me a historical tour with a difference. He wasn't sure of the historical significance of the fortifications and hurried me along to the tomb of the eighteen-metre man. Local legend says that the giant built a nearby mausoleum in one night, carrying the stones from the Red Sea. Kootlebai showed me shells embedded in the stonework which he said, 'prove' that the stone came from the Red Sea. The tomb lies on the top of the cliffs, looking out over sand, scree and salt flats, the seemingly limitless Karakum, merging with a hazy sky. Below the cliffs, I could make out the Charvak settlement: several herds of pin-prick camels, a cluster of small adobe houses, with *yurts* standing at their sides.

The Charvak are no longer real nomads. In the spring, their possessions stay at home and they move their animals to desert pastures. In the autumn the animals return home and live on fodder throughout the winter. As we drove into the village, the women and children scampered inside houses which echoed with nervous laughter. Later the women emerged, concealing their faces with the corner of their veils. Kootlebai's contact welcomed us into his house. A short man, he had a wispy moustache, pointed grey beard and thick creases around his eyes, burnt in by the sun. He was wearing a *telpek*, a large black astrakhan wool hat, whose dreadlocks added several inches to his height, and a huge sheepskin coat, known as an *ichmek*.

Sand formation or possibly a ruin on the fringes of the Karakum Desert

While, in the West, our inclination is to take off clothes when it is hot, the Turkmen dress warmly and the huge astrakhan hat protects the head from the heat.

We sat cross-legged on carpets round a plastic mat, which was soon covered with the local fare: rancid butter, unleavened bread and watermelon jam. His wife placed a *dalla*, a round-bottomed silver jug which the Turkmen call a *kunduk*, on to a ring on the mudbrick stove. The base was submerged in the fire. While the water boiled, Kootlebai explained our purpose and translated the reply.

'People are too frightened to travel by camel. These days, the herdsmen use motorbikes. Camels are raised for their milk and meat.'

'Surely the village *aksakals* [white beards] know the desert.'

'Yes but they don't know the way to Ashkabad. They only know the way to the next village on the fringes of the desert. Only the young lorry drivers know the way to Ashkabad.'

'If he knows the way to the next village, that is fine. If my guide doesn't know the whole route to Ashkabad, he can ask. My main concern is to have a guide, preferably an *aksakal*, who knows the desert.' After a while, we were joined by another man, almost indistinguishable from our host save for a black patch on his hat. 'We would want to travel together.'

Sand dunes in the Karakum Desert

It sounded optimistic. Like Tweedledum and Tweedledee, the short tubby men sat cross-legged, discussing the route and occasionally breaking into fits of conspiratorial laughter as they rediscovered their youth.

'There are only two camels in the village capable of such a journey. The rest do not know how to sit on command.'

'Who owns the camels?'

'Another man. He is coming later. He knows the way.'

Suddenly negotiations began to slip back.

'I don't want to get a sore arse. I am an old man. With nothing to eat for two weeks, I will get bony legs. Why not go by lorry?' asked Black Patch.

'Because it is cheating.'

'It is too far.'

'It is only five hundred kilometres.'

After further discussions about procuring a lorry to return the camels, Black Patch agreed to be my guide. The conversation turned to money. Black Patch began flicking his teacup impatiently.

'What if one of the camels dies? Who will pay for it?' asked Black Hat.

'I will pay for any camels that die,' I replied.

'Red Nose is two hundred and fifty kilometres from here. It is the first settlement you will come to,' said Tweedledum.

'Is that the first water we will come to?' I asked.

'There are many wells on the way, but we don't know if they will be full or not,' explained Kootlebai.

'It is very dangerous,' said Tweedledee.

'What is very dangerous?' I asked him.

'The desert. We need good canisters to carry water,' explained Tweedledum.

'I have very good German canisters.'

The conversation changed tack.

'He's frightened of going to Ashkabad with you,' said Black Hat.

'Why?'

'You might murder him.'

'He might murder me.'

Taking a break from negotiations, I asked to try some camel milk. It was a little watery, much less creamy than cow's milk and had a slightly sharp after-taste. As I was sipping the milk, a dignified man joined us. His beard looked like a huge white apron, which had been stuck on. He was wearing a black *ichmek*, trimmed with red brocade and a 'rasta' hat which the Turkmen call a *telpek*. I felt as though I was part of a fancy dress parade. He had never met a European before, although a Russian man had visited the village in Soviet times.

Tweedledee – my would-be guide with his son

Finally another man with a long grey goatee beard appeared, wearing a grey summer-suit, a black waistcoat and his regulation *telpek* tresses. As the owner of the two camels, he decided that he would only let his camels go to Ashkabad with the man with the apron beard; Tweedledum and Tweedledee were now out of the running. Having scotched the other men's chances, white beard and goatee rapidly lost enthusiasm; Apron Beard didn't seem too keen and grey goatee said he could only lend one of his camels to me.

The sun was setting as we left the house. A hundred camels trotted past, kicking up the pink evening sands. Their young cantered to keep up, stretching out their long necks as they moved. They were herded into pens near the village well. I insisted we try our luck at a farm in a neighbouring settlement where a no-nonsense, short man, dwarfed by a huge sheepskin greeted us at the door. He had a podgy face, a shaven head, mostly hidden by a small *telpek*, and a pointed grey goatee. Durgmoot claimed that he owned the two camels over which we were negotiating that afternoon. Kootlebai explained what I was looking for and how much I was willing to pay. Without any hesitation, Durgmoot said yes, provided that we leave immediately as his daughter was getting married in three weeks and he needed to be back for the wedding.

> ... Afrasiab's cities only, Samarcand,
> Bokhara, and lone Khiva in the waste,
> And the black Toorkmun tents; and only drunk
> The desert rivers, Moorghab and Tejend,
> Kohik, and where the Kalmuks feed their sheep,
> The northern Sir; and this great Oxus stream,
> The yellow Oxus, by whose brink I die ...
> ... But the majestic river floated on,
> Out of the mist and hum of that low land,
> Into the frosty starlight, and there moved,
> Rejoicing, through the hush'd Chorasmian waste,
> Under the solitary moon; – he flow'd
> Right for the polar star, past Orgunjè,
> Brimming, and bright, and large; then sands begin
> To hem his watery march, and dam his streams,
> And split his currents; that for many a league
> The shorn and parcell'd Oxus strains along
> Through beds of sand and matted rushy isles–
> Oxus, forgetting the bright speed he had
> In his high mountain-cradle in Pamere,

A foil'd circuitous wanderer – till at last
The long'd-for dash of waves is heard, and wide
His luminous home of waters opens, bright
And tranquil, from whose floor the new-bathed stars
Emerge, and shine upon the Aral Sea.

Matthew Arnold, 'Sohrab and Rustum', *Poems*, 1853

23

THE BLACK SANDS

Durgmoot's house was a flurry of activity ahead of his daughter's wedding. In accordance with local traditions, the neighbourhood women were helping with the preparations. They had come with an assortment of dishes ranging from meat, sweets, to soggy *millefeuille*, which tasted like fried leather, to give to the men. All the guests kept touching the parcel containing the *millefeuille* and passing their hands over their face, muttering prayers. Many of the women in the room kept their faces covered.

The Turkmen still make carpets; many decorated the sides of the *yurt*, with tassels hanging off the bottom. Durgmoot's daughter was making carpets, an essential part of her dowry. Working quickly, she laid out patterns of coloured wool in concentric circles on a large reed mat. As in Mongolia, the mats are sprayed with water, rolled up and dragged along the ground until the wool is matted together. Durgmoot said that she could make two carpets an hour.

Some time later, Durgmoot showed us into his *yurt* to finalize our arrangements. Although similar in shape, Turkmen *yurts* are quite different from those in the steppe. The main priority is keeping out the sand and flies and consequently, the outside wall is constructed with long woven reeds, which the Turkmen call *kamesh*. There is no need for any layers of felt, as the *yurt* is mainly used in the summertime. A small piece of canvas is drawn over the wheel, which has its own signature pattern. As we sat cross-legged on a Turkmen carpet, the midday sun streamed throughout the half-open roof at the top of the *yurt*, casting a reflection of the crossed canes and spokes of the wheel on the baked earth floor.

Durgmoot readily agreed to $150 plus $50 rental for each camel. I also undertook to pay for a lorry to return the camels from Ashkabad. Durgmoot explained that time was of the essence and warned me at the outset that we would have to walk for eight hours a day and would be rationed to an hour's lunchbreak. As we talked, his son carried bundles of saxaul to the hearth near the door. Within a few minutes, a warm fire was burning and tea was ready. Durgmoot had killed a small astrakhan lamb in

Inside a Turkmen yurt

our honour. Once the fire had burnt out, the ashes were swept up off the baked clay floor and carried outside. To keep me warm on desert evenings, I bought a canary yellow Turkmen sheepskin coat from Durgmoot's wife. It was made from seven sheepskins cured with yoghurt, milk and salt, mixed with a local stone, which dyed it bright yellow. That night we camped on the fringes of the desert, where Durgmoot and his son looked after 850 goats belonging to the village. They took turns guarding the sheep, living in a converted train-carriage in the dunes.

Durgmoot was an early riser and woke me at seven. It was cold, drizzling and a thick mist hung over the desert. We couldn't find the camels. Durgmoot was in his travelling gear: baggy trousers and a long jacket which covered his hands but not his stumpy fingers. The mist finally lifted at ten and we discovered that the camels had been grazing less then a hundred metres away. Not wasting any time, Durgmoot set to work preparing the camels. He made a makeshift saddle, rolling up a long felt carpet into a ring and securing it with string. Grabbing the rope attached to the Bactrian's nose-ring, he tugged hard making loud clearing noises in the back of his throat. Bellowing, it sank on to its front knees, rocking on to its back legs, where it sat chewing the cud. He fitted the ring over the two-humped Bactrian. In the centre of the ring he placed a small mat, to protect the humps. Durgmoot decided I should ride the other camel, a dromedary. Luckily it had a saddle and a small wooden yoke for grip. We draped the saddle-bags over the saddles; he didn't bother tying them down. He joined the two twenty-litre canisters with a piece of rope and draped them over his saddle.

'Do we need this water?' He pointed to the other twenty litres.

'Yes, please.'

I sat astride my camel, which was now so wide that I was practically doing the splits. Without warning it straightened its back legs, lurched forward, throwing me over its neck, and groaned as it heaved itself off its front knees into a standing position. Durgmoot lay on his camel's backside, whipping it with a stick and shouting, 'hoo, hoo'. When it was upright, he scrambled up the back and knelt in the saddle.

We set off at a bruising pace, under an overcast heavy sky, heading southwest along a series of tracks in the sand. Durgmoot rode ahead, swaying with the motion of his camel, whistling and crying 'hoo, choo' and tapping it with a stick. A bucket containing his *dalla*, a small metal jug, clunked at his side. His camel lolloped along, trumpeting plaintively. A light wind teased patches of sand into mini-cyclones, whirling among the saxaul and low tamarisk bushes in the flat desert landscape.

Durgmoot's village

My camel lumbered behind, the jerrycans sloshing with every step. Within twenty minutes my bottom was sore, my legs so stiff I had to use my arms to shift them, and I was getting motion sickness. Durgmoot kept the pace going relentlessly until my camel sat down, turned its head around, stretched its neck out and roared at me. It seemed like a good time to stop; we had been going for about three and a half hours. Our lunchspot, Karim Kaya, lay at the bottom of large white cliffs, which marked the end of the steppe and the beginning of the desert.

We unloaded the baggage and Durgmoot laid out a small carpet as a picnic mat. He collected an armful of saxaul branches and used the small twigs for kindling. It went up with the first match and was soon roaring with a blue flame. I've heard that it takes one hundred years for saxaul to grow to the width of a man's leg. He placed his *dalla* alongside the fire and produced a china teapot, which he had carefully wrapped in a handkerchief. We dined on a tin of sardines, bread and jam. After lunch, I decided to walk. Walking in the sand was heavy-going and I found it hard to keep up with Durgmoot's camel. Finally Durgmoot, who was suffering from indigestion, dismounted and spent much of the rest of the afternoon shuffling along with quick, small steps. He wasn't interested in idle chatter; we had 600 kilometres ahead of us.

At five, we stopped at a well. There had been no rain for a while and it was empty. We camped a few kilometres away from the well. Durgmoot helped me to set up the tents and was intrigued by the design. We dined on leftover lamb, which we fried with potatoes. Durgmoot was not one for singing or stories around the campfire. He stuttered abruptly in broken Russian; his jowly cheeks combined with two missing front teeth producing a cavernous boom to his voice. My few attempts at conversation met with monosyllabic replies.

'How many children do you have?'

'Seven.'

'How many sons, how many daughters?'

'Three boys and four girls.'

As he talked, he picked at half a dozen insect bites on his face. The bruising pace had worn me out and I retired to my tent. Durgmoot sat up for a while wrapped in his huge sheepskin drinking tea, his *dalla* silhouetted in the campfire. I awoke to the sound of Durgmoot, staggering around collecting firewood coughing up mucus, which had built up overnight, and spitting as he walked. I lay still, pretending to be asleep, listening to him say his *Fajr* prayer, the *dalla* bubbling beside him.

In the name of Allah, the Merciful and Compassionate
Praise be to Allah,
The Cherisher and Sustainer of the worlds,
Most Gracious, Most Merciful, Master of the Day of of Judgement!
You alone we serve and Your aid we seek.
Show us the straight way,
the way of those on whom You have bestowed Your grace;
not of those who have earned Your wrath, nor who have gone astray.

The Opening Sura Fatihah
Koran 1:1–7

As poured his tea, he called out, 'Clara. Drink tea!' After six or seven cups and a few spoonfuls of the previous night's lamb, he went to collect the camels. I managed one cup before he hinted that he wanted to get going. Cleaning the pot with sand and swilling it out with a thimble of water, I rolled up the tents, packed the bags and we were off again. I elected to walk, giving my recalcitrant camel a long lead.

At midday, we came to a ruined farmhouse with a well: a large submerged concrete tank which was almost empty. As we lowered our bucket down, a flock of pigeons flapped out. The water was a filthy green-brown, more

Durgmoot silhouetted against the campfire

pigeon droppings than water and full of feathers. The camels didn't mind. Durgmoot cried 'hock, hock' and the Bactrian obediently lowered his long, swan-like neck and sucked loudly, draining the bucket in a couple of seconds. Raising his head, he let out a grateful trumpet and chewed pensively. As he waited for his next bucket, he began to pee, the urine jetting towards his tail.

Owen Lattimore has a wonderful description of why camels take ages to urinate and why its penis is back to front:

> Burkhan (God) created animals but then got tired of recreating them and decided to fit them with an organ to reproduce. The donkey came forward first shouting kei-kei wo, kei-kei wo which means give it to me – and he went off with the biggest, and finally the god was left with one which was poorly made in haste. Who has not come forward? The camel. He cannot be bothered. The camel was summoned. I don't want it. Well you shall have it and Burkhan threw the penis after him and it attached to the camel back to front.

After each camel had drained seven or eight buckets, I took a reading on my GPS and made a note of the coordinates of the well. I had been taking coordinates at every lunch stop and every evening. At least I knew that I could retrace our path.

As I walked along, I stumbled upon many pottery shards and wondered if they had come from the remains of the Khorezmian fortifications nearby. Each time I stopped to examine things, I kept losing dashing Durgmoot who disappeared into dips or behind bushes. I also collected seashells and tortoise shells. Four-toed Horsfield tortoises live in the Karakum, hibernating two metres underground for nine months during the worst of the summer and all of the winter. Although it may seem strange to find shells and tortoises in the desert, the area was submerged several times. One hundred million years ago, the Karakum was covered by the massive Tethys Sea, which disappeared when Gonwonaland collided with the Asian continent, throwing up the Himalayas, the Tien Shan and the Pamirs. The Tethys tipped westwards and formed a series of lakes and inland seas such as the Caspian, the Black Sea and the Aral Sea. Fossils of marine oysters from the Tethys have been found in canyons both in Turkmenistan and in Kazakhstan, while marble has been found at the top of many of the high peaks in the Pamirs. More recently this area was flooded by the Amu Daria, which periodically silts up and changes its course; in this case it flowed into the Caspian Sea. The old course, now known as the Uzboi, was not far away.[41]

Kootlebai and Durgmoot outside
Durgmoot's yurt

That evening we reached a big saltwater lake called Kalector. As we walked, I kept seeing the tracks of large wolves criss-crossing the sand near our campsite, below a rock named Gingi Baba. We had walked forty kilometres that day. Despite my exhaustion, I slept badly. Durgmoot was frightened of wolves and had tethered the camels next to our tents. All night, the camels munched on a bush behind my tent, making crunching noises which sounded like footsteps. Periodically they burped and I kept worrying that they were vomiting after their pigeon-shit water.

At dawn, the sun breathed a warm orange light over the lifeless desert. As the sun rose, our surroundings were bleached into monochrome. A few wispy clouds, which looked like curdled milk, dotted the sky. As the sun came out, Durgmoot became more communicative, stuttering, 'Karakum, no water, no grass,' and shaking his head.

We spent much of that day in salt flats, weaving our way through huge tamarisk bushes, some of which went over the camels' heads. I followed on foot and kept losing Durgmoot, who continued at a cracking pace on his camel. I resorted to reciting my tables to pass the time. It was fine until I got to my sixteen-times-table. I kept stopping to work things out in the sand and fell further behind. After a while I decided to play catch up and got on my camel. I was doing quite well steering it, tapping its neck with a long branch. Just as I was getting cocky, it took off at fast trot in the wrong direction and I realized to my horror that I didn't know how to stop it. Durgmoot taught me the command, which sounds like a Donald Duck 'quack'. Despite my enlarged camel vocabulary, I opted to walk.

Later in the morning, Durgmoot got off his camel and we chatted for several hours about camels.

'Sheep are much better than camels; a ewe will give birth once every five months whereas a cow will give birth once every two years. It is also difficult to sell the camel meat; there are many Uzbeks in Dashoguz who think that eating it gives you grey hairs and women are frightened that it will delay childbirth. Besides, a camel will only produce five hundred grammes of wool and I can get one to two kilos from a sheep.'

'Surely a Bactrian has more than that.'

'No. He has even less wool than a dromedary. The wool from a Bactrian camel is only good for making rope.'

'How many Bactrian camels do you have?'

'Only that one. I don't understand it. Both its mother and its father had one hump, but it was born with two. Its father was very hairy like him. Bactrian

Durgmoot on his camel leading my camel – while I walked

camels are good workers; they are stronger and better when it is very hot and in the cold.'

I told him about a book that I had read which explained a scientific theory that the dromedary is a domesticated Bactrian camel. All camels have two humps when they are in the womb; the dromedary's merge into one hump.[42] This seemed to interest him.

'I used to have thirty camels but eighteen were stolen in one night. The night they stole my camels they took one hundred from the village. I traced the tracks of the lorry to the Kazakh border. The police are in on the racket so there was nothing we could do. The crime is much worse around Merv. My brother was murdered there. He was returning from the bazaar; he had just sold his tractor for five hundred dollars.'

By the afternoon, my legs were aching. We lunched on lamb, which Durgmoot had been carrying in a small churn. Once cooked, the Turkmen cover their meat in a thick layer of congealed fat. It keeps for three days in the height of summer and for two weeks in winter. After lunch, Durgmoot started complaining of pains, which I took to mean heartburn. I gave him some charcoal tablets and hoped that it was indigestion rather than a more serious complaint. That night, I fussed over him, setting up the tents and preparing supper while Durgmoot lay on his sheepskin waving his arm imperiously and barking instructions at me.

'Don't cut the meat like that! Move the pot away from the fire!'

As I followed his instructions, I scalded my thumb, yelped and snapped at him. Despite the criticism, he ate four bowls of stew, burping loudly as the effects of the charcoal tablets took hold. He was soon snoring contentedly.

By then, we were 200 kilometres into the silence of the desert; all I could hear was an eerie wind. Despite the enormity of our surroundings, I felt strangely claustrophobic; perhaps it was the first stages of panic. The camels had nothing to eat and we had already got through half of our water supplies; we had thirty-three litres of water left. As it was winter, I had reckoned on three to five litres each per day but my calculations had failed to take in the enormous quantities of tea which Durgmoot consumed. He sank scalding tea at breakneck speed and got through at least seven litres a day. I thanked God that I didn't let him discard the twenty-litre jerrycan at the start of our journey. That night I woke at 4.30 to the sound of light rain beating on my tent. I scrambled outside, dug a wide, shallow hole and spread out my rain jacket to catch the rainfall. When I got up, there was mugful of sandy water in the hole, which I scooped into an empty flask.

At daybreak, we packed up and continued to plod through boring flats. The saxaul bushes were grey, like embers, which looked as if they would crumble if touched. Eventually we started to follow a track through the dunes. Fresh sheep droppings and a solitary camel suggested that we were not far from water. Sand in my boots had begun to rub the skin into a blister and I decided to rest on my camel. After an hour it had a wobbly, bellowing at me and trying to bite my leg as I clambered off, my muscles frozen stiff.

I spent the day thinking of distracting thoughts; I had already completed my nineteen-times-table; I had thought of the words for everything around us in as many languages as I could and had even made a mental calculation of all my teenage amours. I moved on to a menu of what I would eat when I got home and what I wanted to do; I thought about how nice it would be to catch up with friends in a simple country pub; how nice it would be to be able to confide in someone I could trust, and in my own language, and what a relief it would be to be able to show weakness, without worrying about the consequences – something I had rarely done in over a year. How nice it would be to be looked after and pampered. I longed to soak in a hot bath, have a thorough makeover, put on a dress and behave like a woman rather than an honorary man.

As I walked along, I wondered whether I would look back on the journey as one of self-discovery. I had certainly learned a lot about myself; I had been able tap into a vast reserve of energy that I had not realized that I possessed. I had learned resourcefulness, resilience, adaptability and had made enduring friendships with people whose backgrounds were much less privileged than my own. I knew that I had also developed a well-honed sense of self-preservation which included an ability to make quick judgements about whether I could trust someone. But this also made me more suspicious of people than I would like to have been and when I thought that I might be cornered, I often felt the need to make an early show of strength – a warning that if anyone attacked, I would put up a fight. I had also learned how to survive on my own and I could see that while in some ways that was a good thing, it is dangerous to think that one doesn't need people. I wondered whether I would still be the sociable person that I had been or whether, now that I had acquired a taste for it, I would crave solitude.

We came to another well, but it was empty. The uncovered concrete vat was criss-crossed with deep cracks and filled with rusty poles. It seemed extraordinary that the local herdsmen had made no effort to repair their wells. It used to be done by the central government and since the collapse of communism, the wells had gone the same way. Turkmen used to pride themselves on their well construction. Specialists, often Iranians or Kurds, would be employed to dig down twenty to forty metres and the wells would be maintained and improved over the centuries. Custom dictated that any

stranger was entitled to use the well. The owner and his immediate relatives had priority but if the stranger was already watering his animals, he
would have to wait. While the cost of financing the well was borne by the
owner, everyone was expected to help clean and repair it and help the
owner with tasks such as herding and shearing. I could see that Durgmoot
was concerned.

'There should be water here, there always was. I don't understand.'

We stopped quite late. I reckon we covered about forty-eight kilometres
that day, only five of which I'd managed in the saddle. My feet were blis-
tered, I had pains in the backs of my knees and even my hips were aching.
After unloading the camels and setting up the tents, I no longer had the
energy to cook and Durgmoot indicated that he hadn't the energy to eat.
We each had a hunk of stale bread and retired to our tents. I felt better for
a 'stand-up wash', (five wipes doused in antibacterial wash) and a change of
clothes.

We were off again at quarter past eight. It wasn't worth getting on the
wrong side of my temperamental camel so I walked. Durgmoot sat on his
camel, leading mine and keeping up a furious pace, calling 'hoo, hoo, choo,
choo', and slapping the backside of his lumbering Bactrian seemingly in
time with the clanking bucket and *dalla*. I walked behind at a safe distance
from their knobbly legs. Our pitiful supper the night before had left me
feeling weak and I fell far behind. At lunch I managed to sneak in twenty
minutes' sleep before Durgmoot told me our hour was up. We walked for
another twenty kilometres until nightfall. For the second night in a row,
Durgmoot didn't eat anything and I spent the night fretting about him and
concerned that we now had fifteen litres of water left.

In the morning, Durgmoot set a blistering pace in the direction of
another well which we reached at ten. I shone my torch down the deep,
dark shaft but I couldn't see the tell-tale shimmer of water. I dropped a
stone down the hole and the resounding thud confirmed our worse suspi-
cions. Neither of us rode our camels all day. Both camels had begun
stumbling a lot and at one point my camel fell hard on one knee. The
camels had not been watered for five days and even our water was running
low. I had read that camels can go for ten days without water but I didn't
believe that my camels would survive that long as they were less used to
working and they had had very little grazing.

At midday, we heard the reassuring sound of a bell and several hundred bleating goats. A young, barefooted herder pointed us in the direction of a well, five
kilometres away. I was so grateful that I gave him several polaroids and a
packet of sweets. He gave me a couple of rabbits in exchange. Descending into

The bride and her friend with the London skyline on her dress

a large depression, we came to a pathetic shack surrounded by a black ring of sheep droppings. The well was empty. Durgmoot's face showed signs of panic and he rushed to another well near the farmhouse. It was also empty. I wanted to cry. In the distance we saw a small trough. Lifting up the wooden lid, we peered down the deep well. We couldn't see anything. I dropped a stone down and heard a gratifying 'plop'.

While Durgmoot collected firewood to make tea, I began filling the trough. Bucket after bucket, the camels kept sucking the trough dry; I couldn't keep up. After I'd hoisted about twelve buckets, the trough began filling, the camels still drawing hard but stopping occasionally to dribble and reflect on their ordeal. After filling our containers, I washed my hair and sat down to join Durgmoot in a lengthy tea routine. I was just savouring my second cup when I heard an engine. A lorry was careering down the sand towards us. As it came closer, I realized it was full of women and children. They got out and ran towards us. I counted at least forty women and children accompanied by one male driver. One of the women, dressed in a red robe, was adjusting an elaborate metal head-dress, which jingled like a tambourine as she walked. I wondered if she was going to dance for us. Durgmoot looked equally perplexed.

They gathered around our picnic carpet and began chattering excitedly to Durgmoot. After a few minutes, I asked him why they had come.

'Photos.'

'What?'

'They are relations of the shepherd. He told them you take photos.'

News travelled fast in the desert.

'What is the head-dress for?'

'She is a *devoushka* (virgin). She is soon to be married and wants you to take her photo in her wedding outfit.'

In Turkmenistan, the women wear red wedding outfits to ward off the evil eye. Her head-dress consisted of a highly ornamented helmet with a dowel sticking out of the top, a tear-shape at its apex. A strand of beads and amulets fell down her back and several others draped down her front. The silver amulets on the head-dress represented her ancestors.

I began snapping away. The women knew exactly what they wanted. A woman posed with her red-haired, freckled daughter. The bride modelled with her girlfriends, insisting on a lengthy personalized photo-shoot. As I pulled the photos from the camera, the women snatched them eagerly and giggled as they compared their portraits. Soon every woman had at least one photo. They began squabbling and swapping the group photos like football cards. All the while, Durgmoot lay on his carpet impervious to the idle female chatter, eating bread and drinking copious quantities of tea.

Durgmoot unruffled and drinking tea

One of the women was wearing a purple and green dress with 2001 in bold letters, a woman a year ahead of her time. The London skyline decorated the bottom of the dress.

'London, Anglia,' I said, pointing at her dress. She looked perplexed so I fished out my Russian illustrated guidebook to London and compared the pictures of Big Ben and St Paul's with those on her dress. The women began tittering uncontrollably, leafing through the book and matching the pictures with those on the dress.

The excitement died down. Presenting me with some delicious bread made with flour, sugar and camels' milk, they got back into the lorry and drove off, waving until they were out of sight. The sound of the engine faded, the mirage receded. We plunged back into stillness at our well in the middle of the desert. We looked at each other and laughed. Durgmoot agreed that we could take the rest of the day off. We had travelled 300 kilometres and were exactly half-way to Ashkabad.

It was another punishing walk the next day. Durgmoot trudged ahead on his camel and I followed behind, struggling up and down the large dunes. With every step, my feet disappeared deep into the sand. The camels were still struggling, as they had been watered but still hadn't had much fodder. A young shepherd joined us for lunch, sinking copious quantities of tea with Durgmoot. In the afternoon we followed his bare footprints for miles. In the early evening we found ourselves back in golden dunes; our camels cast long dark shadows on the sands. As we descended from the final crest, we saw the azure dome of a village mosque in the distance. I could make out twenty or thirty simple adobe houses and a smattering of reed *yurts* in a wide plain. The wind whipped up the sand, obscuring the village behind a cloud of dust. As we drew nearer, several dozen children ran out to greet us and guided us to the schoolteacher's house.

As luck would have it, Ak-at-li was the resident English teacher. A corpulent man with strong Turkic features, his camel wool tank-top and long-sleeved shirt made him look like a laid-back academic. He was thrilled to have us to stay. It was the first time he had practised his English in eighteen years! His house was teeming with children, ten of his, a few grandchildren and several nieces. He introduced each one and explained their names.

'This is Strong Boy, this is July and this is my youngest, May He Be Prolific In His Offspring.'

I was sure he'd have trouble signing that on his cheques.

'And what does Ak-at-li mean?'

'With White Horse. When I was born, a stranger rode up to the house on a white horse.'

Two young Turkmen girls

As I walked into a back room, an old man hurriedly hid his *hookah*. The heavy, sweet smell of opium hung over the room.

'You must excuse my father. It is a bad habit. He started to smoke aged forty-two, to relieve his stomach pains and he has been smoking ever since.'

Turkmenistan is an easy, flat smuggling route from Afghanistan. In some villages there is a sixty to eighty per cent addiction rate. The government tries to keep it quiet and aid workers who broadcast the problem don't get their visas renewed.

Later on in the evening, he started smoking again, heating the opium on a small screwdriver and inhaling it through a thin metal tube. We retired to another room and sat down to a feast of rabbit washed down with fermented camels' milk. There were two varieties on offer; one was a revolting watery substance called *chal* which had milky scum floating on the top and the other was pleasant, creamy milk called *agaran*.

Ak-at-li and I had some heated discussions about Turkmen politics. Niyazov's authoritarian regime was increasingly despised by educated Turkmen, many of whom had fled the country since independence. His

support came from the uneducated people in rural areas who are brainwashed by a manipulated press into believing Niyazov's vision of a
Turkmen emiracy. Ak-at-li began reeling off Niyazov's pipe dream: plans
to export Turkmenistan's gas.

Turkmenistan has 8 trillion cubic metres of proven gas reserves and 700
million tons of petroleum reserves but it has no export market. Under the
Soviet Union, Turkmenistan was forced to sell her gas for five to six
roubles per thousand cubic metres, a fraction of the international market
price. Since independence, Gazprom, the Russian state oil giant, has tried
to prevent Turkmenistan from competing in the former Soviet Union and
from opening up her market to the West. The American government,
uncomfortable about their reliance on Middle Eastern oil assets, was looking to secure an alternative source of supply. Wary of the level of influence
that Russia had on the Caspian states, America was using her diplomatic
muscle to encourage a pipeline, which would go under the Caspian Sea,
through Azerbaijan to Turkey. This was a highly expensive proposal,
further complicated by the failure of the six Caspian states to agree on how
to structure such a project. Until such a time, Niyazov's only cashflow
came from selling onward contracts through Iran. The other alternative, a
pipeline through Iran, would have forced Turkmenistan into diplomatic
isolation.

The watering hole in Ak-at-li's village

Camels are a luxurious form of transport in a country where fuel is 1c a litre. The only working camels that I saw in Turkmenistan

However, Niyazov has backed some daring (or perhaps desperate) schemes: with encouragement from Pakistan and initially from America, Niyazov encouraged the Bridas Corporation and later Unocal in their efforts to build a pipeline across Afghanistan, openly supporting the Taliban. When the Americans finally turned against the Taliban regime, Niyazov continued to supply the Taliban with gas. With nowhere to export Turkmenistan's gas, Niyazov had been buying popularity by giving it away. Most villages had free electricity and gas and I read that people were leaving the gas on all day to save money on matches. Transportation was absurdly cheap; petrol was between one and five cents a litre in Turkmenistan and it cost between $1–$5 to fly across the country.[43]

I woke up in time to see the camels being milked. The sun was just rising, casting a warm glow over the desert and silhouetting the camels, lowing beside their tethering poles. Ak-at-li's wife, a bucket around her neck, approached the left flank of a large camel and shooed away its offspring from the teat. Her head came up to the top of the camel's thigh. Running her fingers down the teats, she began squeezing the milk into the bucket and crying 'ha, hur' as the camel fidgeted. After milking three camels, her hands were covered in camel dung and the bucket was half full. She poured the milk into a large churn, containing a little old milk, an agent in the fermentation process. Forty-five minutes later, the milk was ready to drink.

We led our camels through the village to the well. Preparations were under way for winter; large stacks of thick saxaul branches dotted the village and huge piles of green, thorny fodder was piled up on the roofs of the houses. Ak-at-li explained that the village camels came to be watered of their own accord. In summer they normally came every two or three days; in winter every five. The water was pumped up by an old car engine, which turned a rubber belt, whipping up the water into a drinking trough.

Durgmoot was keen to get away. From what I could gather from a mixture of broken Russian, snorts and shivering actions, the old man had snored all night. At first light, he had started shivering, exhibiting the symptoms of opium addiction. He tried to get Durgmoot to accept some of his opium in his tea and had given some to his 13-year-old granddaughter who had a headache. As we left, he was negotiating to sell a baby camel to finance his habit.

The light rainfall of the previous days had already taken effect; green shoots were sprouting up everywhere, which made it look as if the desert had been lightly dusted green. But it wasn't enough for our camels, and despite the generous quantities of fodder that they had been given the previous night, both camels slumped down on their worn kneepads and refused to go on. Durgmoot prepared the rabbit. He wanted soup but I put too much rice in the pot and we ended up with risotto; he wasn't happy. I left him gazing into the fire and went to my tent to listen to the World Service. Guests on *Woman's Hour* were discussing the growing numbers of house-husbands in the West and the psychological damage associated with their feelings of redundancy. I wondered how I could possibly explain these issues to Durgmoot.

Durgmoot was right about the rabbit. I felt queasy throughout the following day. Durgmoot kept up a furious pace, which left me lagging further and further behind. At lunch, he proposed that we stop for two hours to give the camels a chance to graze. Despite his suggestion, he was itching to get away after an hour. We hit the main road into Ashkabad after lunch. Despite the traffic, which unnerved the camels, progress along the road was much faster. However, we were not safe any more. At five o'clock that evening, I noticed a motorcyclist following parallel to us in the dunes, several hundred metres away. I was sure he was watching to see where we camped. I didn't dare say anything to Durgmoot as I didn't want to scare him unduly.

We camped in a small depression in the dunes where our fire would be out of sight. As we were eating supper, we heard the motorbike nearby in the dunes. The engine cut and there was silence.

'He was following us in the sand,' said Durgmoot.

'I know.'

We frantically scanned our surroundings for any sign of him; we couldn't see him but I had an uncomfortable feeling that he was watching us. Seated around our campfire, we were sitting ducks, our giant shadows flickering on the surrounding dunes. Durgmoot's gun was at hand but it seemed unwise to cock it as we didn't know if the prowler was armed. We couldn't see him and I was sure he could see us. After twenty minutes, we heard the engine start up and the reassuring sound of the motorbike receding into the distance. I hoped that was the last we would hear of him.

All night, I could hear the distant purr of a motorbike circling in the dunes. Having reconnoitred our campsite, he'd forgotten where we were; we had been careful to extinguish our campfire and hadn't put up the tents. After we had drunk our tea, Durgmoot dug a hole in the sand, buried the embers and laid the sheepskins over the top. I drifted off for several hours and woke up with a start. I could hear a motorbike coming along the main road. Despite the sounds of other traffic on the road, I knew it was him. My heart felt as if it was going to burst out of my ribcage. I sat up. I couldn't breathe. As it got closer, I heard the engine slowing down. He was looking to find where our camels' footprints had left the road. I heard him turn off the road and several minutes later, the engine cut out. I struggled out of my sleeping-bag and hid behind a tamarisk bush. All I had was my knife and the starter pistol. I could fire a few shots as a warning. If I fired the pistol, it might cause him to fire back. Durgmoot was sitting up. His gun was still folded up on the other side of the fire; it still wasn't even cocked, let alone loaded. We waited for at least half an hour. Durgmoot switched on the big torch and flashed it around, to show we were awake and waiting for him. At one point, he caught a figure in the beam of his torch. He left soon after that. I tried to stay awake, in case he came back, but my eyes grew heavier and I abandoned myself to my fate.

After our ritual four-hour morning march, we crested a hill and looked down on a sea of dunes, whipped up into an angry swell by a strong wind. Below us Erbent was barely visible in the swirling sand which stung my cheeks and streamed into my ears. Folding up my collar and putting on my shades, I kept my head down and trudged on. In Erbent, we sought refuge in a *chaikhana* and persuaded the owner to find some thorn bushes for the camels. We sat on thick quilts, which were laid out around low tables, on a raised platform. In the far corner of the room a group of lorry drivers, *en route* to Ashkabad, were drinking vodka and eating greasy bread and mutton soup. When we had walked in, they had been watching Tom and Jerry. However, Durgmoot turned the other way with a scowl of disapproval as they switched to a semi-pornographic film. I felt mortified. I was the first Western woman that Durgmoot had met or seen. Any good impressions that he might have formed of the West were rapidly being undone by the women on screen, writhing around, their breasts bared.

After lunch, Durgmoot went to water the camels. He returned like the Pied Piper thronged by several hundred children. We set off with our new entourage. Durgmoot walked ahead with the camels and several young boys skipped after him, asking questions about the strange two-humped, hairy camel. I walked with the girls, who squabbled over which of them was to hold my hand. None of the children spoke much Russian. Occasionally we stopped to explain ourselves, drawing pictures in the sand.

'Why is your skin white?'

'Special sun cream keeps my face white.'

'Are you married?'

'No.'

'Do you have an "I love you?"'

'No.'

'Are you sharing a tent with your guide?'

'No!'

'We are going to walk to Ashkabad with you.'

An hour later, the children had spread out over several hundred metres, the young stragglers struggling to keep up. I managed to persuade the older ones to go home. They kept waving until we were out of sight.

After the children left, I had nothing to focus on except the pain in my legs. My knees were very painful and my ankles ached. I could feel the ball and socket joint grating in my hip. My toes were raw and I had two large blisters on the balls of my feet. My hips were so creaky that I had taken to swinging my legs along with the help of my arms. We had been walking the equivalent of a marathon a day for almost two weeks.

The following afternoon, I could make out the Kopet Dagh range, which runs along the border between Iran and Turkmenistan. Up until that point, I had been wishing every day that we'd get there, that I could stop walking and sit down. Suddenly, I realized that Ashkabad spelled the end of my journey and I realized that I didn't want to arrive. Of course, I wanted to see my family and friends but I didn't want to go back to England; it didn't feel like home. I had never set out to 'find myself' but now that I was near the finish, I felt lost. I had walked away from my old life and I knew that I couldn't go back. I had nothing to look forward to. My whole purpose for eighteen months was about to be taken away from me. I wondered how I would look back on the journey in years to come. I felt utterly remote from my former existence in Hong Kong, as though for the past eighteen months I had been living in a parallel world. On my return to England, I knew that my experience in Central Asia would feel distant and unreal and I didn't want to let go.

Durgmoot and I agreed to head for the Tolkuchka bazaar in Ashkabad, a colourful place to finish, full of carpets and camels. No one would be there to meet us – the end had always seemed too far off to plan properly. Now it made it all seem rather pointless. On my last night in the open, we hid in a ditch on the outskirts of Ashkabad. There wasn't room to put up the tents. Bright stars shone like crystals in the dark, moonless sky.

I was tired, but I lay awake thinking about the end of the journey. I'd found freedom in days where my only concern was saddling my horses. If I had had the strength and the financial resources, I knew I would have turned back and done it all again. I'd grown accustomed to the slow plodding rhythm of my caravan. I'd found peace in the restless momentum, which purposefully carried me from one uncertain campsite to the next. I had relished the instability and grown used to the solitude.

I hadn't dozed off for long when we heard prowlers. I heard a lorry pull up near the camels and switch off its engine. I fired a warning shot from my starter pistol and the lorry drove away. Durgmoot tied the camels to a long rope which he held until dawn. I shivered throughout the night and woke up to find a thick layer of frost on the outside of my sleeping-bag.

We walked and walked and walked. At midday, a policeman on speeding duty flagged us down offering us a slice of melon. Half an hour later, we passed a large, concrete sign near a few mud huts saying, 'Asgabad'. Several hours later, azure mosques and Turkmenbashi's flamboyant architectural designs appeared on a dusty skyline. As we entered the outskirts of Ashkabad the camels grew jumpy. Durgmoot was thrown into a state of confusion by the traffic and kept walking in front of cars. We spotted a lorry with a Dashoguz numberplate, loaded with watermelons, which was heading for the main bazaar. Once he had dumped his load, he offered to take Durgmoot and the camels back some 600 kilometres to Turkmenbashi for $25!

By the time we got to the bazaar, it was closed. A few stragglers were packing up their containers and most people didn't notice our camels. Luckily I found a tea service which made a good wedding present for Durgmoot's daughter. We tied up the camels outside a *chaikhana* and I ordered a feast. When the food arrived, Durgmoot protested; he wanted to get going. As I sorted out his money, he managed a couple of spoonfuls of *plov* and a few sips of tea before he was off to sort out his camels.

The author and her camel – nearing the finish line

The dromedary ambled into the truck; the Bactrian roared with disgust and spat a mixture of bile and old grass down my front. Durgmoot wasn't having any tantrums and the poor camel had a half-lacerated bottom by the time he lumbered into position. A few wooden planks separated the camels from the road. Durgmoot set about immobilizing the dromedary, tying its legs together and passing a rope over its back and under its legs. I handed him his money, my starter pistol and the tea set. He seemed bemused that I should be giving him more than we had agreed. Smiling, he shook my hand, got into the truck and it rattled out of the bazaar, kicking up a trail of dust and sand.

I didn't feel ready to leave. At any moment, I could hail a passing car which would transport me to the centre of Ashkabad where I would be five or six hours from Heathrow. Back in London, the sharp edges of my current reality would become blurred. I couldn't bear to make the transition. I sat in a quiet corner on my bags for at least an hour watching the remaining people pack up their stalls and the hum of activity die down. Camouflaged in my dusty velvet-green Turkmen dress and floral head-scarf, I faded into the anonymity of the bazaar. Soon there were only a dozen people left. A group of chattering portly women, weighed down with worn plastic bags, waited in line to board a local bus. A Turkmen with a half-smoked cigarette hanging out of his mouth stood in the back of a truck, barking orders at young men who were swinging heavy sacks of flour on to their backs. As he shouted, he choked on his smoke and irritably he flicked his cigarette out of the back of the truck. A couple of young men with long, aquiline faces hoisted a heavy carpet on to their shoulders and strapped it on to the roof of a waiting Volga. A large lady, half hidden under a thick grey *babushka*'s shawl, leaned heavily on a pram containing half a dozen rounds of flat bread as she wheeled it out of the main gate. A couple of emaciated dogs trotted several paces behind the creaking wheels, hoping for a crust. The bazaar was empty.

NOTES

1. John Massey Stewart, *The Nature of Russia*, 1st edn (Boxtree, 1992)
2. Charles Bawden, *The Modern History Of Mongolia* (Kegan Paul, 2002)
3. Paul Ratchnevsky, *Genghis Khan His Life and Legacy* (Blackwell, 1991)
4. Leo De Hartog, *Genghis Khan, Conqueror of the World* (I.B. Tauris, 1979)
5. Gabriel Ronay, *The Tartar Khan's Englishman* (Cassell, 1978)
6. David Morgan, *The Mongols*, 2nd edn (Blackwell, 1999)
7. Robert Marshall, *Storm from the East*, 1st edn (University of California Press, 1993)
8. Karl Menges, 'People, Languages and Migrations', in *Central Asia: A Century Of Russian Rule*, ed. E. Allworth (Columbia University Press, New York, 1967)
9. John Wyld, 'The Legend of Prester John' (*Royal Society for Asian Affairs Journal Vol XXXI*, Part One)
10. Peter Jackson and David Morgan, *The Mission of Friar William of Rubruck*, 1st edn (Hakluyt Society, 1990)
11. Ibid., p. 49.
12. Thomas Winner, *The Oral Art and Literature of the Kazakhs of Russian Central Asia* (Duke University Press, 1958)
13 Massey Stewart, op. cit., p. 86.
14 Morgan, op. cit., p. 138
15 Gabriel Ronay, *The Tartar Khan's Englishman* (Cassell, 1978)
16 Marshall, op. cit.
17 Edward Allworth, *Central Asia, His Life and His Times* (University of California Press, 1998)
18 Morris Rossabi, *Khubilai Khan, His Life and His Times* (University of California Press, 1998)
19 Marshall, op. cit.
20 Karel Van Leeuwan, Tatjana Emeljanenko and Larisa Popova, *Nomades in Central Asia, Animal Husbandry and Culture in Transition* (Amsterdam, 1994)
21 *Newsweek*, July 2003
22 Rene Grousset, *The Empire of the Steppes* (Rutgers University Press, 1970)
23 Ahmed Rashid, *The Resurgence of Central Asia: Islam or Nationalism* (Zed Books, 1994)
24 John De Francis, *In the Footsteps of Genghis Khan* (University of Hawaii Press, 1993)
25 Ahmed Rashid, *Jihad: The Rise of Militan Islam in Central Asia* (Yale University Press, 2002)

26 Allworth, op. cit., p. 30–5

27 Ahmed Rashid, *The Resurgence of Central Asia: Islam or Nationalism* (Zed Books, 1994)

28 Knobloch, Edgar, *Monuments of Central Asia: A Guide to Archaeology, Art and Architecture of Turkestan* (I.B. Tauris, 2001)

29 Tiziano Terzani, *Goodnight, Mr Lenin*, 1st edn (Picador, 1993)

30 Ratchnevsky, op. cit.

31 Knobloch, op. cit.

32 Beatrice Forbes Manz, *The Rise and Rule of Tamerlane* (Cambridge Canto, 1999)

33 Terzani, op. cit.

34 Knobloch, op. cit.

35 Fiztroy Maclean, *To the Back of Beyond: An Illustrated Companion to Central Asia and Mongolia* (Little, Brown, 1975)

36 Ahmed Rashid, *The Resurgence of Central Asia: Islam or Nationalism* (Zed Books, 1994)

37 Bernard Lewis, *The Assassins* (Weidenfeld and Nicolson, 2001)

38 Maclean, op. cit.

39 Geoffrey Moorhouse, *Apples in the Snow*, 1st edn (Hodder and Stoughton, 1990)

40 Morgan, op. cit., p. 316

41 John Sparks, *Realms of the Russian Bear* (Little, Brown, 1992)

42 Sparks, op. cit., p. 136

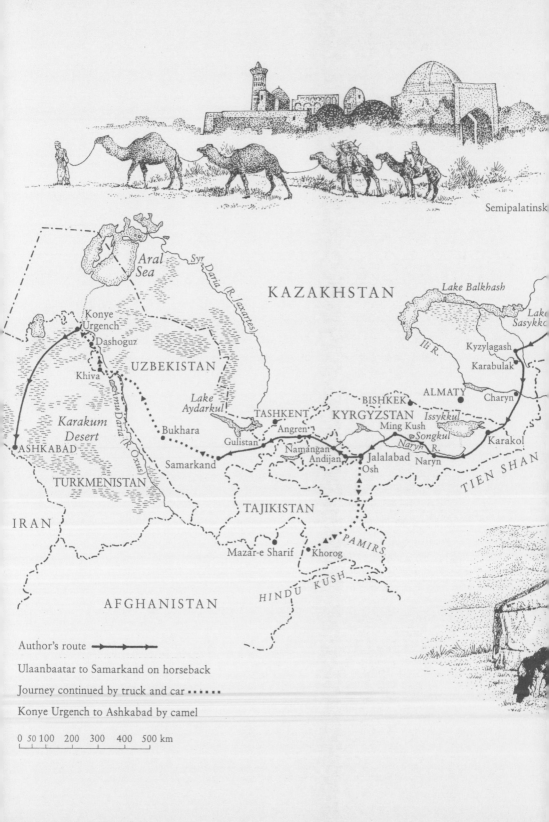

Semipalatinsk

*Aral
Sea*

*Syr Daria
(R. Jaxartes)*

KAZAKHSTAN

Lake Balkhash

*Lake
Sasykko*

Konye
Urgench

Dashoguz

Khiva

UZBEKISTAN

Ili R.

Kyzylagash

Karabulak

ALMATY

Charyn

*Karakum
Desert*

Amu Daria (R. Oxus)

*Lake
Aydarkul*

Bukhara

TASHKENT

Angren

BISHKEK

Issykkul

KYRGYZSTAN

Ming Kush

Songkul

Karakol

ASHKABAD

TURKMENISTAN

Gulistan

Samarkand

Namangan

Andijan

Jalalabad

Osh

Naryn

Naryn R.

TIEN SHAN

IRAN

TAJIKISTAN

PAMIRS

AFGHANISTAN

Mazar-e Sharif

Khorog

HINDU KUSH

Author's route ➤➤➤

Ulaanbaatar to Samarkand on horseback

Journey continued by truck and car ●●●●●●

Konye Urgench to Ashkabad by camel

0 50 100 200 300 400 500 km